GLOBAL PERSPECTIVES ON VIOLENCE AGAINST WOMEN AND GIRLS

ABOUT THE AUTHOR

Tamsin Bradley is a social anthropologist and Professor in International Development Studies at the University of Portsmouth. Her previous works include *Women and Violence in South Asia* (2015) and *Challenging the NGOs* (2012), as well as the edited collections *Interrogating Harmful Cultural Practices* (2015) and *Dowry: Bridging the Gap between Theory and Practice* (Zed 2009).

GLOBAL PERSPECTIVES ON VIOLENCE AGAINST WOMEN AND GIRLS

Tamsin Bradley

BLOOMSBURY ACADEMIC
LONDON • NEW YORK • OXFORD • NEW DELHI • SYDNEY

BLOOMSBURY ACADEMIC
Bloomsbury Publishing Plc
50 Bedford Square, London, WC1B 3DP, UK
1385 Broadway, New York, NY 10018, USA
29 Earlsfort Terrace, Dublin 2, Ireland

BLOOMSBURY, BLOOMSBURY ACADEMIC and the Diana logo
are trademarks of Bloomsbury Publishing Plc

First published by Zed Books 2020
This paperback edition published by Bloomsbury Academic 2022

Copyright © Tamsin Bradley, 2020

Tamsin Bradley has asserted her right under the Copyright,
Designs and Patents Act, 1988, to be identified as author of this work.

Cover photo © Vlad Sokhin/Panos Pictures
Cover design by Burgess & Beech
Index by John Barker

All rights reserved. No part of this publication may be reproduced or transmitted in any form or by any means, electronic or mechanical, including photocopying, recording, or any information storage or retrieval system, without prior permission in writing from the publishers.

Bloomsbury Publishing Plc does not have any control over, or responsibility for, any third-party websites referred to or in this book. All internet addresses given in this book were correct at the time of going to press. The author and publisher regret any inconvenience caused if addresses have changed or sites have ceased to exist, but can accept no responsibility for any such changes.

A catalogue record for this book is available from the British Library.

ISBN: HB: 978-1-7869-9414-1
PB: 978-1-7869-9415-8
ePDF: 978-1-7869-9416-5
ePub: 978-1-7869-9417-2

Typeset in Plantin and Kievit by Swales & Willis Ltd, Exeter, Devon

To find out more about our authors and books visit
www.bloomsbury.com and sign up for our newsletters.

*Adventurous and strong, aware yet still.
Qualities I have grown thankful for.*

CONTENTS

List of figures | xi
List of tables | xiii

    Introduction..1
    Setting the global context 1
    Review of common approaches 5
    The importance of a gendered lens 11
    Women's economic empowerment 16
    Structure of the volume 19

1 Social norms, positive deviancy and cultural capital................. 25
    Introduction 25
    *Social norm change, positive deviancy and cultural
       capital in the context of VAWG* 26
    Women fighting violence in Nepal 36
    Women fighting violence in rural Rajasthan, India 41
    Conclusion 46

2 Measuring attitudes around harmful cultural
    practices: the continuum approach... 48
    Introduction 48
    Measuring change: introducing the continuum 50
    Overview of FGM in the UK 52
    *Applying the continuum: attitudes towards FGM
       in Portsmouth and Southampton, UK* 54
    Digging deeper into different viewpoints 55
    Conclusion 60

3 The intersections of gender, religion, culture,
    sexuality and violence..62
    Introduction 62
    Cultural relativism as a critical lens 64
    The links between religion and FGM 71
    The links between sexuality and FGM 75
    Challenging Western hegemony 77
    Conclusion 80

4 Women, work and violence in Nepal: experiences
from the construction sector 81
Introduction 81
Methodology 83
Data analysis 84
Interview findings 85
The role of autonomous women's networks
   and organisations 96
Conclusion 98

5 Applying the intersectional lens: the experiences of
professional middle-class women in Nepal
and Pakistan.. 101
Introduction 101
Different work contexts: comparing Nepal and Pakistan 104
Key themes emerging from the data 108
Female entrepreneurs in Lahore and Islamabad 117
Conclusion 121

6 The experiences of home-based workers in Pakistan 126
Introduction 126
Reviewing the country context 127
Work and living conditions of home-based workers 132
Details of HomeNet Pakistan 135
Findings 137
Women's experiences of violence 145
Conclusion 150

7 The global drive to end female genital mutilation:
is an end in sight?..153
Introduction 153
What do we know about why FGM happens? 155
The importance of understanding context 158
The medicalisation of FGM 166
FGM in Sudan 168
Conclusion 174

8 Violence against women and girls in conflict settings...............177
Introduction 177
Review of research on VAWG in conflict settings 181
The context of South Sudan 186

Digging deeper into the normalisation of VAWG in South Sudan 192
Access to justice in South Sudan in the context of VAWG 195
Conclusion 200

9 Embedding a violence against women lens in development.. 202
Introduction 202
What does a VAWG mainstreaming tool look like? 203
Applying the model to the lives of women in refugee contexts 206
Conclusion 217

Conclusion: towards a more nuanced theory of change..220

Notes | 225
References | 227
Index | 243

FIGURES

1. The gender lens 13
2. The ethnographic web model 31
3. The attitude continuum on HCPs 51
4. Women, work and violence: a theory of change 224

TABLES

1 Design phase questions 204
2 Operational questions 215

INTRODUCTION

Setting the global context

Ending violence against women and girls (VAWG) is a major challenge in the global pursuit to achieve social equality and justice for all. In 2015, the United Nations (UN) listed 17 Sustainable Development Goals (SDGs), the fifth of which is focused on achieving gender equality, and Target 5.2 is as follows: "Eliminate all forms of violence against all women and girls in the public and private spheres, including trafficking and sexual and other types of exploitations" (UN, n.d.). But statistics relating to reducing the prevalence of VAWG suggest that progress has so far been slow. According to UN Women (2018):

- One in five women and girls aged between 15 and 49 reported experiencing sexual and/or physical violence by an intimate partner in the 12 months prior to data collection.
- The global figures on homicides committed by a family member recorded that in 47 per cent of cases, women were the victims, in contrast to 6 per cent of cases where men were the victims.
- Forty-nine countries have no legislation protecting women from domestic violence.
- Thirty-seven countries exempt a perpetrator of rape if they are married to (or subsequently marry) the survivor.

In relation to Target 5.3, which is focused on the elimination of harmful cultural practices such as female genital mutilation (FGM), forced marriage and child marriage, UN

Women (2018) cite a number of statistics that illustrate the situation so far.

At least 200 million girls have undergone FGM. While prevalence rates have decreased by 30 per cent over the past three decades, this is not universal across all cutting countries. In these countries, populations are set to grow, meaning that the figure is likely to increase significantly if current trends continue.

Over 750 million women were married before the age of 18. Progress on this has been slow, with data from 2000 and 2015 showing a small decline in the number of women married before the age of 18, from 22 per cent to 19 per cent, and for girls married under 15 years a reduction from 11 per cent to 8 per cent (UN Women, 2018). A key challenge recognised by UN agencies such as UN Women is that data on the prevalence of different forms of VAWG are still very patchy, and breaking these down into the full spectrum of different types has proven challenging. The data gaps, both in terms of quantitative and in-depth qualitative understandings, are such that international donors have not only put funding into interventions, but have also begun to fund applied research. A strong and comprehensive evidence base must be the foundation of well-positioned and designed activities to end all forms of VAWG. What the data above clearly reveal is that we are still a long way from ending VAWG, despite an unprecedented global drive and the allocation of significant resources to do so.

Given the current global drive to end all forms of VAWG, this volume intends to provide detailed insights into some of the many different contexts in which this violence occurs. It offers new evidence relating to the extent of the issue, and current interventions to end it, as well as considering why it persists. The volume presents an overarching argument that stresses the critical importance of understanding the complex and diverse contexts across the globe in which VAWG not only continues, but seems to flourish. Gathering this level of understanding must be considered a systematic starting point in the design of any interventions and policies that intend to end VAWG. This argument is supported through different case examples which emphasise that, despite contextual differences, certain things need to be in place if activism and projects that seek to confront and address this violence have any chance of working. At the national level, a strong network of civil society women's organisations, linked and supported by robust and committed government departments that themselves have women well represented at all levels, is essential. National efforts must then link to international donor programming and resourcing that works with policymakers, implementers and local activist organisations. A final piece of the puzzle is the involvement of peer networks, and indeed acknowledgement that women, in many different ways and at multiple levels, organise organically to resist and build capital, such as they can, to challenge the barriers that inhibit their freedom and limit their well-being. This chain of stakeholders needs to be sensitive to and build upon the capacity that already exists through such peer networks that have emerged through the shared experiences of violence and hardship.

While it is not possible to cover every country context, the volume offers case studies of a range of countries selected because they each offer unique and useful insights and new data that help to build the evidence base that supports the arguments presented above. The detailed case studies included are of Nepal, India, Pakistan, Sudan, South Sudan and the UK. However, each chapter takes a comparative approach and draws on various other examples, where relevant, in order to provide a more global perspective. This range of political, economic, social and cultural environments enables a number of key points to be made: first, greater understandings of individual country contexts are crucial in order to end VAWG globally; and second, compiling insights that are useful in policy and programme circles requires the application of clear and targeted theoretical frames. Several such frameworks will be woven together here and consistently applied, enabling similarities and differences between the contexts studied to emerge. Methodologically, this volume combines a political economy analysis with the conceptual framework of the ecology of violence, which is applied in each case study along with much more microfocused insights gathered through a combination of qualitative research approaches, including in-depth interviews, life histories and ethnography.

As stated above, the volume presents new research from across South Asia, Africa and the UK, combining a consistent theoretical frame that seeks to offer nuanced and complex understandings of the "why" and "how" violence remains so prevalent across the globe. The originality comes in four forms, the first of which is filling knowledge gaps by providing in-depth, context-specific insights. The second is the application of a range of different but interlocking frames, creating a critical lens geared towards drawing out the lessons regarding "what works" to end VAWG. This lens comprises three frames: the ecology model, the intersectional approach and a spectrum designed to help identify the range of different forms of VAWG in a given context. The third is the overarching argument that activists on the ground working for and with survivors are fundamental to achieving the goal of ending VAWG. And fourth, the range and types of violence covered are also original, including harmful cultural practices from FGM to early child marriage, dowry and bride price-related harassment, intimate partner violence (IPV), other forms of domestic violence, stranger rape and work-based harassment.

In short, this volume is timely and much needed as it combines an innovative theoretical lens with original country context insights offering a critical narrative on "what works" to end violence against women and girls. Understanding the ecology of violence across the globe requires such a combination of approaches because political, economic, social and cultural contexts shape and sanction specific violent behaviours. Processes of normalisation function to lock women and girls into environments that are harmful, while concepts of honour and shame are so pervasive and dominant that access to justice (ATJ) mechanisms often fail to bring an end to centuries of violence. While the global- and country-level pictures look bleak, we are also at a moment of great optimism. The global movement to end VAWG is arguably stronger than it has ever been, with resources flowing into both research and programming. It is vital that this momentum is maintained, and as such this volume is intended to contribute to better understanding – and ultimately ending – VAWG. There is hope in achieving this goal because we are at a unique and important moment in the history of social movements against VAWG. At the forefront of this is the critical work of local women's organisations, but to succeed they must be supported by the more in-depth understanding of VAWG that this volume seeks to provide.

Review of common approaches

Programming to end VAWG falls into a number of broad categories: *behavioural change* programmes often focused on engaging men and challenging violence as part of a hegemonic masculinity; public awareness campaigns designed to break down social norms perpetrating violence; public health projects focused on drawing attention to the negative medical implications of particular forms of violence, such as FGM; and advocacy and ATJ programmes attempting to build the infrastructure necessary to end VAWG. *One-stop centres* (OSCs) are also now seen as offering an efficient and cost-effective approach to responding quickly to violence. These centres house medical and forensic facilities and legal and counselling support, as well as providing shelter and police protection. By getting in early, targeting younger generations provides some hope for reversing patterns of aggressive behaviour towards women and girls and challenging beliefs that such violence is normal and to be expected. These types of child- and youth-focused programming, particularly *school-based interventions*, endeavour to work alongside schools by integrating gender-healthy curricula into lessons. Finally, with the growth of social media, the creation of new social movements for change is also seen as carrying potential in terms of challenging normative views on violence and opening new spaces for reflection and discussion on VAWG.

Stepping Stones is an example of the *behavioural change approach*, and is designed to encourage groups of men to critically self-reflect on their use of aggression towards women. The programme usually consists of a number of sessions (around ten) and is intended to promote healthy and equal gender relationships. Gibbs, Jewkes, Willan and Washington (2018) present findings on the effectiveness of the Stepping Stones intervention following their research based on a cluster randomised control trial (RCT) in 34 informal settlements in South Africa's eThekwini Municipality. In the intervention group, a significant decline in IPV behaviour was observed when compared to the control group (from 50 per cent at baseline to 33 per cent at end line). Other related and recognised triggers also declined, including alcohol use. A less predictable change was that income generation also increased, helping to address poverty, which is another key trigger of IPV. The evaluation of this particular implementation of Stepping Stones shows the potential benefit of engaging men in this way. However, it is as yet unknown whether these changes in violent behaviour will hold and endure into the future. Life in poor communities is vulnerable to shocks that can cause tension and stress, leading to positive changes in patterns of behaviour being reversed.

Public health campaigns focus on communicating the problematic medical implications behind forms of violence. Chapter 7 discusses the health messaging that is being used to end FGM. Another example is HIV/AIDS, which has been a key focus of sustained international public health campaigning. In *The Role of Public Health in the Prevention of Violence*, the UK Faculty of Public Health (FPH) stated that:

> Violence is a major public health problem. We believe it has been given insufficient attention and priority in the arena of public health policy, partnerships and interventions. A public health approach to violence prevention involves, measuring health needs arising from violence, determining causes and solutions to problems, advocating effective interventions and mobilising partnerships to improve health and prevent or control the harmful effects of violence. (FPH, 2016, p. 3)

The statement also reported that there are 2.5 million violent incidents in England and Wales each year, resulting in 300,000 visits to hospital emergency departments and 35,000 emergency admissions, which together cost the NHS an estimated £2.9 billion a year. The overall cost to the UK economy of responding to violence ranges from £29.9 billion to £41 billion per year. But when violence occurs in conflict zones, the costs are even greater. The FPH reports that 1.3 million deaths occur each year due to violence, and in conflict zones deaths and injuries are accompanied by long-term consequences for health and adverse social and environmental consequences at the national level (FPH, 2016, p. 6). Public health campaigns seek to denormalise violence in all its forms while also publicising where survivors can go to seek medical support.

In recent years, one-stop centres (OSCs) have become increasingly popular as a way of responding holistically to the needs of survivors in one place. In particular, the humanitarian sector sees this model as effective in delivering cost-effective and high-quality services to survivors in post-conflict situations:

One-Stop Centres provide multi-sectoral case management for survivors, including health, welfare, counselling, and legal services in one location. They are linked as well to the police through referral pathways. These crisis centres are typically located in health facilities, including the emergency departments of hospitals, or as stand-alone facilities near a collaborating hospital. These centres can be staffed with specialists 24 hours or can maintain a core group of staff with specialists on call. Unlike SARTs and SARCs that focus on sexual violence, one-stop centers may focus their services on the issue of domestic violence, or they may address both domestic violence and sexual violence. (Ward, 2013, p. 224)

The OSC model originated in Malaysia and is now also used in countries across Asia and Africa. The advantages of it are that OSCs can quickly deliver counselling, legal and medical support to survivors in a safe space (for detailed discussion of the OSC model, see Askew & Keesbury, 2010; Clarke & Haque, 2002; Grisurapong, 2002; Kilonzo & Taegtmeyer, 2005; Kilonzo et al., 2009; Vaz, 2008). An OSC called ISANGE (meaning "feel welcome and safe") located in Kigali, Rwanda, has received much attention. ISANGE was founded through a partnership between the Rwandan National Police and Health Services and the UNFPA, UNICEF and UN Women. The centre offers a range of services in line with the practices of the model used elsewhere, including protection from further violence, crime investigation, medical and forensic testing, court referrals, and treatment for physical and psychological trauma. The national health department has also committed to providing offices in all government-run hospitals for women to be seen by the police in safe conditions. Given that the lack of forensics is often problematic in seeking a prosecution in rape cases, the government has also committed to collecting medical evidence within the crucial 72 hours post-incident.

School-based interventions are now seen as a way to address and potentially reverse the early normalisation of violence in the mindsets and behaviour of boys and girls. An example can be seen in the work of Right to Play, an organisation in Pakistan that uses sport as a way to combat peer violence and corporal punishment while promoting mental health and healthy relationships. One intervention of the programme in schools in Hyderabad in the Sindh Province recorded in the baseline evaluation that 85 per cent of girls and 94 per cent of boys had experienced peer violence (both perpetration and victimisation). As a result of the sports curriculum, significant improvements were measured in terms of reductions in these figures, but there were also improvements in other measures of well-being and in challenging other forms of violence, both at home and at school (for more information, see Jewkes, Karmaliani & Mcfarlane, 2018).

The Girl Generation is an example of an emergent social movement that is part of a growing trend towards maximising the potential of social media and on-the-ground campaigning in order to build energy, momentum and focus around a specific issue. The Girl Generation describes itself as follows:

> We are The Girl Generation, an Africa-led global collective of members and partners brought together by a shared vision that FGM can – and must – end in this generation.
>
> The Girl Generation is a platform for accelerating social change, bringing together hundreds and thousands of voices under one positive identity, which challenges the social norms that hold FGM in place.
>
> We achieve this by contributing to the growth of the Africa-led movement to end FGM, by strengthening social change communications, sharing inspirational stories of change, and leveraging resources.
>
> Through our collaborative efforts positive change is happening. Across the African continent and beyond, people

are coming together to abandon this form of violence against women and girls. (The Girl Generation, 2016)

Social movements, then, are designed to drive the creation of activist platforms from which pressure can be exerted on governments and donors in order to release the support and resources needed to bring about change. In Sudan, as discussed in Chapter 7, a national movement known as Saleema was launched as a way of promoting a concept of a "whole and uncut" girl as healthy and empowered. This approach often draws on advertising techniques looking to communicate key messages through any available media, including radio, T-shirts carrying slogans, posters and street plays, to name a few. Evidence suggests that these approaches are effective in opening up spaces for conversations that begin a process of denormalising harmful practices, such as FGM in the case of Saleema (for more information, see Johnson, Evans, Badri, Abdalla & Donahue, 2018).

Access to justice programming (ATJP) is implemented as a way of building or bolstering the necessary infrastructure in order to support survivors, but it also sends a clear message that violence will not be tolerated. As Chapter 8 illustrates, with a focus on South Sudan, justice systems often operate dualistically, with "traditional" forms of arbitration existing alongside policing, legal and court structures. Legislation is the cornerstone of ATJP because it creates the framework within which violent behaviours can be challenged and controlled. But the difficulty with bringing about meaningful change through such legislation is in ensuring that it is effectively implemented. Here, we see challenges across the globe in realising legislative justice; in many countries, the male-dominated elitist system seems to work against making progress towards a fair and gender-equitable approach to applying the law.

The importance of a gendered lens

The common types of interventions to end VAWG listed above have emerged alongside a set of theoretical approaches that seek to understand how power dynamics in relation to gender map out at the community level. Gender mainstreaming as an approach in development has been around since the 1980s, and was at its inception heralded as a way to understand and respond to social inequalities. While gender is now broadly considered to be a necessary part of the design of all development programmes and interventions, as well as monitoring and evaluating them, the extent to which it is truly "mainstreamed" is questionable (Mukhopadhyay, 2016). Whether gender is now mainstream or not, gendered violence persists. Gender relations, and how power weaves through them, undoubtedly underpin the legitimisation of VAWG. Accordingly, the adoption of a gendered perspective when attempting to end VAWG is critical.

Gender shapes the context in which VAWG flourishes, and – as already stated – this volume will be making the consistent argument that understanding this must be the starting point. I argue that we need to go back to the beginning and critically assess the limitations of how gender is currently being applied in development programming, and look to deploy new tools that can better link gender, power and violence across cases. Forthcoming research by Bradley and Byrne (2019) discusses this perspective in terms of a "gender lens," arguing that it is important to treat gender not simply as an additional component of development to be mainstreamed or tagged onto the design of projects. Instead, it should be a lens that stays in place at all times, and through which development programmes and projects are both designed and critiqued. The gender lens:

- captures contextual details on how gender and inclusion present themselves in different sites across a single country;

- understands how and why specific programming has been designed and implemented, and considers if it responds to the contextual challenges and barriers;
- supports greater understanding of what works to promote gender equality and social inclusivity; and
- reaches a realistic and achievable understanding of what gender-inclusive outcomes might look like in different contexts.

A gender-inclusive lens should drive data collection and analysis in a way that is more consistent and coherent, and should map these data to the key areas listed above, with a specific focus on how and where violence intersects with gendered issues (e.g. who has resources, freedom of movement across public and private spheres). The gender lens unpacks both the features that we would expect to see in a gender-equal inclusive society (i.e. agency and decision-making) and those that we would hope to see improved through effective programming (i.e. access and vulnerabilities).

At a basic level, gender influences the likelihood that the survival needs of a man, woman, boy or girl will be met. For example, do wives and husbands share food equally or do some family members systematically get less because more is given to others? Are boys given more than girls to eat because their gender value/status is higher? Understanding these types of power dynamics is critical if we are then to address issues of survival and security and identify levels and reasons for vulnerabilities. The gender lens offers a practical means of sensitising development actors to the multiple impacts that gender has on and for programming and achieving positive outcomes. It supports the analysis of disaggregated data, as well as facilitating responsive and adaptive programming, because through it, activities that work to improve gender and inclusivity can be better identified and a greater focus can be placed on them. The lens allows us to gather evidence feeds into generating realistic expectations regarding what can be achieved in relation to gender inclusivity by asking: What is feasible? What does success look like?

The gender-inclusive lens

Figure 1 The gender lens

The lens, as depicted in Figure 1, is shaped by four dimensions: access, agency, decision-making and vulnerability. By viewing various aspects of programme design, monitoring and evaluation through these, it is possible to ensure that gender becomes embedded within and is a fundamental part of project implementation. Below are top-level definitions of each dimension with some examples of the questions that they raise.

Access

This is defined in terms of participation in different activities and resource opportunities. Understanding the barriers that prevent men and women from accessing opportunities is critical if activities are to encourage equal gender participation, which is a core goal of gender mainstreaming approaches.

- Which groups are the most marginalised before, during and after interventions?
- What are the challenges and barriers to open and equal access to resources and opportunities?
- Do intervention activities involve and benefit all groups of men and women equally? If not, who is the activity targeted at, and why?
- If groups are excluded, is this problematic? Does it trigger a negative consequence?

- Is there scope to widening access? What are the barriers?
- What might be the implications of involving men and women equally (e.g. trigger a backlash if traditional domains are crossed)?

Agency

This is defined in terms of the ability, confidence and strength people have to vocalise how they feel about their situation, the injustices they face, and the barriers to a better life they experience, as well as their views regarding the relevancy of specific activities in addressing these issues.

- Are all groups of men and women able to voice their feelings, and are they heard within families and at the community level?
- What platforms, spaces or opportunities (if any) are available for men and women to express agency?
- Are all groups of men and women likely to speak up and act if they feel they are being marginalised (e.g. from resources allocation or if they suffer injustice)?
- How is it (or might it be) possible for interventions and activities to increase agency?

Decision-making

This is defined in terms of the level of influence men and women feel they are able to exercise over decisions at both household and community levels.

- What are the main processes for decision-making at the household and community levels?
- Are decisions gendered, and do only men or only women make decisions in specific domains?
- What opportunities exist for women to influence community structures?
- If women are given a place on community committees, what are their experiences, and are they able to exert real influence and affect change?

- At the household level, are women able to retain control over resources?
- Does decision-making power build resilience to violence and other injustices?

Vulnerability

This is defined in terms of the levels of violence to which men and women are exposed. It also refers to general levels of insecurity, including through lack of food or healthcare or insufficient access to education or economic resources.

- To what extent will an activity positively impact vulnerability, or is there a risk of unintended harm?
- What are the main vulnerabilities, and are they felt equally by different groups of men and women?
- Do interventions and activities aim to remove these vulnerabilities, and will the positive impact be felt equitably?
- Do livelihood schemes build resilience equally for men and women?
- Is it possible that an intervention will increase the vulnerability of a particular group of men or women (e.g. if income activities only focus on women, does this bring tension into the home)?

Viewing these four dimensions through a gender lens builds a picture of where and how women and girls may experience more or less intense exclusion, which in turn may render them vulnerable (or not) to violence. It enables an assessment of when and how particular activities and/or interventions may in fact be working towards building agency and resilience to forms of violence. As such, the lens can help to pinpoint particular ways in which resourcing and support may effectively reduce levels of violence. Chapters in this volume consider a number of different interventions and programmes; in particular, Chapters 4, 5 and 6 look at the intersections between women earning an income and their experiences of different forms of violence. The lens is helpful in understanding how income may increase agency and decision-making in some areas but might not necessarily reduce all vulnerabilities. In fact, in some cases, a backlash against women's increased agency and financial independence has been observed.

Women's economic empowerment

Specific programmes designed with a view to empowering women so that they may take greater control over all aspects of their lives have tended to favour particular entry points. Among these, improving or increasing women's economic engagement is a common approach. For example, women's economic activity is encouraged through employment or self-employment, which is sometimes supported by microfinance. Women's economic *engagement* refers to participation in activities that generate an income, but this does not necessarily equate to *empowerment*, which is a holistic concept denoting a process whereby an individual is able to access resources and build their own power and agency. This normally means increasing decision-making power, building self-efficacy and self-esteem, gaining control of assets, and generating positive outcomes. Economic engagement is not *ipso facto* empowering, not least because market forces often reproduce rather than decrease inequalities (Kabeer, 2012). The market discriminates in terms of wage rates, hiring practices and so forth, which – in terms of gender – results in a tendency for women to be offered only less-skilled (and therefore lower-paid) jobs (Anker, Korten & Malkas, 2003). In conflating economic engagement and empowerment, some common but highly problematic assumptions arise, including:

- women who earn incomes can necessarily maintain control over them;
- women have recourse to social and legal support if their earnings are taken away by others; and

- financial independence makes leaving abusive relationships viable (ignoring social and perhaps even legal contexts).

Economic engagement therefore becomes empowering when it contributes not only to economic income, but also to the enhancement of women's power and agency, and also the transformation of social norms (structure) that prevent the exercise of agency. Economic engagement (income generation) has a complex and often thorny relationship with VAWG. While positive impacts are well known (and perhaps at times overemphasised) (Peterman, Pereora, Bleck, Palermo & Yount, 2017), research that has been conducted tends to present contradictory findings (Vyas & Watts, 2009). As chapters in this volume reveal, women's experiences of violence often increase when they have jobs because they face sexual discrimination, intimidation and violence in the workplace, as well as in public spaces during their commute. For some women, the violence experienced at home may also increase due to male backlash, as discussed below. And as noted earlier, this is likely to be linked to differences in the sociocultural contexts of the various studies.

We know that negative masculinities structure workplace cultures in many contexts (e.g. see Gibbs, Jewkes & Sikweyiya, 2017; Jewkes & Morrell, 2017). These culturally defined gender concepts "are reinforced by organisational norms, the behaviour of managers and leaders, a lack of codes of conduct and workplaces dominated by men" (Taylor & Pereznieto, 2014, p. 13). Patterns of horizontal segregation (job roles/sectors in which women dominate) ensure that women are often confined to specific sectors with higher violence exposure (e.g. domestic work, assembly line manufacturing, teaching or nursing) The "world of work" also encompasses women's experiences on their way to and from work, and therefore incorporates the harassment that women in all countries face (albeit to varying degrees) in public spaces, including on public transport (Cruz & Klinger, 2011).

As Chapter 6 shows, women may choose to work at home as a way of avoiding some of the violence and problems associated with going out to work. However, even working at home brings certain risks and potential tensions. A consistent cross-cultural indicator for VAWG is the contravention of local gender norms (Jewkes, 2002) and the failure to maintain cultural expectations of masculinity/femininity. The transgression of traditional gender norms, which can include taking up employment or earning money, may actually lead to increased oppression at home, in part due to violent "backlash" that seeks to redress the power balance (Goetz & Sen Gupta, 1996).

Relative resource theory suggests an inverse relationship between men's economic resources and VAWG (Goode, 1971), and – even more importantly – an inverse relationship between spousal economic disparities and IPV. That is to say, the greater the difference between a husband and wife's material resources, the greater the chance of violence (Gartner & Macmillan, 1999; McCloskey, 1996). In India, for example, one study has found that "where wives are better employed than their husbands, physical violence is higher" (Panda & Agarwal, 2005, p. 834), and another highlights the "frustrations that men felt at their inability to fulfil the socially expected sole breadwinner role [and] the frustration felt by many men was magnified when they perceived women to be 'getting ahead' or doing well" (Donnelly, Goodall, Neville & Williams, 2014, p. 16). This cultural perspective may help to explain the vastly inconsistent findings of studies that have examined the relationship between women's economic engagement and VAWG in various locations (for an overview, see Vyas & Watts, 2009).

As Chapters 1 and 3 argue, gender norms intersect with other issues, including other social divisions such as class and caste, life histories, legal frameworks, religious institutions/ideology, local economic structures, and marriage patterns, creating varied experiences of violence within countries and cultures. This intersectional focus remains a consistent analytical consideration for my research in each country, and by applying the four dimensions of the gender lens, it is possible to identify, understand and monitor the impact of changes in context and to evaluate the interventions designed to empower women.

Structure of the volume

Chapter 1 explores the global realities of violence as a normalised part of women's lives. Associated with social norms are a series of mechanisms through which forms of violence become sanctioned and legitimised, and stigma in particular is used to ensure that people conform to a particular status quo, which usually operates to maintain the privilege and status of a few. I unpack particular theories of social norms and the associated concepts around mindset change by presenting a web approach depicting numerous interlocking strands. I argue that there is a need to maintain a relational approach to the study of violence in terms of how it maintains itself through a web of strands and is often hidden from view; it is accepted as part of what it is to be female. Power is a necessary driver for violence, and is therefore central to how gender relations reproduce and are preserved by either actual instances of violence or the threat of it. This chapter also explores the concept of "positive deviancy" as one route to challenging the normalisation of violence.

Chapter 2 outlines an approach to measuring attitudes specifically in relation to what are commonly termed "harmful cultural practices" (HCPs). The attitude continuum is presented as a useful, practical way of understanding the range of opinions existing within a community or group towards HCPs. Changing mindsets that support behaviours deemed harmful to women is now a global priority. For example, as mentioned above, SDG5 seeks to end all forms of violence against women, including HCPs. However, we know that the process of changing world views that endorse practices such as female genital mutilation (FGM) and dowry (which often triggers violence against wives) is far from straightforward. Additionally, demonstrating the success of interventions or changes over time on attitudes towards HCPs poses an even greater challenge. The chapter goes on to demonstrate the usefulness of the continuum in relation to a research case study on attitudes towards FGM in Hampshire, UK.

Chapter 3 explores and tackles the problematic territory of representing and retelling the narratives of violence of different women across the globe. In other words, the process of listening to and then reproducing the violence endured by other women is a challenge faced by researchers working to end such injustices. As an anthropologist, I must also face the critiques launched at my discipline, in particular the accusation of using a cultural relativist approach, which can potentially contribute to constructing essentialised and racialised images of women as victims. I will explore these critiques, arguing through the example of FGM campaigning that cultural relativism is a useful tool that can support the sensitive and accurate understanding of why and how abuse is normalised and continues.

Chapter 4 is the first of three chapters that look specifically at the links between violence and women's economic engagement. As noted earlier, economic empowerment is considered critical to ending violence, but the path to change is far from straightforward. This chapter documents and analyses the experiences of women working in Nepal's construction sector. Nepal's construction industry has grown significantly in recent years, which has in part been driven by the need for rapid reconstruction following the earthquake of 2015. Many men and women have been forced to migrate to Kathmandu in order to find work and housing after being displaced by the earthquake and/or the Maoist insurgency, and many men and women migrants have found employment in the informal construction sector. This chapter seeks to capture and explore the experiences of female construction workers in particular. I wanted to understand how they viewed earning an income, even in a physically harsh environment such as a building site. Does having an income make any difference to how they see themselves in relation to their husbands and other family members, and does increased income equate to increased decision-making power and resilience to violence?

What I found through qualitative interviews was that violence is endemic in women's daily lives and across spaces. The participants talked about constant and ongoing experiences of violence on the way to and from work, while at work, and also at home. But despite the constant presence of violence in their lives, they all stated how earning an income gave them a greater sense of self-confidence and self-esteem. However, translating this increased autonomy into action that leads to ending violence against them seemed far more complicated. Evidently, a number of dimensions need to come together in a holistic approach if violence in all forms is to end. One important element that emerged was membership to a local peer network and/or organisation within which violence could be talked about safely and where support could be gained. Building the capacity of such organisations and networks may represent a critical entry point in the movement to end all forms of violence against women.

Chapter 5 builds upon Chapter 4 by exploring the links between work and violence among middle-class and professional women in Nepal and Pakistan. Nepal and Pakistan represent very different contexts, which makes for an interesting and revealing comparison. The chapter captures and presents the experiences of women working across a number of employment sectors, including business and non-governmental organisation (NGO) sectors, as well as those who are self-employed as entrepreneurs. The importance of including a chapter that captures the experiences of women from seemingly more privileged and wealthier backgrounds is that a clearer intersectional view emerges through which violence is revealed as a barrier to the empowerment of all women, not only those at the lower end of the socio-economic scale. However, the impact is not equally distributed among all women because, as the gender lens brings into focus, particular vulnerabilities, including those relating to poverty, mean some women are at a greater risk than others.

Chapter 6 extends the intersectional lens to consider the lives of female home-based workers in Lahore, Pakistan. This chapter provides important insights gained through a number of qualitative interviews into the specific challenges and forms of violence that they, as a group, confront in their daily lives. This group must work out of economic necessity, but their lives are still policed by strict conservative gendered values which stipulate that income generation is the preserve of men. Navigating the difficult line of earning money for survival while not triggering hostility as a backlash is challenging, and it carries a heavy psychological burden, in addition to the abuse suffered as part of daily life. This chapter also highlights that home-based workers are a critical part of Pakistan's economic development, but they are largely invisible; existing in the informal sector without any legal protection makes responding to the vulnerabilities of women working in homes even harder.

Chapter 7 focuses in on the specific harmful cultural practice of female genital mutilation (FGM). In particular, the chapter reflects on how successful global campaigning has been in bringing prevalence down. In keeping with the volume's core argument, the chapter reviews and compares FGM in three country contexts: Sierra Leone, Sudan and India. This comparison helps to show that while there is some crossover in terms of why and how the practice occurs, there are also fundamental differences that need to be understood if interventions to end it are to be effectively positioned and implemented. The chapter then presents a review of evidence and what we know about prevalence rates, and looks at some of the most common interventions that have been designed to end it.

Chapter 8 considers one of the most talked about forms of VAWG globally: sexual violence during conflict. This issue has arguably risen to the surface following the celebrity publicity it has received. The chapter reviews what we know about why sexual violence occurs during conflict periods and which forms it takes. I argue here that while rape is indeed used as a weapon of war, it is still IPV that represents the most prevalent form of VAWG both during and post-conflict. Understanding the complexities of how VAWG materialises during conflict is obviously crucial if we are to correctly and effectively respond to it.

Chapter 9 argues that given the global evidence now in existence (not least that presented in this volume), greater sensitivity to VAWG as an embedded and normalised part of the lives of women and girls is now urgently required. The chapter will argue that in order to address VAWG, gender needs to be embedded into how development interventions are designed, implemented and monitored, because – as we see with regard to women's economic engagement – we cannot assume that interventions will magically build resilience to and reduce violence. In fact, if local context is not adequately considered, the reverse can happen. Applying a VAWG framework can act to mitigate against harm and ensure that a "do no harm" approach is taken, regardless of the sectoral focus of the development programme.

The *Conclusion* draws comparisons between the different contexts discussed in the volume and identifies the key lessons that can be gleaned from them. I review and critique the overly simplistic theories of change that often underpin development programmes and look to present one that is based upon the evidence presented here. In doing so, the conclusion returns to a recurring theme: the significance of vibrant women's organisations that operate at the local level and within civil society spaces. It is when such spaces exist and are able to support the work of local activism that we see the greatest impact in terms of supporting survivors back to well-being and a higher chance of justice being seen. In these spaces, normalisation of violence can be challenged effectively, and we have seen encouraging indications that they can also contribute to resilience being built among the most vulnerable.

1 | SOCIAL NORMS, POSITIVE DEVIANCY AND CULTURAL CAPITAL

Introduction

This chapter will focus on unpacking one of the main barriers to reversing trends in violence against women and girls (VAWG), namely social norms. As stated in the Introduction, violence in many forms has been accepted across contexts as a "normal" part of a woman's life and one she must accept as part and parcel of what it is to be female. The normalisation is so strong that women themselves also perpetrate the view that a woman must expect violence, especially if she does not perform well in her gendered role. The problem for activists trying to end VAWG is that even when the groundwork has been done and legislation is in place to criminalise perpetrators of violence and outlaw practices such as female genital mutilation (FGM), at an individual level people still hold the belief that violence is a necessary part of the lives of women and girls. This chapter will look at how social norms operate within a wider system of sanctions and disciplining through the concepts of honour and shame. This analysis will help us to unpack why specific forms of violence continue, providing a foundation from which to consider the discussions that follow in subsequent chapters.

Arguably, we know more now than ever before about why perpetrators abuse and how survivors respond, but these insights are largely focused on the individual and tend to draw on public health and psychology frameworks. Gendered violence in particular is largely characterised as an individual behavioural problem that can be treated by specific interventions. As a result, the ways in which behaviour is shaped by context and is indeed subject to constant change is often missed. Inroads have been made globally in achieving gender equality, as demonstrated by higher levels of female economic engagement and greater access to education for girls, and to higher levels, but these gains have not translated into the kind of reduced levels of violence we might expect. The drive to end violence is now focused on changing the cultural, religious, political, economic and social attitudes or norms believed to underpin violent behaviour. And as demonstrated in the Introduction, there is now an increased urgency to tackle violence, and we are perhaps at a critical moment with momentum and resources at a high.

Social norm change, positive deviancy and cultural capital in the context of VAWG

Before going further, I need to pose the question: What, then, is a social norm? According to Ball, Paluck, Poynton and Sieloff (2010), "A social norm is a perception of where a social group is or where the social group ought to be on some dimension of attitude or behaviour" (p. 9). Norms are linked to sanctions that are put in place at various levels and that operate to maintain a collective normative view or perception. As already noted, a critical focus for campaigns to end VAWG has been – and still is – the question: How are norms changed? According to Harper and Marcus (2014), it occurs when a new norm becomes more widely adopted than an old one. But understanding what is needed to trigger the rise of new norms is far from clear. For many working in the end VAWG space, understanding these triggers has become the most critical issue (e.g. see Heise, 2011). This is because many VAWG programmes are founded on the belief (or rather the *hope*) that if we understand the causes of violence better, we can then act to end it. This knowledge–attitudes–practice (KAP) strategy is focused very much on changing individual behaviours, but research has shown that this linear process of individual change simply does not materialise (e.g. see Westoff, 1988, p. 225).

Rates of VAWG remain stubbornly high. New forms of violence frequently emerge, such as in the form of a backlash against women achieving well in the workplace or assuming roles traditionally in the domain of men (see True, 2012). This backlash often operates in subtle ways, and some of these will be explored in detail and in the chapters to come that focus on women, work and violence in Nepal and Pakistan (see Chapters 4, 5 and 6). Knowledge alone is not sufficient; perpetrators of VAWG continue their violence even in contexts where there is a high level of acceptance that violence is wrong. FGM is a pertinent example; a family may commit publicly to stopping it but then go on to cut their daughters in private. I have seen in my research countless examples across multiple contexts of women who remain in violent situations despite having the knowledge and even attitude that violence is "wrong" and that it is not "normal" (see also Bank, Dutt, Horn, Michau & Zimmerman, 2015). Many examples of this normative view in relation to specific contexts will be given throughout this volume.

Another focal point of the end VAWG global movement is reversing patterns of normalisation around violence, and changes are measured in terms of shifts in social norms. Interventions and campaigns are assessed according to how and to what extent changes in normative views about VAWG have occurred. Clearly, though, this assessment is not straightforward. As I have already argued, individuals can – and do – change their views or can even hold multiple views at the same time. As such, evidencing that there have been clear and sustainable shifts in social norms is complex, and it could be argued that we do not really yet know how to generate this evidence robustly and at scale. For this reason, in Chapter 2, I present a continuum approach as one way of capturing shifts, even slight ones, in viewpoints over violence.

I agree with those scholars who have stated that understanding the link between social norms and violence is critical (e.g. see Heise, Ellsberg & Gottmoeller, 2002). However, I argue that caution must be applied when using some of the approaches found within social norm theory. Individual behaviours are identified and classed "normative" because they are observed by a significant number of people within a given context. The behaviours are then linked to cultural views around why they continue. For example, that a man hits his wife because he believes that all men do is a social norm, while believing that not to do so would bring his masculinity into question is a cultural view. Sanctions also operate to ensure that particular "accepted" behaviours can flourish without conflict or contradiction. For example, violence exists because women do not want to report it, as doing so would bring shame to their family. Instead, women accept the abuse as normative rather than risk shaming those with whom they live closely and on whom they are often dependent. Mackie's (1996) analysis of the role of sanctioning to preserve FGM and footbinding showed the importance of moving beyond a focus on individual behaviours in order to consider the interdependence of decision-making processes. He argues for a greater focus on the powerful role of social sanctions and moral judgements that operate to maintain a collective, dominant view that suppresses deviancy at an individual level.

I would go further. Even this is insufficient because it fails to appreciate the complex ways in which power operates at multiple levels. Connell (1995) was critical of sex role theory, claiming that it did not adequately capture power that is exerted by those in authority in order to maintain a structure in which they benefit. Codes of behaviour and conformity are presented as morals in order to ensure compliance. To deviate or challenge such codes will bring sanctioning that few are willing to risk. This lack of attention to power is evident in approaches to social norm or mindset change, which bypass issues of authority. Yet structures of authority exist to maintain a system in which an elite minority benefit often at the expense of many. In other words, I am arguing that attention has to also be focused on the way that power layers itself through each dimension of life. Individuals will only be successful in bringing about change if they can work to counter the power that suppresses them through the legitimisation of violence. This often means that actors need to work together and at various levels, as depicted by the ethnographic web model illustrated in Figure 2.

Attempts to reverse norms take two main approaches: first, the creation and use of social movements to drive a different discourse and transformation; and second, the promotion of role models. These can range from celebrities to community and/or religious leaders, who – through their adoption and promotion of new norms – are thought able to bring about influence across their community. These two approaches are presented in a highly optimistic light. For example, UNICEF, in its report on social norms (Mackie, Moneti, Shakaya & Denny, 2015), stated that when programmes are holistic and community-based, enshrining human rights, then transformation of social norms is likely to occur. This again implies a rather linear set of processes that will magically generate the change desired. But the more likely reality is that embedded power relations will maintain ways of thinking through a complex system of violently imposed sanctions and stigma that adapts to political and economic change. Attention needs to also focus on the influence of the political and economic context because even when new ideologies emerge that support an end to localised violence, transformation is often slow or non-existent. Violence will only end when commitment is secured at all levels, from the global to the national and local.

An excessive focus on social norms/mindsets is unable to come to grips with what sustains or can end violence because such approaches cannot unpack the dynamic interaction of social relationships, power, institutions, and the environmental dimensions that shape perceptions, attitudes and behaviours. We know that violence exists both in a structural institutional sense, through the exclusion of women from many domains and positions, and in a physical sense, through various acts of abuse across public and private spaces (see the data presented in the Introduction). As such, mapping the various locations and levels of violence is important, but to go beyond this I suggest a combination of approaches and models. For example, Bourdieu's (1977) concept of *habitus* pushes us to focus on the dynamics of the different spheres and types of relationships that sustain violence (see Bradley, Martin & Parliwala, forthcoming). *Habitus* conceptualises social life as a constantly changing series of relationships held together by structures that are imposed by norms, power and authority. *Habitus* can be both an organising tool and a theoretical lens through which to understand the social realities for different groups of women and to capture how change manifests and impacts. Understanding the complexity of how different forms of violence feed from each other and link to symbolic, structural and behavioural dimensions is critical if violence is to be replaced with gender equality. In drawing on the idea of *habitus*, however, I recognise the need to exercise analytical caution to move beyond linear or circular assumptions. Contradictions can be seen at all levels, including individual viewpoints and ideologies – both are constantly in flux. For example, governments will shift commitment on human rights depending on economic priorities and political will. An individual woman may challenge violence in the workplace but accept her husband beating her at home. Appreciating how and where individual agency emerges in a sustained form and feeds into collective action for change is critical.

In this chapter, and indeed throughout this volume, I present a collection of examples from around the world to argue that the links between violence, gender inequalities and social transformation

SOCIAL NORMS, POSITIVE DEVIANCY, CULTURAL CAPITAL | 31

cannot be seen as a series of linear steps or stages. There are many theories of change that focus on ending violence against women, and many of these link financial independence to empowerment (e.g. see Taylor, Bell, Jacobson & Pereznieto, 2015). But it has been demonstrated that simply opening up women's access to income-generating opportunities does not magically lead to a reduction in violence. The reductive framework of social norms or mindset change models overlook the web-like nature of our lives, in which layers of different strands intersect and then realign to constantly shape and reshape the contexts of lives. Rather than a linear theory, we need to step into a web to both understand why violence occurs and to work through effective entry points for change.

Figure 2 depicts a web of spheres and dimensions, all of which weave and combine in multiple ways. Violence is reflected at each intersection and in each space. Appreciating this web of complexity helps us to understand why violence still flourishes. In this volume, and in this chapter in particular, I draw attention to the significance of social and cultural capital. This is because

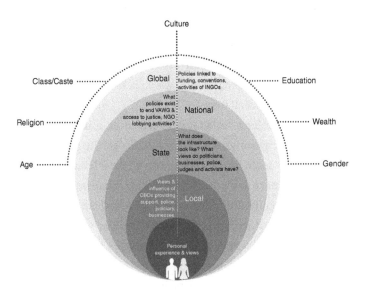

Figure 2 The ethnographic web model

while these forms of capital exist in all contexts to some extent, in my work I have encountered constant examples of peer networks, women's networks and groups of local advocates working together to build resilience to violence. There is evidence of defiant collective agency being produced and/or transformed through these networks and the discourses within them.

Violence plays out in multiple ways and in almost all the spaces that women occupy – be it at home, on the way to and from work or school, while at work or school, or in other community spaces. The only spaces that seem to be free from risk are female-only peer networks or the safe confines of dedicated women's organisations. In highlighting this collective agency, I recognise once again that even when these possibilities to engender change are present, they cannot be taken as given, even when mobilised. However, a range of scholars (e.g. Appadurai, 2013) have argued that "development" policies and programmes have tended to miss the opportunity represented by social and cultural capital. As a resource, this type of capital is often undervalued or overlooked entirely by stakeholders, and ironically it is often free. In short, I believe that approaching an end to VAWG through a lens that combines *habitus*, a web approach, and the concept of social and cultural capital will make a significant contribution to achieving SDG5, which is committed to gender equality and ending all forms of VAWG.

When researching VAWG, we need to be wary of projecting passive representations of agency, especially of women's agency. The women I have spoken with all show levels of agency in trying to make their lives better with whatever resources they have available. But despite this agency, there remains for many women a degree of acceptance of violence as an integral part of their social world. Applying Bourdieu's (1977) theory, we start to see certain gendered behaviours and perceptions as symbolic violence because of how they ultimately render women as inferior and vulnerable. Returning to Connell's

(1995) argument regarding the need to appreciate how power operates, power relations are often hard to see and violence may not manifest itself in clear acts that can be singled out as abuse. Relating the experiences to *habitus* makes it possible to understand the intersections of the symbolic and physical realities of how violence plays out, regardless of how and when agency is exercised. In other words, the symbolic and physical realities become embedded in the *habitus* of individuals, leading them to accept violence as an integral part of society, and potentially perpetuate it further.

Gendered violence may not necessarily be related to specific norms, but, as the web suggests, multiple factors weave toxically together. In the contexts I have studied, certain gendered constructs dominate. For example, the notion that men should be the main breadwinners, meaning that women can only work in lower paid roles that require less skills, and thereby cannot challenge the breadwinning status of husbands, is pervasive. That women who travel in public without husbands are considered shameful and likely to cheat, and are therefore asking for harassment, is a widely held belief. And that women should expect to be beaten if they fail to perform their household chores correctly, regardless of whether they also work, is often taken for granted. We can continue to draw out the norms that clearly do need to change if transformation is to occur, but understanding how and why these expectations are maintained requires much closer consideration of context. Behaviours might be expressed at the individual level, but they are enforced and reinforced by wider spheres and structures and by the relationships that bind different spheres together (see Figure 2).

Not least in this is a wider prevalence of political and ideological structures that practise or subscribe to violence more generally, and gendered violence specifically, and within which shifts in gender or sociocultural relations are a threat to the status quo of the political economy. In Myanmar and Sudan, any challenge to the status quo will bring suspicion, and the risk of military brutality is still very real, propped up by the prevailing influence of extreme Buddhist nationalists in Myanmar and highly conservative Islamic values in Sudan. In India, women who are deemed too vocal in public can become targets for the Hindu right wing currently in power (see Bradley & Kirmani, 2015). VAWG is symbolised through manipulated discourses of all or any type (social, religious, cultural, political and economic) that offer both sanction and legitimation for abuse. The relationships between ideological, religious and political spheres and the household cannot be overlooked. Attempts to disrupt these relationships have moved the end VAWG sector into engaging men more systematically. As detailed in the Introduction, working with groups of men in specific locations is now popular with donors, and many interventions now follow the Stepping Stones behavioural change programme. However, the evidence that such programmes bring sustainable change is flimsy because, I argue, they do not necessarily manage to alter the domination of discourses that sanction patriarchy and endorse VAWG (see Gibbs et al., 2017). In other words, the web helps us recognise that even when individual views change, it may only be momentary if it is not supported by changes at other levels.

I firmly believe that the "underpinning" norms will shift only when women have resilience and a collective agency strong enough to respond to the backlash that change often brings. The strength of relationships within peer networks is critical to their success as a vehicle of resilience and support. While violence exists globally, the specific ecology in which VAWG flourishes will differ from place to place. Religious and cultural practices will play a stronger role in promoting violence in some parts of the world than in others, and the same will be true of political, economic and secular social ideologies. Applying *habitus* and notions of social and cultural capital helps both to consider how and where change might be possible and to ensure (from a programming perspective) that sufficient resilience exists to withstand the likely backlash. It also stresses the importance of relationships between people within and across levels of society. I argued at the start that the existence of so-called "positive deviants" is important in creating and maintaining networks and peer support. In the last few decades, positive deviance has emerged as a useful concept in understanding the nature of – and potential solutions to – complex social problems. The term "positive deviance" has emerged from the concept of deviance. For years, studies on deviance have predominantly focused on negative forms of deviance. Negative deviance is described as behaviours or conditions that do not conform to acceptable social norms, therefore eliciting negative evaluations from a social group (Heckert & Heckert, 2002; Paternoster & Tittle, 2000). In reverse, then, positive deviance emerges when an individual goes against normative attitudes and behaviours, rejecting them on the grounds that they are harmful, and examples of it can often be found in contexts of change. These individual leadership figures are not celebrities, and are usually not very visible outside of their immediate context. However, they should be seen as critical catalysts for social change and an invaluable resource in the struggle to end VAWG.

The remainder of this chapter considers these theories in relation to two distinct South Asian contexts: Nepal and India. In each case, I begin by presenting a summary of the political-economic landscape within which women are fighting violence. I then present data that reveal much more of a micro-picture of how women experience and navigate these unique circumstances. By applying the ethnographic web, I intend to draw out some of the complexities around how violence might be challenged in each of the contexts. Much of the analysis presented in this chapter will be picked up in greater detail later in this volume.

Women fighting violence in Nepal

In Nepal, I have spoken with women in a range of income positions, including the construction sector and the informal entertainment industry (see Bradley & Sahariah, 2019). Many women have migrated to the capital, Kathmandu, because of displacement due to the Maoist conflict and also the earthquake of 2015. In the construction sector, women work in the lowest-paid, least-skilled positions (e.g. carrying large baskets of cement) while their male peers occupy the higher-paid, more skilled positions of masons. A summary of research into the experiences of women working in Nepal's construction sites will be provided in Chapter 4. The research found that there is a high level of harassment at work, women fear violence when commuting to and from work, and violence at home – particularly from partners – is widespread. Social norms clearly shape and limit women's income-earning opportunities and sanction the use of male violence against women both at work and at home. Some women talked of how violence at the hands of their husbands was just what happened. However, most of the women interviewed also talked about how they worked together with their female peers to offer each other protection, travelling together to and from work to mitigate violence (for more details, see Chapter 4).

In the context of Nepal's growing informal entertainment sector, women shared horrific tales of past violence both at the hands of the Maoists but also perpetrated by husbands and other family members. It may seem ironic, but the women interviewed all said they would rather endure the ongoing violence at the hands of their clients, most of whom were policemen and politicians, rather than return to their violent husbands.

Murthy and Seshu (2013) noted that sex workers may have a sad story to tell, but they are not "frozen in sadness." They argue that several tenets of patriarchy are challenged within sex work, not least because women's decision-making power is significantly increased at home, giving them a sense of control and independence that would otherwise be denied. They point out that while there has been a large body of writing on sexuality, labour and trafficking, there is comparatively little on sex as work or the business of sex. They go on to stress that there is a greater need to understand sex work from the perspective of sex workers in order to gain deep insight into the empowering impact it may or may not bring. Bradley and Sahariah (2019) argue that unravelling these difficult questions can be helped by both listening to the experiences and stories of female entertainment workers directly and through the application of concepts of empowerment (see also Chapter 4). But does the income earned represent a resource that enables these women to leverage enough confidence to act in order to bring about other changes? To some extent, this question can be answered by the interviews summarised below. For example, as one woman interviewed shared, "Yes, I have autonomy and a freedom I have never experienced before. Whilst we still face violence it is not on the scale of past suffering" (Bradley & Sahariah, 2019, p. 34).

A further critical question remains as to what extent sex work itself should be seen as a form of violence against women. While there is a consensus that violence is inherent in sex work and that it commodifies a woman's body by bringing them to the marketplace to be exploited by men, there is, however, a greater need to look at the sex industry and its allied activities (e.g. dance bars, exotic dancing, escorts, cabin restaurants) from a broader social, economic and political perspective. This is necessary because as sex work is largely shaped by global and regional sociocultural contexts, but understanding of this is somewhat limited (Busza, 2004; O'Connell Davidson, 2006).

Ditmore (2014) (cited in Monto, 2014), while examining the lives of women engaged in the informal sex industry in Cambodia, states that they suffer varied and extreme violence (see also Farley, 2003; Jenkins, 2006). However, Ditmore stops short of calling the industry itself violent because the women engaged in the industry do not want it to be abolished. Rather, they demand better working conditions that are free from harassment, violence, and exploitation by pimps, businesses, police and other actors. Despite limited choices of alternate employment and despite their marginalisation and exclusion, many prostitutes interviewed by Ditmore work to uphold culturally valued social obligations, such as paying off debts and supporting their families (Monto, 2014). The sex industry, then, offers a lucrative means of earning an income that can in turn support families. The question then arises: If other lucrative earning options existed, would women still choose to work in the sex industry?

Recent efforts to address the harm associated with prostitution (Healy & O'Connor, 2006), as well as less recent feminist theory (Dworkin, 1993, 2004; MacKinnon, 1987, 1993), have gone so far as to define prostitution as violence against women. Such pronouncements obscure a more complex relationship between the sex industry and different forms of gendered violence (Weitzer, 2005). Monto (2014), who reviews four studies on Cambodia, asserts that the role of violence, the forms it takes, and its likelihood differ dramatically from context to context. He argues that defining prostitution as violence results in "a tautology in which the cause, the effect, and the definition of violence are all conflated" (p. 77). He asks:

> How often is violence or the fear of violence a motive for entering or participating in prostitution? Is violence in the sex industry related to violence against women more generally? If prostitution is violence, important questions such as these become irrelevant. (p. 78)

In the context of the women spoken with in Bradley and Sahariah (2019), the violence represented through their profession must be seen in its correct context – as relative to the extreme violence they have suffered in the past – which in most cases leads to their decision to work in entertainment. The position of women in Nepalese society has been traditionally weak because of dominant patriarchal systems. Harmful cultural practices such as child marriage and dowry, along with lack of education, tend to further disempower women and expose them to violence (Basu & Dutta, 2009; Chapkis, 2003). Also, years of internal conflict between Maoists and government forces have displaced thousands and driven internal migration, resulting in many women and girls landing in highly exploitative environments, including entering commercial sex work in order to meet their survival needs (YPP, 2010, cited in Harman, Kaufman, Menger & Shrestha, 2016). However, as the stories below attest, the exploitation of the industry leaves less of a traumatic imprint than the oppression and abuse of their past.

In the context of Nepal, Liechty (2005a) highlights how Kathmandu emerged as a hub for prostitution and male entertainment in the early 1990s. Globalisation resulted in the emergence of "restaurants of dance," potent symbols of a new modern culture. These new zones of entertainment became hotspots where bodies lose their caste-based moral meanings and become anonymous parts of a "free market" of commercial exchange. Thamel, which emerged as the central tourist district of Kathmandu, in that context allows women a certain sense of anonymity within the boundaries of a highly commercialised sphere (Liechty, 2005b, 2010; Marimoto, 2010, cited in Caviglia, 2017). Kabeer's model of empowerment raises the question of agency and resilience, and will be explored in chapters to come in the context of Nepal's informal entertainment sector. But here, it is worth considering the issue of empowerment, which in this context is difficult to unravel. For example, to what extent can empowerment be seen as having occurred through women in this industry gaining access to income?

Basnyat (2014, p. 1045) asks similar questions, and concludes that women in this sector are not agency-less, but rather negotiate within the marginal space in which they find themselves. I argue, in this chapter and those to come, that the room to bargain and express resilience must be supported by an enabling environment with strong peer ties that serves to bolster individual agency and drive collective action. In the research documented by Bradley and Sahariah (2019), being able to earn enough money to stand independently was described by some women as liberating. However, and once again, while this moment of realisation is of critical importance, it will not translate into sustained structural change unless individual women are backed by collective agency and organisational support that has the strength and leverage to push for change outwardly through the various spheres as depicted by the web model. This can be seen in the passage below:

> "We have each other, we work together to ensure we are safe." All the women interviewed stated that contact with a local women's organisation increased their confidence and helped them process the violence they had and continued to suffer. For example: "without organisations like Raksha Nepal I know I would have sunk into a deep depression and then what would have happened to my children?" (Bradley & Sahariah, 2019, p. 33)

Support in the informal entertainment sector is provided by a network of localised organisations mostly run by women who themselves once worked in the sector. These female leaders could be described as positive deviants; they have turned their backs on patriarchal convention and also campaign for safe and dignified lives for the women who have sought independence by working in the sector. The founder of one of the most successful organisations working in the sector is a good example of this notion of positive deviancy. I asked her to describe how and why she decided to dedicate her life to social change. She responded:

> I just decided that my life would be different. I refused to let myself struggle as my mother did. Then a cousin rang and said, "Why don't you come to the city [Kathmandu]; there are so many more opportunities here." So, I left, unmarried and alone, and came to the city. After experiencing daily abuse singing in dance bars, I decided again that this would not be my life, and nor should other women put up with such violence. So, I set up my own organisation and made it my life's duty to push for change and see women live secure and good lives.
>
> (interview conducted by author, January 2017)

In terms of changing the structures of the *habitus* in which women live, these figures are critical but cannot operate in isolation. Identifying these empowered figures and building their capital to reach out and support the resilience of others is critical in the fight to end violence against women. So too is the need to place their experience within a web of interlocking strands, including the political economy context. This enables gaps in the necessary enabling environment to emerge and to be plugged, hopefully by the kind of linked consensus outlined in the Introduction that sees national governments working with international actors and local organisations.

Women fighting violence in rural Rajasthan, India

In the context of my second example, rural Rajasthan in India, the day-to-day lives of women in the villages of the Thar Desert is unsurprisingly very different to the lives of women in Nepal's construction and entertainment sectors. However, the common theme in all of their lives is the experience of constant daily violence. A second common theme I will unpack in this section is the way in which women form organic peer networks to reach out to those who share similar experiences and as a way of processing the trauma violence. The example of women in rural Rajasthan also highlights the extent to which women will draw on whatever resources they have available in order to build resilience and determination to find a way through. The example that follows illustrates this in relation to religious ritual, specifically the Hindu daily practice of puja.

I offer now a summary of my experiences in the early 2000s while living with a number of women in an area of the Thar Desert about three hours from Jaipur. Each day, a number of the women I lived closely with performed a ritual as part of their daily puja. The ritual was something they had constructed between them, and it brought them together even when they did not perform it as a group. The ritual was dedicated to Sita, who in Hinduism is presented as the ideal female role model and wife of Rama, a symbol of hegemonic masculinity (see Bradley, 2006). Rama and Sita are presented as images of what men and women and boys and girls should aspire to. Sita is often presented as passive and obedient, while Rama is presented as strong and commanding. Their story is told in the Hindu epic Ramayana. One of the parts most often retold focuses on the time when Sita was kidnapped by Ravana, an evil demon. She then had to be rescued by Hanuman, the monkey god. On her return, Rama doubted that she had been kidnapped, accusing her of an affair with Ravana. Sita then had to undergo various fire tests to prove her fidelity. At the time of my fieldwork, there were two schools of thought on Sita: on the one hand, those scriptural scholars who saw Sita as a less than perfect role model for young girls as she complied with patriarchy; and, on the other hand, scholars, such as Sutherland (1989), who highlighted, in Valamiki's version, how Sita subtly challenged Rama and subverted patriarchy by demonstrating how unjust it was. She endured the pain of the fire test as a way of showing how inhumane Rama was being. For the women I observed worshiping Sita, she was strong.

They felt linked to her because they also suffered from violence, and they asked her for strength and guidance to help them resolve their own situations.

The two women I spent most time with took different actions in response to the violence they experienced. Prem remained separated from her violent husband. Devi, after a while, moved back, but felt sure she had demonstrated to him that she could leave, and would again if he continued to hit her. I learnt an important lesson: agency is expressed in different forms; sometimes conformity is an act of defiance. When a woman or girl seems to behave subserviently, it is important to question if even that is in fact protest:

> Indian women take the image of Sita into their inner world and inject it with meanings they require to reflect their individual subjectivities. Through personal interpretations of Sita, women confront and voice their rejection of those devaluations of female sexuality and assert themselves as active creators of their own personal identities. (Bradley, 2006, p. 123)

Puja gave Devi and Prem the space within which to shape their own narratives based on experiences they knew they could not ignore, but needed to process. Despite having to endure intimate partner violence, neither Devi nor Prem lacked agency, and both had the self-determination to work through their situation. As is the case with the women in the informal entertainment sector in Nepal, to some degree, strength is gained by working together.

I left Rajasthan clear that I needed to challenge any image of rural women as passive victims, as this is not what I had found. This view is also emphasised by the anthropologists Gold and Raheja (1994), who recorded the folk songs and performances of groups of women, also in rural Rajasthan. They argued that through the collective process of performing – and indeed composing – songs, women were able to tell their stories:

Through the songs imagined conversations, these stressful situations and relationships are eased and opened up; grievances expressed, dominance defied, love declared contact established. At the same time no risks are taken even on the level of imagined discourse, for choral performance superimposed harmony over dissonance and the unemotional delivery inherent in the times and singing styles masks the emotional chords that may be struck by the words. Chorused conversations submerged discord between the sexes even while they suggest behavioural alternatives that may blatantly controvert dominant ideas about how women should act. (pp. 42–43)

In other words, women were able to think differently about their lives and imagine radical alternatives to the violent norm. This process of thinking and imaging should be seen as a form of resilience in which the status quo is not just accepted, but seen to be flawed and in need of change. Unlike the Nepalese context discussed earlier, aspects of religion and culture, as well as peer networks, represent vehicles for the expression of agency and resilience. It is important to understand that in applying the web model, the specific strands that are more or less relevant to a context can be identified.

Rates of violence against women in India remain very high. An International Center for Research on Women study of Indian women found that 52 per cent of those interviewed had experienced IPV, while an even greater number (60 per cent) of male respondents said they had inflicted violence on their partners (ICRW, 2014). This statistical reality illustrates once again the importance of understanding violence in terms of a series of relationships and processes that operate institutionally, socially and individually. Transformation must happen at each level if violence is to end, and should build upon resources already being used. In India, the rise of Hindu fundamentalism has not helped to reverse trends in violence. Bradley and Kirmani (2015) argue that the election of the right-wing Hindu Bharatiya Janata Party (BJP) has made the *Hindutva* ideology a much more visible presence of in everyday life. *Hindutva* literally means Hindu-ness and projection of Indian culture through Hindu values and belief, and it is a central part of the BJP's ideology. During their campaign, the BJP had been critical of the governing party, the Congress Party, for the secular approach it had adopted.

Hindutva can be understood in gender terms because it sets out strict roles and responsibilities for men and women that are determined by gender. Fulfilment of these duties are seen as an individual's dharma. For women, this means conforming to a domestic and reproductive role and assuming a subservient position in all life (see Bradley, 2011; McKean, 1991). Groups such as the Rashtriya Swayamsevak Sangh (RSS), Vishva Hindu Parishad (VHP) and Hindu Sena have been documented as using force to challenge behaviours they see as contrary to the values of *Hindutva*. This monitoring and disciplining of digressions seems to be largely focused on the behaviour of women. Bradley and Kirmani (2015) cite examples of incidences when women have been physically attacked by groups associated with these right-wing organisations. The attacks occurred because the attackers considered the women to be dressed "inappropriately" or saw them indulging in activities, such as drinking in bars, that are deemed un-Hindu through the conservative application of *Hindutva*. The impact of this level of religious fundamentalism can clearly be measured in gender terms. It highlights again the importance of taking account not just of the social norms surrounding VAWG, but also the wider political-economic context in which it occurs. For example, governments that endorse highly conservative gender codes are unlikely to be proactive in protecting women from the full spectrum of violence. In the case of India, while legislation exists that criminalises violence against women, the implementation of these laws has historically been weak (see Bradley, 2017).

This can also be seen in the context of Sudan. Chapter 7 gives an overview of programme approaches to ending harmful cultural practices, including FGM/C in Sudan, where DFID have funded a specific programme of interventions. But in this chapter, it is relevant to highlight that understanding why the high prevalence rate remains also needs to take into account – again – the political economy. Sudan also has a highly conservative and Islamic government, and – as previously stated – we know that in conservative environments, VAWG flourishes because it is seen as a mechanism to enforce a status quo that is heavily gendered. In addition, the Sudanese government under President Omar al-Bashir has gradually withdrawn government funding of the state health system. As a result, coupled with the international sanctions that have crippled the economy and the brain drain of highly qualified medical practitioners fleeing to take up better-paid jobs elsewhere, the system is on its knees (see Malik, 2014). Sudan has a long and proud history of training medical doctors and other health professionals, many of whom were committed to working within the state system. But now it is very difficult for a doctor or any medical professional to make a living from a state position, which has resulted in the growth of a private sector offering a range of medicalised procedures, including laser FGM. In terms of the language used to advertise the procedure, it is uncomfortably conflated with cosmetic plastic surgery. A smoother, more beautiful look is offered through the application of laser technology. State-trained midwives are also having to boost their poor salaries by performing FGM for families privately. The economic need is such that even the anti-FGM training specifically targeting midwives is not enough to prevent them from conducting the practice privately.

Conclusion

This chapter has shown that changing social norms surrounding violence have to take into account a much wider and more holistic set of factors, from culture and religion through to the specifics of the political economy. Norms are enforced and reinforced for a number of reasons, which needs to be understood through careful analysis and appreciation that a number of factors are likely working together. I have offered two examples of very different political, economic and cultural contexts in order to support the argument that understanding why and how violence in different forms flourishes requires a nuanced and relational approach. Violence continues because it is supported by multiple processes and institutional relationships that combine with deeply ingrained social and cultural norms regarding gender. When these are combined with specific political and economic ideologies, a heady mixture emerges, the consequences of which play out on and through women's bodies. To date, approaches to intervention and bringing about change, though well meaning, are still not nimble enough to weave between these layers and push open spaces to hear and see the challenge that change agents are experiencing and voicing on a daily basis. Existing resources that take various different forms, ranging from religious rituals to peer networks or local women's organisations, need now to be given greater recognition and support. Top-down campaigns capture global attention and funding, but will not transform social norms unless they are responsive to the work already going on and are able to harness the agency of women who battle and navigate violence on a daily basis.

2 | MEASURING ATTITUDES AROUND HARMFUL CULTURAL PRACTICES: THE CONTINUUM APPROACH

Introduction

In the previous chapter, I explored how social norms operate to embed certain values and beliefs that legitimise the use of violence against women and girls (VAWG). I also stated that the effectiveness of interventions designed to change, reverse and transform these norms also needs to be measured. In other words, evaluating interventions requires approaches that can capture even the slightest of changes in attitudes and behaviours with regard to the full spectrum of violence. The approach needs to be able to identify certain groups that may be more easily persuaded against violence and who are more ready to accept that violence is not normal and should be challenged. Understanding where people are in terms of their experiences of violence (either as perpetrator or survivor) and their views needs to run alongside activities that seek to end it.

In this chapter, I present a practical tool that can be used to measure social norm change. As addressed and discussed in the previous chapter, the established view among those working to end VAWG is that in order to see it end in all forms, entrenched attitudes towards violence and other related norms and values need to be transformed. Given the levels of development and aid funding now channelled into this issue, measuring and demonstrating impact is critical if resource levels are to be increased or even maintained. While VAWG is currently a global priority enshrined within SDG5, we cannot take for granted that this will always be the case. The application of approaches and tools to capture data that can reveal the nuanced and often small movements towards change has never been more important. I will present here a continuum that maps out the range of views and attitudes present in a given context and/or community in relation to specific forms of violence. As it is a continuum, it tracks changes at different levels, both individual and community, and marks any shifts in viewpoints. This can include views that endorse the use of violence moving towards ambivalent standpoints, and from ambivalence towards views that may be seen as deviant in that they explicitly reject harm towards women and girls.

In measuring shifts in attitudes, it has become clear that in some contexts, practices have become further embedded as the wider social-cultural-religious contexts have become more conservative. Actors in the global context in which development security policies are being framed seem unaware of the negative knock-on effect on the lives of women, and specifically the prevalence of harmful cultural practices (HCPs). Ironically, the development agenda is fast becoming reinvented as one of "human security," which, according to Nayyar (2012), must respond to and eradicate gender-based violence (GBV), including all HCPs. Those of us working to end VAWG likely care less about how and why resources are directed and flow towards ending VAWG, as long as the commitment to end it remains. What is clear, though, is that when taxpayers' money is being spent, the sustainability of this commitment is dependent upon providing evidence of impact.

This chapter presents and tests a continuum approach to measuring change, with a focus on FGM in the UK. It begins by introducing the concept of an "attitude continuum" as a way of measuring changes in attitudes, following which data on the prevalence of FGM in the UK are presented. The third section brings these two themes together, applying the continuum through a piece of research conducted in Hampshire in the UK, and the final section then digs deeper into the various viewpoints that emerge and reflects on what they tell us in terms of mindset change around FGM. The conclusion argues that the continuum is a useful tool for evaluating the effectiveness of interventions designed to end FGM.

Measuring change: introducing the continuum

As stated in the introduction, this chapter proposes the adoption of an approach that enables activists and policymakers to monitor shifts in attitudes surrounding HCPs. The approach will be summarised here and then tested out in the following two sections of this chapter in the context of FGM in the UK. However, it should be noted that this approach is designed to be used to measure shifts in relation to any form of VAWG, from intimate partner violence through to work-based harassment. I argue here that an attitude continuum is a valuable tool for capturing cross-generational and intergenerational differences in perceptions held by individuals. The continuum should be used alongside an intersectional analysis of qualitative data. In combination, the intersectional approach and the attitude continuum act as an effective way of drawing out patterns and nuances in how people retell their experiences of, for example, FGM. It allows for the influence of class, ethnicity and other social constructs to be considered, and for their role in shaping specific narratives around the practice to be identified. But most significantly, in terms of measuring the impact of eradication programmes, it challenges the assumption that people's views remain static throughout their lives. For example, as research in relation to dowry has shown, it is possible – and indeed seems to be rather common – for a woman to hold radically different views as a young married woman and later as an older mother-in-law (e.g. see Bradley & Pallikadavath, 2018). A frame is therefore needed to capture any shifts in attitudes; eradication programmes can only claim to have worked if people hold their "anti" views throughout their life cycle. As found in relation to dowry in India, young women are more likely to be opposed to harmful practices as their experiences of trauma are still very strong in their memory. However, as women get older, and particularly if they bear a son, their status changes and they acquire greater authority within the family and wider community. In line with this more assured positioning, many women become more conservative in their views and often switch to supporting practices that they once saw as problematic (Bradley & Pallikadavath, 2018).

The research presented in this chapter highlights this by using an attitude continuum in the analysis of women's responses to HCPs, specifically attitudes to FGM in the UK. At one end of the continuum are women who hold firm to the belief that the practice needs to be maintained because it is an expression of cultural identity and carries practical-economic functions. As they see it, this enables a smooth transition for women into marriage. At the other end are those women who fervently believe that these practices must be eradicated because they are harmful. The research found that many women position themselves at the midpoint: they know the practices to be harmful and abusive, but they also say that they feel unable to challenge them. From an activist standpoint, views and attitudes clearly need to shift towards the liberal end of the spectrum if HCPs are to disappear, and measuring this shift (if there has been one) is a vital part of the fight to influence such change.

Culture remains an important part of the analytical web helping to unpack "why" HCPs remain embedded in the lives of women

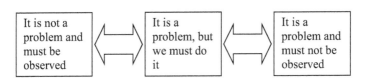

Figure 3 The attitude continuum on HCPs

even as other aspects of their lives change (e.g. as they access education and employment). However, explanations for "why" HCPs continue cannot be reduced to cultural accounts; instead, the frame used to analyse them must reflect a web of interlocking factors. Crenshaw (1989) coined the term "intersectionality" to describe the various social factors that produce the social inequalities women experience. In the critical analysis of HCPs, a gendered lens is the most useful perspective, but intersectionality does much more than just pinpoint the root of oppression – it explores the interrelationships of various dimensions, including gender, age, class, race and ethnicity, which come together in varied and complex ways to shape the different forms and degrees of discrimination to which people find themselves subjected. Culture and religion also need to be placed alongside these factors, which in turn shape a person's positioning, identity and experiences in relation to HCPs.

In the rest of this chapter, I will demonstrate how the continuum and the intersectional approach should be applied in the context of FGM in African diaspora communities in the UK. Before going further, let us review what we know of the prevalence of FGM in the UK.

Overview of FGM in the UK

FGM/C is practised among a variety of ethnic and religious communities in at least 28 countries in sub-Saharan and Northeast Africa, Asia and the Middle East, with national prevalence rates ranging between 0.6 and 98 per cent. The practice is also increasingly found among migrant populations originating from these areas in other countries. According to UNICEF (2013), an estimated 125 million girls and women aged over 9 years have undergone FGM/C and 3.3 million girls are at risk of undergoing the practice each year (Diop, Johansen, Laverack & Leye, 2013). Research conducted by The Girl Generation states the following:

Combined information from surveys in 29 countries where FGM is more commonly practised (and data are available) with information from the 2011 census about women who had migrated from those countries ... found that the highest prevalence rates in the population were in London boroughs, with the highest number being 4.7% of women in Southwark and 3.9% in Brent, compared to 0.5% in England and Wales as a whole.

Outside London, Manchester, Slough, Bristol, Leicester and Birmingham have high prevalence rates, ranging from 1.2 to 1.6%. Other authorities, including Milton Keynes, Cardiff, Coventry, Sheffield, Reading, Thurrock, Northampton and Oxford had rates of over 0.7%. For the most part, people born in countries where FGM is practised tend to be concentrated in urban areas, but there are likely to be affected women and girls living in every local authority area. (Dorkenoo & Macfarlane, 2015, p. 4)

Alison Macfarlane, Professor of Perinatal Health at City University London, whose work is quoted above, also estimated in her report that 132,000 women in the UK had undergone FGM. The following statement from her is published on the Trust for London website:

The figures in this report are estimates, based on numbers of women living in each area, who were born in countries where FGM is practised, and the prevalence of FGM in those countries. They suggest that women who have undergone FGM are living in virtually every part of England and Wales. The support they need may have to be organised differently in areas where only small numbers of women are affected, compared to areas with substantial populations of affected women. Support is needed for these women during pregnancy and childbirth and may also be needed for older women, because of long term complications of FGM. It is important not to stigmatise women who have undergone FGM, or assume that their daughters are all at risk, as many families have given up FGM on migration and attitudes have changed in some of their countries of origin. On the other hand, others may have not given up FGM and it is important to safeguard their daughters. The women concerned are very diverse. Although some have had little education and have limited knowledge of English, many are university graduates, or at least have completed secondary school. As a result, the estimates in this report should be used as signposts to guide professionals in planning services for affected women and in engaging with them. (Trust for London, n.d.)

It has taken some time in the UK for the extent of FGM to be understood and to be seen as a nationwide issue that requires a multi-agency approach. This chapter presents a contribution to the goal of reaching a greater, more in-depth understanding of how and why it goes on in the UK, as well as offering a way of measuring mindset change through the use of the continuum.

Applying the continuum: attitudes towards FGM in Portsmouth and Southampton, UK

The research summarised here was led by a leading regional women's organisation (for the full report, see Bodian, 2015).[1] Prior to this research, no data – qualitative or quantitative – on FGM/C in Hampshire existed. The project aimed to get an understanding of how different women and men from so-called "cutting communities" perceived FGM. Collecting data was seen as an essential first step in order to ascertain if FGM/C was perceived as a concern for women and their children. It was hoped that the report would support the development of an evidence base that might, in turn, be used to establish some general directions for the development of effective policy and the identification of potential training needs.

The methodology

The research adopted a qualitative methodology, and therefore did not attempt to produce quantitative estimates on prevalence rates. The approach was ethnographic, both in the way that research participants were located and also in the interview technique applied. Although a list of questions was constructed and used in order to be clear with participants about the nature and purpose of the conversation, the approach was open-ended. Answers to the questions were sought through a general gentle conversation on and about cultural identity and tradition. The question list also operated as the consent form, and each participant signed to indicate that they were happy to proceed. Fifty-five semi-structured interviews were conducted with adult women from the "at-risk" African communities in Portsmouth and Southampton, which includes those from the following countries: Guinea, Somalia, Tanzania, Zanzibar, Zambia, Ghana, Gambia, Senegal, Nigeria, Sudan, Eritrea, Mali, Togo, Liberia, Ivory Coast, Kenya and Uganda. The extent to which FGM/C is practised differs across these countries in terms of being more prevalent in some compared with others. A strict ethical and child protection protocol was in place, and while there was no indication during the research that any girl was at risk of being cut, it was made clear to the participants that should this have arisen, action would have been taken.

The attitude continuum was applied in order to ascertain if a significant number of informants hold to a positive view of FGM/C. The data were also analysed in order to draw out common attitudes towards the practice. The attitude continuum, as illustrated in Figure 3, depicts views ranging from those who strongly agree with the practice of FGM/C to those who strongly disagreed. The purpose, then, of using a continuum is to see how pervasive views that support the practice are, and to draw out overarching patterns in terms of the influence of age and culture on these perceptions.

Digging deeper into different viewpoints

Women opposed to FGM/C

Most of those interviewed expressed very directly that they view FGM/C as abuse. The strongest reason given was that women suffer long-term health complications as a result of the practice. Interestingly, as highlighted in the interview passage given below, women who support the practice pointed out that they did not suffer any complications, suggesting – unsurprisingly – that if a woman experiences significant and prolonged pain that she can connect to FGM/C, she is more likely to hold firm that she is against the practice.

Many commented that the hygiene of cutting has improved, but this did not deter those in this category from seeing it as abuse. There was also significant support for legislation as a way to send a clear message to communities that FGM/C is abuse.

Women with ambivalent views

Fear of FGM/C being carried out on daughters during a family holiday in their country of origin came up in a number of the transcripts. For example, one Kenyan woman, who is clear that she views the practice as mutilation and child abuse, stated:

> It could happen to my daughters if I go back with them. They won't ask my consent. My community will have more power – there is nothing I can do when I go to their territory.

A Gambian woman, who was also adamant that the practice is abuse, similarly stated:

> My daughter is safe in the UK; she will be snatched when I take her back home. I am powerless outside of the UK. I am concerned.

And one Guinean woman said:

> All women in my community are circumcised. I was 11 when it was done to me. I was taken on holiday back to Guinea and it was done. I don't think they should do it but they [my community] feel it should be done. I blame my mother and grandmother and culture for doing this to me. I don't think

it should be done anymore, but it is part of tradition. No one should go to jail for it – I've been raised to believe it is important.

Women supportive of FGM/C

Those interviewed whose views placed them in this category claimed that the practice is not a problem because it is an important and embedded part of their cultural identity. For example, a Gambian woman stated:

> I went through FGM when I was 5 years old back in Gambia; it was very traumatic. I can still recall it now. I do not blame my mother, but just accept it is part of my tradition. It is very painful and problematic for women, but if I have a daughter I would put her through it because it is part of our cultural identity.

A Guinean woman also stated:

> It is not problematic, but part of my culture. I have been cut myself and I am fine. I have given birth to three kids and did not have any complications. It has become problematic because people are talking about it – it is topical. It is a ritual that honours girls. I don't like the term "mutilation" – it is political. I support circumcision because it is part of a girl's initiation process. The government should leave us in peace and deal with priorities; they will never bring anyone to justice because they don't have a clue where and who operates it.

A second Guinean woman shared a similar view:

> Most people from my village who live in the UK have been circumcised. We were about 7 when we were cut, but now they tend to cut as young as 18 months. I didn't think that it was problematic until I watched a documentary about it. To be honest, it is not a bad practice. It is a problem now because people have no knowledge about African practices and are condemning it. I don't agree with that. People should not criticise our customs, because that is what makes us who we are. We are Africans, and out rites and practices should be respected.

Giving her opinion on why FGM happens, a Somali woman stated:

> It happens in Somalia to prepare women to become good wives.

The Guinean community were particularly conservative and supportive of the practice. As one woman put it:

> Every Guinean woman is basically cut, even girls born here. I don't think it is child abuse; it is an action to protect your child. You could be a victim if you are not circumcised. I don't want my daughters to go through it, but I worry.

Fear of social marginalisation as a motivating force for the practice was given in a number of the interviews. For example; a Gambian woman stated:

> The problem is that if girls don't go through it, they won't be perceived well by society.

Women in the "for" category and also some in the middle "ambivalent" category expressed the view that while it was wrong, they may have little choice. Many expressed fear that if circumcision was not performed, their girls would not be protected from the ills of the modern world. For example, one Guinean woman said:

> As a mother, you get worried about your daughter having sex at a young age and you want to circumcise her. If you do it, the organ will never be replaced, and you may not satisfy your husband. Women who are circumcised can be faithful; others who are not cannot handle themselves. Educate them so that they do not jeopardise their future. FGM could protect the girls. Back home, you can be in your twenties and not know a man. We all know FGM is not good, but we want to protect our kids.

A Somali woman also stated:

> Most families go back to Somalia to do it. Some private doctors are doing it in the UK. I strongly support it. It is good because it prevents diseases such as HIV. If circumcision is performed, sexual life will be hard for her; therefore, she won't catch [any] diseases. Those women who complain haven't had it done properly. However, I am against those who do it without medical training. The term "FGM" is misleading; this is not mutilation, but circumcision. I don't think it's child abuse. Abuse is negative, while circumcision is done because of love. Parents want their children to be part of Somali culture.

Another Somali woman said:

> I don't think it's problematic. Maybe people see their own culture that way. I have never had complications, so I don't share the health argument. It's an honour for the girl and her family. Circumcision is done out of love; it cannot be seen as cruel. I will never accept the word "mutilation"; that's an insult to everyone who practises circumcision. It's a decent practice, believe it or not.

The analysis of the research data indicated very clearly that the vast majority of African women from the affected countries interviewed for this study opposed the practice of FGM/C. Of those who did not, there were only 12.7 per cent who wholeheartedly supported it, while the other 27.3 per cent were ambivalent; they recognised its negative impact on girls and women, but also felt obliged to conform with community expectations and traditions.

As was recognised in the report, the research study was small and did not set out to establish any statistical data, so wider conclusions cannot be drawn concerning the whole of the African diaspora communities in Portsmouth and Southampton. However, the following key points did emerge within this study:

- The level of trauma associated with a woman's own experience of the practice was highly significant in shaping her attitude to FGM/C.
- The level of cultural conservatism and the particular community that the participant was from was highly significant in shaping attitudes.
- Women did not know where to find information about FGM, nor where to seek help, should they need it.
- Age made no significant difference to the views expressed.
- Many women and men would welcome policies and services to support them in eliminating the practice of FGM/C from their communities and families.

The interviews among women who are strongly against the practice reveal that the lasting trauma over the medical implications of the practice acts as a key trigger for long-term mindset change. Those women who hold to the cultural importance of FGM often claim not to have experienced lasting pain or do not associate difficulties they may have encountered with the practice.

Conclusion

This chapter has presented an example of how an attitude continuum can be used as an innovative and practical approach to measuring the weight of different viewpoints in relation to HCPs, applied in this instance to FGM in the UK. As stated in the Introduction, we have in recent years seen a renewed global push to see an end to all forms of VAWG, including FGM, child marriage and honour killings, to name a few. However, it is widely recognised that ending these harmful practices requires those that observe them to change their views. In an ever-pressurised donor environment, demonstrating value for money (VfM) is critical, and as such implementers of global and national programmes must demonstrate that their actions are generating results. When the intervention is about behavioural change, the approach to capturing positive evidence needs to be focused at the level of mindset change. As I have argued here, an attitude continuum can be used effectively to analyse a cross-section of viewpoints at the start, middle and end of an intervention. This approach will give all stakeholders (including community members) a good sense of whether views are shifting. It will also bring into view the complex dynamics that emerge as people shift between different stances as they get older or mix in different groupings, or become educated and employed, for example. It also helps to draw out the contradictions, those that hold parallel views that seem not to make sense. With this insight, we can move to a better understanding of the difficult positions many women, and particularly change agents, find themselves in. Actions can be targeted in order to support change agents and present women and girls with safe alternatives, rather than having to submit to practices that ultimately cause them harm.

3 | THE INTERSECTIONS OF GENDER, RELIGION, CULTURE, SEXUALITY AND VIOLENCE

Introduction

In this chapter, I explore the intersections between gender, religion, culture, sexuality and violence, and – as might be expected – I argue that they are far from straightforward. Unravelling the linkages is made yet more difficult due to the tricky theoretical terrain to which studying the religion and culture of different groups leads. The work of feminist anthropologists can be – and often is – accused of being reductionist, essentialist and Eurocentric either because research seems to tolerate harm in other places, which the researcher themselves might not tolerate, or because the research appears to isolate a single practice as being violent, thereby casting moral judgement over the entire culture and/or religion that is held responsible for it (e.g. see Mohanty, 1988; Narayan, 1997). The application of postcolonial critiques adds another fraught dimension to studies, often accusing anthropologists of generalising negative depictions of women and playing into the hands of Western power and ideologies that wish to denigrate entire cultures as justification for their own brutality. For example, images of burqa-clad women in Afghanistan have been projected globally in ways that can be used to support Western liberation narratives that legitimise the War on Terror (Ayotte & Husain, 2005; Povey, 2003).

Similarly, we see this in relation to the global movement to end female genital mutilation (FGM). Stories accompanied by harrowing images have been used to exert pressure on governments to ban it while also encouraging donors to pour money into interventions to support survivors and bring about an end (Bedri & Bradley, 2017). These movements bring feminist anthropologists into an uncomfortable dialogue with resurgent colonial narratives that place the white liberated woman in a binary against her "poor" developing other. However, as an anthropologist, feminist and activist, I argue that all forms of violence against women must be ended. And, as such, I have had to find a path through the obstacles that these ethical critiques create in order to forge an approach that is respectful and sensitive to difference while also supportive of grassroots change. In navigating this terrain, I have found the lens of cultural relativism a useful and important critical tool, coupled, of course, with a strong political-activist-ethical commitment to be responsive to harm when it is articulated. I argue here that the cultural relativist-ethnographic lens broadly enables two critical things to happen: first, in-depth contextual understanding of the "why" and "how" violence flourishes can emerge; and second, it supports the identification of local spaces and platforms that have been created and used to push for the rejection of violence.

As a feminist anthropologist, the links between gender, sexuality and violence are central themes in my research, but these cannot be separated from the wider ecology of violence in which they are located and that is shaped by many intersectional factors, such as religion, culture, political economy and history. In the context of one so-called "harmful practice," FGM, I explore in this chapter what the cultural relativist lens can bring and then apply it to a number of key strands (namely religion, culture and sexuality) in an attempt to draw out the web that holds the practice almost intact in the lives of so many women.

This chapter is structured as follows. First, I set out my stall, or at least offer more of an explanation as to why I believe cultural relativism needs to be reborn as a critical tool as it has much to offer different fields of activism. Second, I explore the links between religion and FGM, and how these links have been made by Islamic scholars, activists and the wider NGO community. The third section then digs into the different ways in which so-called "cut" women express and experience their sexuality. My insights, which I argue are deeply personal, are made possible because of the application of a relativist lens, and what this approach shows us as outsiders can be uncomfortable but also revealing. In the conclusion, I return to my central argument, which is that as anthropologists, we still have some way to go in arguing and demonstrating the value of our discipline in shaping and linking global movements with the grassroots change agents who will undoubtedly be the ones to bring about an end to violence.

Cultural relativism as a critical lens

As anthropologists, we are all well aware of the tortuous self-reflexive turn our discipline has taken (Clifford & Marcus, 1986). We have had to acknowledge the often complicit role the anthropological approach played in furthering colonial narratives, the way in which ethnographic data were used to prove the uncivilised nature of "others." The introduction of cultural relativism has enabled us to step over the line of outsider into a space in which we are not insiders, but at least are able to communicate respectfully and build understanding with groups of people who lead very different lives. We have also seen the emergence of approaches such as peer ethnography, which seeks to go even further in developing an insider perspective (Hawkins & Price, 2002). However, in stepping over, we have been accused of endorsing – even celebrating – traditions that from the outside seem harmful to women. I argue in this section that, on the contrary, the relativist lens supports an understanding of difference which entails drawing out the complexities of why and how practices such as FGM continue. This lens must take into account the way in which "harmful" issues rise to the surface because the global political conditions demand that they do – for example, the way in which the veil of Muslim women has been used as the symbol of their oppression at the hands of Islam, and how, in turn, such images have been used to justify war and invasions (Cloud, 2004; Mahood, 2009). Similarly, female circumcision, or – as the activist community terms it – mutilation or FGM, is another example of a practice used to brand others problematic and in need of Westernised change. FGM is now the focus of global campaigns that have been launched to see it end. But in both of these examples, the bodies of women become objectified and manipulated through Western liberal narratives that seek to brand "other" cultures as immoral.

Abu-Lughod (2013), focusing on the burqa of Afghan women, talks about how it has become a global symbolic focus in the War on Terror, in part justifying the need to evade Afghanistan. She states:

> The issue the burqa raises is how to deal with cultural "others," how are we to deal with difference without accepting the passivity implied by the cultural relativism for which anthropologists are justly famous – a relativism that says it's their culture and it's not my business to judge or interfere, only to try to understand. Cultural relativism is certainly an improvement on ethnocentrism and the racism, cultural imperialism, and imperiousness that underlie it; the problem is that it is too late not to interfere. The forms of lives we find around the world are already products of long histories of interactions. (p. 11)

What I argue here is that cultural relativism needs to be reframed as a tool and used – in the context for international development – to draw out deep understandings of why a particular practice that seems harmful continues. Research on violence against women, by its very nature, should be applied and feed into efforts to end harm. Cultural relativism is the first stage in a much longer process that, on the one hand, respects difference and, on the other, supports processes of social and political change that are committed to end violence and abuse. In making this argument, I hope that it settles the fears expressed by Abu-Lughod (2013), for example, when she states:

> Implying that we should resign ourselves to being cultural relativists who respect whatever goes on elsewhere as "just their culture," I have already discussed the dangers of "cultural" explanations; "their" cultures are just as much part of history and an interconnected world as ours are. What I am advocating is the hard work involved in recognizing and respecting differences – precisely as products of different histories, as expressions of different circumstances, and as manifestations of differently structured desires. We may want justice for women, but can we accept that there might be different ideas about justice and that different women might want, or choose, different futures from what we envision as best. (p. 47)

These arguments are also made by Ong (1988) and support my argument that anthropological research cannot stop at cultural relativism, but instead must be accompanied by a responsive and longitudinal commitment to different approaches to action, change and indeed visions of what it is to be an empowered woman. A further statement by Abu-Lughod (2013) articulates the political position that feminist anthropologists today should be ethically occupying:

> Could we not leave veils and vocations of saving others behind and instead train our sights on ways to make the world a more just place? The reason respect for difference should not be confused with cultural relativism is that it does not preclude asking how we, living in this privileged and powerful

part of the world, might examine our own responsibilities for the situations in which others in distant places have found themselves. (p. 67)

I agree, of course, with Abu-Lughod. A cultural relativism that stops at the point of depicting difference is morally questionable, especially when the reality being "uncovered" can easily fuel ethnocentric and racial justifications for yet more violence. I argue here that cultural relativism is an important entry point for opening up understandings of the links between many dimensions and how they are shaped by political economy and historical legacies. Later in the chapter, I move on to present insights from ethnographies that give us a depth of knowledge into links between religion, gender, sexuality and culture, and I argue that by adding a critical layer to the relativist lens, accompanied by an ethical stance of respect for others, it is possible to support grassroots activism that navigates history and contemporary political tensions in ways that outsiders simply cannot.

It is important, given the presence of well-funded global programmes such as the end FGM movement, that feminist anthropology be clear that it has moved into a more ethically sound place in which relativism supports change that has been initiated from within. The recent controversy the anthropologist Bettina Shell-Duncan has found herself in nicely illustrates how little those outside of anthropology understand about the ethnographic lens, what it is, and the value it can bring, not just in terms of insights, but also in directing practical action. Shell-Duncan has spent many years conducting ethnographic research that documents Rendille women's experiences of FGM in Kenya. She is also a lead academic working on UK Aid's research programme on FGM, led by the Population Council in Kenya. In an interview with *The Atlantic*, she talked about the understanding she had gained through her research into the "why" and "how" women can seemingly (from the outside at least) submit to such a brutal practice. For example, in that interview, she argues:

The sort of feminist argument about this is that it's about the control of women but also of their sexuality and sexual pleasure. But when you talk to people on the ground, you also hear people talking about the idea that it's women's business. As in, it's for women to decide this. If we look at the data across Africa, the support for the practice is stronger among women than among men.

So, the patriarchy argument is just not a simple one. Female circumcision is part of demarcating insider and outsider status. Are you part of this group of elder women who have power in their society?

One of the things that is important to understand about it is that people see the costs and benefits. It is certainly a cost, but the benefits are immediate. For a Rendille woman, are you going to be able to give legitimate birth? Or elsewhere, are you going to be a proper Muslim? Are you going to have your sexual desire attenuated and be a virgin until marriage? These are huge considerations, and so when you tip the balance and think about that, the benefits outweigh the costs. (cited in Bodenner, 2015)

These insightful comments were possible because momentarily, while living with and observing Renville women, Shell-Duncan adopted a relativist perspective. Without it, she would not have come close to this level of insight, yet her critics misinterpreted the purpose of her lens and accused her of being an apologist for the practice. One such critic lists a number of Shell-Duncan's statements, claiming:

Here's some of the statements that Shell-Duncan makes in celebrating, or at least excusing, FGM:

The bride came out and joined the dancing. I almost died. I thought she must be on codeine, but she wasn't. She was joyful. I didn't understand the joy about this.

But later I remembered that when I gave birth to my first son, I had a very difficult delivery. After my son was born, everyone in the delivery room popped a bottle of champagne. I felt like I had been hit by a Mack truck and they were toasting champagne. But it was a good pain, and that's what this was. This girl had become a woman.

When I went back two years later, the girl came to me and gave the [pain] pills back. She said, "You don't understand, this is not our way. And if I didn't do that, I wouldn't be a woman now."

I understood why. And I respected her. (Khazan, 2015)

As an anthropologist reading this passage, I feel deeply touched by the closeness she was able to achieve with the women she spent time with. Such relationships come out of trust and respect for difference. If Shell-Duncan marched into the women's village demanding that they all see circumcision as mutilation, she would have failed to understand why the practice remains so prevalent and appreciate that while patriarchy and misogyny may well be driving it, women are actors in its continuation and are certainly not passive. Understanding this is important if millions are not to be wasted on ill-thought-through interventions that may assume that women are victims and men are perpetrators, and that all women see FGM as mutilation. Evidently, as I come on to highlight through work on FGM and sexuality, this is not the case. The reason for the slow progress of end campaigns is precisely because FGM is not experienced as abusive by all those who have endured it. Shifting attitudes around FGM requires supporters to no longer see it as a fundamental part of what it is to be a woman, but to instead adopt the view that it represents abuse.

Some who read the work of Shell-Duncan see her narrative very differently from me. For example, one critic, American biologist Jerry Coyne, summarised his view on his blog *Why Evolution Is True* as follows:

> There's more, but you get the ambivalence. We have a conflicted feminist who sees that FGM is harmful, and is trying to stop it, but at the same time is trying to justify the practice ... I applaud Shell-Duncan's initiative to reduce FGM, but one can see her being drawn into a form of cultural relativism that has the danger of diluting her opprobrium of FGM. At least she's doing something about it. (Coyne, 2016)

This is clearly not what Shell-Duncan is doing, but the passage highlights how little is understood about the cultural relativist lens today and the important role it plays in drawing out more complex and nuanced understandings. The lens helps us see the "why" in more complex ways than can be sought using any other social science methodology. Cultural relativism, when applied and used as a tool to draw out understanding, rather than as a position, supports the visibility of the unexpected. This, when it comes to such an extremely violent practice as FGM, can be difficult to hear, to see and to acknowledge.

However, the critiques made of particular colonial and essentialist representations of women's lives and bodies are deeply problematic and can block the goal of gaining deep experiential understanding. To return to the critique made by Abu-Lughod (2013) in relation to the global manipulation of the image of "the veil," she argues:

> Two points emerge from this fairly basic discussion of the meanings of veiling in the contemporary Muslim world. First, we need to work against the reductive interpretation of veiling as the quintessential sign of women's unfreedom. What does freedom mean if we accept the fundamental premise that humans are social beings, always raised in certain social and historical contexts and belonging to particular communities that shape their desires and understandings of the world? Is it not a gross violation of women's own understandings of what they are doing to simply denounce the burqa as a medieval imposition?

Second, we must take care not to reduce the diverse situations and attitudes of millions of Muslim women to a single item of clothing. Perhaps it is time to give up the Western obsession with the veil and focus on some serious issues with which feminists and others should indeed be concerned. (p. 78)

The ethnographic lens is critical because it supports a multi-stranded analysis (see Figure 2 in Chapter 1) that then renders such oversimplification impossible. It highlights the links between practices, values, beliefs and behaviours, and understands the significance of joy and pain in reinforcing identify and agency. It also reveals a hard reality for activists, which is that many women see practices such as FGM not as brutal abuse, but as an integral part of their sexuality and identity and as a vehicle for self-identification that some describe in terms of empowerment. In studying violence, applying the ethnographic web model helps to guard against an essentialist or reductionist analysis. It also helps to generate answers to key questions that underpin the success of the global movement to end violence, not least: Why, after so many decades of campaigning, does violence still flourish? The very complexity of the web means that I cannot analyse each and every strand of it here. Instead, I have chosen to focus on religion and sexuality in the context of FGM, partly because they are among the most talked about and also the most sensitive in relation to this particular practice.

The links between religion and FGM

In my work, I argue that religion does play a role in perpetrating HCPs, but it is not straightforward (Bradley, 2010a). Religion, or rather religious ideas, are of course far from homogenous, but they are gendered and carry a certain authority that can feed into the construction of a social ecology that renders women inferior to men, and ultimately vulnerable to different forms of violence. The extent to which religious beliefs and values support and promote forms of violence against women is unclear. If we take FGM as an example, while there is relatively little literature exploring the links between Islam and FGM, what does exist clearly highlights that the lines between religion, culture and practices such as FGM are blurred and need considerable unpacking. The lack of clarity also leaves the relationship open to multiple interpretations, some of which may be manipulated in order to gain political and/or social capital.

In research conducted by Van Raemdonck (2016), the controversy over the relationship emerges because of one Hadith in which Muhammad is recorded as saying to a woman known to carry out the practice, "If you cut, do not overdo." Islamic discourses surrounding FGM are diverse – some recognise the religious dimension; others do not (unlike the transnational discourses, which tend to only refer to FGM as "cultural"). Of course, in somewhere such as Egypt, where FGM is observed by both Muslim and Christian communities, attempts to make strong correlations become increasingly difficult. UNICEF's 2013 report exploring the impact of the global FGM campaign reported that in Egypt, over half the population considers FGM to be a religious requirement (UNICEF, 2013). In Egypt, the origins of the practice can be traced back to recordings by the early Christian Church, who reported that its purpose was to curb sexual desire (Berkey, 1996).

The Koran (seen as the literal word of God) does not mention female circumcision. In the Hadith narratives of Mohamed's sayings, in fact, the Koran states that the body was created by God, and is therefore perfect and not to be altered. This has been used by some campaigners as evidence that FGM should be stopped:

> God does not create the organs haphazardly without a plan. It is not possible that He should have created the clitoris in a woman's body only in order that it be cut off at an early stage in life. (Abu-Sahlieh, 2001, p. 105, cited in Van Raemdonck, 2016, p. 34)

THE INTERSECTIONS OF GENDER, RELIGION, CULTURE | 73

But as previously noted, in the most famous Hadith, Muhammad is reported as saying to a woman who cut girls that if she did so, she should "cut a little and not over do it because it brings radiance to the face and it is more pleasant for the husband" (cited in Van Raemdonck, 2016). Links have also been made with other Hadiths that talk of the need for cleanliness rituals that are associated with both male and female circumcision. Regardless of whether we can provide evidence of scriptural links to FGM, the relative influence of religious leadership is another critical dimension when trying to understand why FGM persists.

In Sudan, for example, attempts by activists to see changes in legislation have made only limited inroads despite Sudan being the global focus for the UK Aid FGM programme. Sudan is, in effect, the pilot country, with various approaches being tried out in the hope that the "solution" to the problem of FGM can be found and then rolled out. The National Plan of Action on FGM (endorsed by the Ministry of Health in 2001 and led by the National Council for Child Welfare) and the chapter on FGM included in the Reproductive Health Strategy (published by the Federal Ministry of Health) are intended to support the work of advocacy groups. The Sudanese Network for Abolition of FGM (SUNAF) is a key actor in the national-led movement to end FGM, and at the federal level attempts have been made through a steering committee to coordinate other advocacy groups and stakeholders who are committed to end FGM. At the state level, there are councils and steering committees motivated to end FGM. At the community level, we see the work of grassroots organisations bringing women's groups together with religious leaders, midwives, community leaders, and youth and children's groups in order to push for behavioural change on this issue.

Media campaigns have also been used as a vehicle, utilising radio and broadcasting in different languages (UNFPA, 2011). Out of the National Action Plan emerged a clear strategy that was endorsed in 2008, feeding into the global push to end

FGM within a generation. As part of how the global push has been translated into the Free Sudan programme, the National Council on Child Welfare (NCCW), along with other key institutions and councils, drafted a Child Act Bill (2009), which included an article rendering FGM illegal on the grounds of health and social reasons. Unfortunately, Article 13 of the law, which prohibits all forms of FGM/C, was removed by the Council of Ministers from the Act following a fatwa of the Islamic Jurisprudence Council that called for a distinction between the various forms of FGM and for Type I, known as Sunna, not to be banned (Medani, 2010). Since Sudan follows a federal system, states are permitted to have their own legislation and formulate their own Child Acts. The first states to ratify the Child Act were South Kordofan in 2008 followed by Gadaref State in 2009. The process of ratifying the Act in both instances followed a series of activities coordinated by NGOs and other key actors. A workshop opened the dialogue and focused on presenting the statistics, and then went on to present the views of Sudanese religious scholars who felt FGM must be abandoned. These arguments were made on religious grounds, or rather by stating that FGM is not in fact a religious practice. Extensive roll-out of workshops then took place, with the aim of orienting NGOs, advocacy groups and ministry officials in order to prepare them for the drafting and implementation of the legislation. Reports on the process highlighted the importance of presenting prevalence data as a means of framing the problem that the new Act must address. Other states followed in drafting legislation, including Blue Nile, Kassala, River Nile and South Darfur.

The flip side to seeing religious leadership as a problem or obstacle to change can be seen in an influx of development programming that has attempted to engage them as agents of change. The theory lying behind these programmes is that local religious communities listen to their leadership and will follow the advice they give, making them powerful actors in bringing about social change. As Jones and Petersen (2011) state, "Religious leaders are perceived to be vessels of authority and are consequently being reduced to a means to achieve desired change that can be utilized by policy makers and development practitioners to 'do development better'" (p. 1291).

Research was conducted by Østebø and Østebø (2014) into such an approach in Ethiopia, where leaders (both Christian and Muslim) were engaged in a programme to end FGM. They argue that the instrumental use of religious leaders is informed by a unidimensional and static conceptualisation of power. These views, they claim, obscure the intrinsic complexity of power and power relations. A conceptualisation of power as relational and closely intersected with performance and confidence better reflects realities on the ground. These views resonate with those of Connell (1995) (as summarised in Chapter 1) in relation to the operation of power through gender relations. Interventions using religious leaders appear to be underpinned by assumptions of religious homogeneity within Islam that move us further from effective action to end FGM. Østebø and Østebø (2014) go on to argue that if religious leaders are to be true agents of change in such processes, they need to appear as more than instruments in the hands of national and global actors; they need to prove their independence and committed involvement.

A cultural relativist lens supports efforts to understand why such an approach simply will not work, not least by highlighting the multiple dimensions that shape social worlds. Turning now to sexuality, in recent years we have seen the publication of some very challenging ethnographies that counter the Western feminist view that FGM mutilates women's sexual organs to the point that pleasure is no longer possible.

The links between sexuality and FGM

Once again, Abu-Lughod's (2013) observations and highly critical and reflexive questions are a useful starting point:

First is the acceptance of the possibility of difference. Can we only free Afghan women to be like us or might we have to recognize that even after "liberation" from the Taliban, they might want different things than we would want for them? What do we do about that? Second, we need to be vigilant about the rhetoric of saving people because of what it implies about our attitudes. (p. 88)

Malmström (2016), in her ethnography of Egyptian women's experiences of FGM, shatters post-Freudian Western understandings of sexuality to which the clitoris is believed to be crucial to sexual lust and circumcised women are assumed to be frigid and mutilated. Malmström recorded that in Egypt, men are considered to have weaker libidos than women, and so circumcision modifies and equalises, which is thought to increase sexual pleasure for both men and women. Contrary to Western readings of the impact of FGM, her research records that sexual pleasure is thought to be an important and fundamental part of marriage:

> We let our girls become circumcised to keep them, if not, they will be highly sexed and more turned on than their husbands. But they will not be cold after marriage, before I did not feel sexual feelings very much, but after our marriage I really enjoy [she blushes]. After you marry the lust will come, from below and from the feelings you hold for your husband. The sexual desire comes from the inside of the 'room' and the husband will open it up ... A woman feels pleasure and she can feel that she is hot. But she has control because she has been circumcised. (p. 106)

What this reveals, according to Malmström, is that women feel empowered by their ability to control their libido. Norms around sexuality clearly exist, and part of them projects a strong sense of female agency. In other research conducted by Malmström and Van Raemdonck (2015), they analyse a saying heard numerous times during their fieldwork: "the clitoris is in the head!" Their work documents Egyptian women angrily accusing Western women of having a patronising and limiting understanding of sexuality. They felt their sexual pleasure was increased by the practice and challenged what they saw as the assumption that pleasure can only occur if your clitoris is intact.

Clearly, what this research reveals is that there are differing narratives around the sexuality of so-called "cut" women. It also makes apparent how muted these viewpoints are within the wider (and now global) end FGM movement. As in the work of Shell-Duncan, these experiences and viewpoints are very difficult for activists opposed to FGM, such as me, to hear. Yet hear and listen we must if we are to understand why women themselves often fight to continue with a practice that many see as brutal. Anthropology has a critical role in ensuring these voices are heard, no matter how challenging they may be. And anthropology also has an important role in critiquing the dominance of narratives that stifle the experiences of those most affected, in this case by FGM.

Challenging Western hegemony

In my own research, I have documented the views of women from so-called "cutting communities." Many of these women are very sure about what they believe is happening as a result of the growing anti-FGM movement: "When it comes to discussion surrounding FGM it's not about women of colour having autonomy over their own bodies but rather creating a space where white women can find self-actualisation through women of colour's struggles" (Bedri & Bradley, 2017, p. 33).

At the local level, spaces must be made for survivors and grassroots activists to emerge who will be capable of approaching community conversations around FGM using language that is informed by a closer cultural reading of the practice and why it persists, but without accepting the practice (see also Easton, Monkman & Miles, 2003). This is certainly the view of the women from so-called "cutting communities" who I spoke with after the Girl Summit 2014 held in London. For example:

> I have been on this campaign for many years to try to redirect people's attention away from the imagery of FGM that they are being caught up in, especially these past few years due to the international communities pouring millions of pounds into anti-FGM campaigns. The discourse is extremely racist, reductionist and condescending. For the most part, the discourse is dominated by white feminists, but sadly more and more black women are voicing the same dialogue, which is very disheartening. (interview conducted by author, May 2014)

It is also evident in the sparse engagement with community groups. For example, in an interview with the director of a pan-African community group who attended the Girl Summit 2014, she stated:

> The conference did not give any space to the grassroots. It was just a platform for the big and powerful to try to look like they care. Certain figures have risen to prominence in the FGM eradication movement. They are claiming to connect with the grassroots, to understand and to voice the concerns of those affected. However, as a community group and African, no one is interested in what we have to say. No one is engaging with us or supporting our work. It was even pretty impossible to get an invite to this conference. What does that say? (interview conducted by author, August 2014)

This view was also voiced in an article written by a leading FGM activist and founder of FORWARD:

> Despite the presence of organisations and individuals from all over the world, there was very little visibility for diaspora and community organisations or individuals. They are

the ones who have fought hard to get these issues on the agenda, when large NGOs and the British government were still silent. These are the individuals who've faced rejection from their communities or have described losing their jobs in order to focus on the cause. They have been portrayed mostly as victims and not survivors and agents of change.
(Otoo-Oyortey, 2014)

In Sudan, similar views have been voiced by local activists who are concerned that ongoing work, which precedes the latest wave of programmes, could be sidestepped rather than built on. In particular, the growing urban-based youth movement could well provide an already energised and determined platform for change. In other words, there is no real need to start from scratch, but to instead identify what already exists and how capital could be built through resourcing it. Social media already supports the natural emergence of networks in which issues such as FGM are widely discussed by the young and educated. As one such activist articulated:

> I don't understand why international actors think they need to start from the beginning. It may be muted and cautious for obvious reasons, but there are many young people, men and women, who want a different Sudan, who endorse conceptions of human rights and see practices such as FGM as abuse.
> (interview conducted by author, May 2015)

Another local activist based in Khartoum stated:

> Social media such as WhatsApp is often vibrant with discussions about FGM. The young are not afraid to voice their views, both pro and against. I would say, though, that there is a clear move towards rejecting FGM, while there is a continuing commitment to stay true to Sudanese values and traditions in other ways. (interview conducted by author, February 2016)

This view highlights again the importance of respecting and acknowledging local spaces in which a new generation of change agents are voicing their dissatisfaction with the continuation of practices such as FGM. Anthropology's role can be found in increasing the audibility of these opinions and ensuring that they are heard by global campaigners.

Conclusion

So, how can activism be positioned in response to these differing narratives and discourses? As a feminist anthropologist, I see my role as one of exploring at a grassroots level the spaces in which harm and violence are being challenged. I want to understand how intergenerational conversations are now beginning to more openly challenge practices that are seen as harmful, such as FGM. I would like to think that one of the main successes of the global movement is in pushing for these conversations to be had more often and more publicly. Tensions undoubtedly exist in households in which some members of the family support the practice while others do not. Understanding the impact and results of these conversations is important. This chapter has considered some of the broad issues relating to understandings of FGM, but the complexity of the practice and its impact warrant further attention, and so it will be discussed once again in Chapter 7, with more detail of the specific and high-prevalence context of Sudan.

4 | WOMEN, WORK AND VIOLENCE IN NEPAL: EXPERIENCES FROM THE CONSTRUCTION SECTOR

Introduction

This chapter presents new data focused on understanding the impact of increased economic engagement on women who work in the construction sector in Nepal. In particular, the chapter seeks to explore the potential financial independence it brings to women in terms of building (or not) their resilience to different forms of violence. Violence against women and girls (VAWG) in Nepal is a major problem, with the most recent available statistics putting national rates in line with global figures. It is estimated that one in three women in the country suffer from intimate partner violence (IPV), the most common form of violence against women worldwide (Dalal, Svanstrom & Wang, 2014). In terms of economic activity in 2014, 83 per cent of women participated in the labour force, compared to 89 per cent of men (WEF, 2014). But despite this high level of workforce participation, the workplace often is not a safe place for women. One ILO report recorded that 53.8 per cent of women employees reported having experienced workplace violence (ILO, 2004, p. xiv), though much of the sexual harassment that women face "at work" from colleagues actually takes place outside the premises (Saferworld, 2014; Shrestha, 2015). Sexual harassment in public spaces is common, especially on public transport, where it is said to be endemic. Generally speaking, women's free (unaccompanied) movement in public spaces reflects badly on the *ijjat* (honour) of their families (Roomi & Parrott, 2008) and could well leave them exposed to domestic violence.

The informal sector, which construction works falls into, makes up 92.6 per cent of the workforce, and only 1.5 per cent of employed women work in the formal sector (ILO, 2010, p. 9). Women who work in the informal sector are likely to be far more vulnerable to ongoing harassment with no recourse to state support. As such, the extent to which working reduces or perpetuates forms of violence is both unclear and complex, not least because it must also be considered alongside many other factors. With this context in mind, over the past decades, Nepal has made significant policy and programme advancements. For example, in 2006, the Nepal Gender Equality Act amended 56 discriminatory provisions in law and clarified and expanded definitions of violent crimes against women, including rape and homicides. Later, in 2009, the government of Nepal also passed the Domestic Violence (Crime and Punishment) Act, which makes it illegal for one family member to commit a violent act against another, and nationally there are many more resource and support centres dedicated to working with women who suffer from violence. But given the scale of VAWG and the high percentage of women actively engaged in work in the country, as well as the government measures to improve gender equality, a deeper insight into women's experiences of work, public spaces and the home is needed. In order to contribute to this, the research underpinning this chapter focused on capturing the experiences of women working in Nepal's informal construction industry.

Nepal's construction sector is booming, not least because of the need for rapid reconstruction following the devastating earthquake of 2015. Many men and women have migrated from rural areas in search of work in Kathmandu's construction sector and have set up home in informal settlements on the city's outskirts. In making this move, many joint family units have been disrupted when only a married couple and their children have moved. The impact these shifting family structures have had on women's experiences of income and violence must also be explored. The analysis of data draws out how female construction workers regard earning an income, and the importance of it for their sense of well-being and agency is explored. The data also allow us to see a wider, more complex picture and to pick up on other dimensions that need to be in place in order to drive greater gender equality. In particular, the data revealed that local women's organisations and/or mobilisers who are trained to end violence are critical in bridging the gap between increased income and increased resilience to violence. The picture that emerges is non-linear, with women working in construction recording many forms of violence (according to global definitions) while not always regarding them as such. The normalisation of violence remains deep-rooted, even in cases where IPV is experienced daily. Understanding how and where income can feed into a process of positive change is vital if we are to construct a holistic and workable approach to ending VAWG and at the same time economically empower them.

Methodology

The data for this chapter were collected through semi-structured interviews with women and some men in Manohara (a municipality in Kathmandu District of Nepal) between November 2015 and March 2017. Thirty-two in-depth qualitative interviews were conducted with women working in the construction industry who work largely as unskilled labourers, and eight interviews were conducted with men from the same community who also work in construction, mostly as masons. The women and men interviewed were aged between 19 and 55, and most were or had been married. Of the female participants, the majority had married at 15 years, some had married at 14, and only a small number had married between 16 and 18. In most cases, their husbands were only a few years older, and the marriages had generally taken place in rural districts prior to internal migration. The marriages were usually arranged, a few had been forced, and some were described as "love marriages." Most participants were Hindu or Buddhist, and a few were Christian, and they came from a range of castes and ethnic groupings, including the Gurung, Lama, Chettri Bhandari, Limbu, Pariyar and Dalit ethnic/caste groups. Almost all had migrated from rural districts within the last 10 to 12 years, and only a few were born in Kathmandu. Educational levels were low, with only two of the women having achieved the High School Leavers Certificate. Many had not been to school at all or had only completed a few grades, and of those who did go to school, most finished between grades 5 and 7. The educational level of husbands was about the same, with some achieving a few grades higher than their wives. The sample was mixed in terms of women still living with their husbands and those who were now on their own due to husbands working elsewhere (including in the Gulf) or having been abandoned.

Data analysis

In the analysis of data, a number of well-established approaches were adopted and applied. The social ecology framework is endorsed by numerous development institutions, including the UK Department for International Development (e.g. see DFID, 2012). It presents a picture of violence as inherently multifaceted, produced by the interaction of numerous elements of everyday life at various levels, including household, community and nation. Its focus is on how the "embedded" nature of violence is extremely important, and emphasises that structural changes (such as legal reform) and even community-level interventions are unlikely to meet their full potential unless efforts are also made to work on and within the broader cultural systems in which they are located, interpreted and enacted.

An intersectional approach complements the social ecology framework as it recognises that gender is by no means an isolated social category. Rather, it acts to constrain women's freedoms in diverse ways by interlinking with additional categories such as race, caste, class, disability, sexual orientation and age, which contributes further to social, economic and political power inequities. It aims to analyse the "differential ways in which social divisions are concretely enmeshed and constructed by each other and how they relate to political and subjective constructions of identities" (Yuval-Davis, 2006, p. 205). The VAWG spectrum builds on a legacy stemming from Kelly's (1988) work *Surviving Sexual Violence*, which sought to demonstrate that violence against women should not only be analysed as episodic or deviant acts of cruelty, but rather must be seen as normative and functional within a broad spectrum of abuse.

This chapter is structured as follows: the first section presents the findings from the interviews and is divided into subsections according to the key themes that emerged; the second section draws out the evidence that points to the importance of women's networks and organisations; and the conclusion offers reflections on where Nepal is in relation to the promotion of women's rights, and argues that civic women-only spaces must be protected and nurtured.

Interview findings

As outlined in the methodology, this research focused on capturing the experiences of women (and some men) working in construction. Semi-structured interviews were conducted, each lasting between one and two hours. The interviews with female construction workers found no direct relationship between earning an income and greater resilience to all or any forms of violence. In applying the gender spectrum, all the women interviewed had suffered at least one form of violence within the last year. The types of violence they talked about included IPV (e.g. marital rape), sexual harassment and physical intimidation at work, harassment travelling to and from work, and high levels of anxiety around getting home safely.

Importance of income for self-esteem

All the women interviewed felt that earning an income was important not just for their survival and that of their children, but also for their self-esteem and confidence, but degrees of willingness to challenge violence differed among them. Women who belonged to a local organisation that worked specifically on ending violence were much more vocal in their determination to recognise a wider spectrum of violence and also to challenge it.

Broad support for women working

In the interviews with men, there was widespread acceptance and support of women working, though there were also some contradictory views. For example, many of the men talked, on the one hand, about women being equal in respect to working, but only a few said that they shared the domestic and childcare work with their wives. In some of the interviews, the pressures on men to earn enough to support families was a very clear and heavy burden. Earning a good wage was certainly seen as an important dimension of masculinity.

Women who have migrated from rural districts are expected to work, and this is widely accepted by husbands and extended family, and women born into rural families have a long tradition of working in the agricultural sector. Commitment to and investment in the education of their children was very high, and no difference in relation to girls and boys was detected. Many of the women were paying for children to be educated in private boarding schools, and the women expressed that they hoped for their children to out-achieve them.

Overburdening and the glass ceiling

The overburdening of women is very clear. For example, accounts of the working day such as the one that follows were common:

I go to do labour work. I wake up at 4 a.m., cook food, pack it, and go to work. I work until 10 a.m. After 10, there is a lunch break until 11 a.m. Then again, I start working. After starting to work, I rest for a while when the employers are not there. When the employers are there, they will say, "You don't work, you lazy people." Then I come home at around 6 p.m., I cook food, eat, and sleep. Again, in the morning, I wake up at 4, cook food, pack it, and go to work.

One woman recounts her husband's frequently expressed view:

Yes, he thinks that only women have to do all the household chores. "The household work is for women, otherwise why get married?" This is his view.

Many women talked about a glass ceiling in their work and a lack of opportunities for skill development and progression. Some women had received training to become masons, but none of the sample actually worked in this position. They all acknowledged the pay gap even between men and women working in the same unskilled sector. They talked of men being seen as stronger, and therefore more productive, and so they were paid more highly. Women also spoke of the role of the mason being easier and much better paid (three times more per day). When asked if they would like to be a mason, they said yes because the work is easier and better-paid. However, they also said that even with the training, they would not be able to go for such work due to fear of harassment. The job of a mason is seen as a man's role, and women who try to break into it are looked upon very harshly. The difference in pay between men and women doing the same job was put down to men being stronger. This gendered mindset was held by a significant number of the men, but it was also shared by the women interviewed. That said, a number of the participants challenged this view:

> Actually, we [women labourers] are the ones who do the work. It is more difficult than the work they [masons] do. We have to prepare the mixture [referring to cement, sand and water], carry bricks and carry sand. They only build the walls; still, we are paid less. I do not know why.

All female participants recognised that the construction sector offered them the highest possible daily rate for unskilled labour, but the relatively higher wage came at the price of having to work in a harsh and male-dominated environment. For example, one woman told me:

> Some [contractors] are arrogant. They speak badly, speaking rubbish words without thinking how other people feel about it. Some are of a dominating nature and think that they [contractors] can say and do anything to us [labourers].

And in answer to the question "Why do you think they dominate you?" she replied:

> Maybe because I am a woman. Some are of a dominating nature while some are good. If we are working with new contractors, then they try to dominate us [labourers]. They think that we should be continuously doing our work. Instead of helping us, they try to be the boss and threaten us to bring the materials required for them to do their job, making life easier for them.

In many of the interviews, women talked about how they worked together in order to challenge the unfairness they experienced. In one case, a group of women joined together and confronted a contractor who had not paid them, one of whom described the confrontation as follows:

> I got tense when I heard that the contractor ran away without paying us. We used to go to his house to find him in the

mornings without having a meal, only to find out that he was not home. Once we waited from morning to evening, and then finally met him and threatened him that we would call the police if he did not give us our money. Many of us were there.

Earning an income increases confidence

All of the women interviewed stated that they would work even if they did not need to. They talked about the material necessity, the need to earn money in order to buy food and pay for school fees, but most of the women also said that earning an income increased their confidence and meant that they could influence decisions at the household level. This control and financial independence was considered vital and worth the hardships of working. Some of the women retained control over their income and did not hand any of it over to their husbands or other family, while some women talked of pooling their income with their husbands. Only a few women stated they handed all of their income to their husbands. An example of the psychological benefit of earning an income can be seen in the following comment:

> To me, even if it is not difficult, working is better because it is satisfactory to my body too. It "exercises" my body. If any good work comes through my husband, I am ready to do anything – be it carrying loads or anything else. I am ready to work.

The link between income and decision-making power was acknowledged by many of the women. For example, one woman interviewed stated:

> It is a very obvious thing that if one earns, others will not say anything. But if one doesn't, then others try to dominate you.

Health implications

The perceived benefits (such as greater financial stability and provision of food, clothes and school fees) are seen by the participants to far outweigh even the negative health implications of construction work. All the women interviewed shared that they suffered health problems that could be linked to their work. Access to affordable medical care was very limited and was a drain on their salaries, and a number of the women stated that they used alcohol to numb the pain after work. For example:

> It does harm sometimes. There is the excessive discharge of white fluid [from the vagina]. When it happens, I go to Manohara clinic to get medicine, and that instantly works and makes me feel better. When I ask about it, they say the white liquid is discharged because of lifting heavy loads, and they prescribe me medication.

Recognising and challenging violence

The women's responses varied in terms of how they recognised the wide spectrum of violence, which included work-based harassment, and also in their willingness to challenge it. Some of the women maintained that husbands beating their wives was "just what happens – if a wife does something wrong, she should expect to get beaten."

Sexual harassment at work

Sexual harassment at work was the type of VAWG most often brought up, but it was not necessarily categorised by the women as violence. While accounts of physical harm on the sites were few, all the women recounted instances of male workers and contractors using "rude" language towards them. One participant described the situation as follows: "It is heard that contractors assault the woman labourers physically. It will happen if masons and contractors do not have morality." Another woman interviewed stated, "It is usual that workers use rubbish words at the workplace." However, some women did see the harassment they suffered at work as violence. For example, one woman said in relation to men "speaking harshly and rudely and also touching and teasing" that "I think this is called violence."

Strategies for avoiding sexual abuse

Many women talked about the strategies they employed in an attempt to avoid sexual comments, touching and "teasing" from male workers and contractors. These strategies included working closely together and making sure that none of them were left alone. Some of the participants felt that a few women encouraged attention from male contractors, and this impacted negatively on female workers in general by giving the impression that all female workers are easy. A significant number of the women talked of times when female workers sought the affections of the contractors as a way of increasing their chances of being paid. As one woman put it, "Well, maybe the contractors think women cannot speak. I heard that they give to those who flirt, smile and talk with them."

Feelings of being unsafe travelling to and from work

Many women felt very high levels of anxiety when travelling to and from work. For example, one woman disclosed, "I just feel scared. I walk hastily on the way. It is problematic to cross the way under the bridge up to Dial [the name of the community school in the Manohara settlement]." Another participant stated:

> I mostly do not walk at night – I feel very troubled while walking outside at night. Those who see women walking late at night might say something. I feel afraid thinking people might tease me when walking alone at night.

Rape was commonly cited as the form of violence women mainly feared while travelling home from work and in the dark. This concern was particularly present while women walked in the dark from bus stops to the edge of their community. Once they were inside the boundary, they felt more secure because they knew many people who they felt would come and help them. The interviews did not reveal personal experiences of rape on the way home from work, but many of the women talked of a reported incident that was obviously playing heavily on their minds and feeding their concerns.

Strategies to reduce risk when travelling to and from work

The interviews revealed a number of strategies used by women to try to reduce their risk of harm while travelling to and from work. These included walking quickly from bus stop to community, travelling to work in pairs or groups, or carrying a pin as a weapon to be used if harassment takes place on public transport. Some women claimed they would hit out if threatened. Those women who worked alongside their husbands felt a much lower level of harassment and anxiety around travelling to and from work; they felt the presence of their husband offered them protection.

Experiences of intimate partner violence (IPV)

Many women gave extreme accounts of being beaten by their husbands. For example, one woman shared her harrowing story of extreme abuse as follows:

> He started talking to the other girl again, then he beat me up, saying that there was nothing wrong with him just talking to her. So, I stayed at my parents' house for a week. He had said that he did not need me and that I should get out of his house. If I say anything about his affair, then he beats me! I have so many bruises on my body.

Those women who still remained in a marriage with a violent husband talked of regular beatings as a normal occurrence between man and wife. While they did not like to be beaten, they said they would not do anything about it because it is "just what husbands do."

Those women who attended sessions run by a women's organisation stated that they would discuss instances of violence with other women there. They also said this helped them work through what to do and felt they were not alone. As shown below, many women also talked about the role of the social mobilisers. None of the women talked about sharing experiences with their husbands or other family members.

Alcohol as a trigger

A number of the women talked about their husbands drinking as a trigger for beatings. As one participant recounted:

> When he was here, he used to work as a labourer. He used to earn money and spend it on alcohol. And then he started to fight with me and call me names such as *raddi* and *bhalu* ["bitch" and "prostitute"]. I had to work hard and manage the household, but still I could not have food in a peaceful environment as he used to beat me.
>
> I tried many times to leave, and he would beat me whenever he found me. I tried to separate from him by calling my parents, but he would ask for forgiveness from them for his mistakes [from his mother-in-law, father-in-law, brother-in-law and sisters-in-law].

Another participant stated:

> I was actually married, but my husband had married another woman and brought her home. Then he kept beating me very badly, so I stopped living in that house. Even others advised me not to live like that. Since my husband had another wife, I did not stay there.

These stories reveal a range of actions taken by women. One chose to stay in her marriage and considered it inevitable that she is abused, whereas the other stepped out of the abusive situation. Understanding what triggers a woman to act to end violence against her is important. As already stated, membership and regular attendance at women's groups that are focused on ending violence seems to be a key factor. This is important to note because all the women did talk about sharing problems with their friends and female work colleagues, but this sharing is not itself enough to mobilise a woman to leave a violent husband.

Some of the women interviewed, independently of any formal group, had actually set up their own saving groups. They claimed it was critical that they saved for the future.

The role of the social mobilisers

The role of the social mobiliser (local community leader trained to respond to issues of VAWG) was highlighted by a significant number of women who talked about them as the first point of contact if violence at home became too much. The passage below also suggests that the mobiliser can influence actions, and in this particular instance it was the intervention of the mobiliser that encouraged the woman to stand up to her husband:

> I did not want to leave my husband – I used to rather think that I should die. Once I spoke about this issue to the social mobiliser of this place, she came and asked him not to repeat such acts in the future. But the very next day, he beat me again; he had beaten me in the middle of the road in front of other people. Then I threatened him that I would file a case against him and get a divorce.

Also, the importance of the link between mobilisers and women's groups comes through in this passage:

> If it happens nearby here, we say to the social mobiliser of this place [referring to the elder sister]. They belong to the same

savings organisation. There will be discussion at their place, and then reporting happens.

Lack of faith in the justice system, particularly the police

Only a few women who had suffered violence said they had reported it. Very little faith was expressed towards the justice systems and mechanisms. The perceived ineffectiveness, in particular of the police force, which is seen as being indifferent to the needs of women, acted as a deterrent to report. In one interview, a woman stated, "There is no point reporting violence to the police; they don't do anything. Anyhow, they don't care about us living here."

Interviews with men

As previously stated, the interviews with men highlighted that husbands largely support their wives going out to work. However, it was clear in a number of the interviews that it would not be appropriate for wives to exceed their earning potential in relation to their skill level. In other words, most of the men interviewed were masons, and when asked most did not feel that being a mason was a job for women. The perception coming through was that only men possessed the capacity to do such skilled work. Unsurprisingly, this view was not held by the women interviewed, who felt their work was much more challenging.

Most of the men interviewed were unaware of the level of sexual harassment women faced while working and also the fear women had travelling to and from work. Most men felt that husbands and wives working together was the best approach but was not always possible. Some of the men interviewed disclosed that they used force on their wives, and felt this was legitimate if they did not "fulfil their chores correctly." Most of the men felt that domestic chores were the remit of their wives, even if they worked.

The role of autonomous women's networks and organisations

If we apply our various analytical frames to the data, a number of conclusions can be drawn. First, in the context of the ecological frame, at the household level there is a clear overburdening of women, with domestic duties being shared only in a few cases. Work is accepted and expected, but is also highly gendered, and women are not encouraged to progress into skilled positions, despite training opportunities being available. Decision-making is – on the whole – shared, with most women retaining at least a proportion of their salary, which many save.

Moving outwards to the community level, there is evidence of women supporting each other through informal networks encouraged by the presence of local organisations and social mobilisers. All the women interviewed knew who to turn to within their communities, but at the state level most women did not trust the justice apparatus and considered it to be corrupt and ineffective. These perceptions also stretched to government levels, from which they felt generally alienated, despite having the right to vote.

A clear link can be drawn between engagement with local women's organisations that focus specifically on ending VAWG and women who are defiant and prepared to challenge violence. As already stated, many women are active in saving and are part of saving schemes, but being a member of such schemes does not seem to have any bearing on their willingness to challenge violence.

Two dimensions emerge as key factors in women challenging violence. The first is a mindset that recognises the range of violence that women suffer, which includes denormalisation of, for example, IPV and domestic violence, and harassment in the workplace and while travelling to and from work. The second is access to a supportive network or organisation that provides safe spaces where women can share their experiences and receive advice, and can work through the process of recognising the forms of violence they are exposed to. Shifts in attitudes towards violence and membership to organisations or networks seem often to go hand in hand. The recognition of violence may also be aided by the discussions and mutual sharing that take place in women-only spaces. The courage to face it and to talk about it may come about due to mutual support among women (Alvarez, Chuchryk, Navarro-Aranguren & Sternbach, 1992; Keck & Sikkink, 1998; Weldon, 2006).

Additionally, theories around social and cultural capital are relevant here (e.g. see Bradley, 2010b; Nussbaum, 2000), but better understanding is needed of the informal mechanisms women use in this sector to talk about violence and challenge each other's acceptance, as well as how this relates to such theories. Also, more insight is needed to reveal how women work together and with local actors to challenge violence. This understanding could help to strengthen collectives and to build social capital. Belonging to a women's organisation or network seems significant for women in terms of building resilience to, challenging, and ending VAWG. Through these, women seem to automatically draw on and from each other in order to strategise and implement solutions.

The findings discussed here support the results of an extensive secondary quantitative study conducted by Htun and Weldon (2012), which argues that autonomous women's organisation working to end violence are critically important. They list three reasons why women's autonomous organising is so important. First, "women organising as women generate social knowledge about women's position as a group in society" (Htun & Weldon 2012, p. 553; see also, Mansbridge, 1995; Mansbridge & Morris, 2001; Weldon, 2011; Young, 2000). The specific contextual understanding of violence that emerges from these groupings is needed to direct action towards relevant entry points to bring about transformation. These entry points cannot be assumed to be the same for all groupings even within the same cultural context. Second, as the review of literature in Chapter 1 highlights, ending VAWG requires a shift in the unequal gender structures underpinning societies across the globe. This restructuring will not happen within pre-existing political institutions or parties, where the so-called "gender issue" may struggle to make it onto the agenda in any sustained and meaningful way. All too often, as Htun and Weldon (2012) point out, VAWG is marginalised in public debate. Autonomous organisations that are committed to and focused on ending VAWG are the only realistic hope. Third, women's organisations represent safe spaces within which women are able to vent their frustrations at their marginalisation and vulnerabilities and seek support and strategise collectively or individually.

This research found that work, not just economic resources, is vital for women and has an incredibly important empowering effect that also raises self-esteem. The construction site, however, does not represent a safe space for women, and though a degree of resilience to violence at work is navigated through peer networks, violence at home is more challenging, making support from mobilisers critical.

Conclusion

It is very clear from the literature that gender norms intersect with other issues. This includes social divisions such as class and caste, life histories, legal frameworks, religious institutions and ideologies, local economic structures, marriage patterns, and so on, and these factors create varied experiences of violence within countries and cultures. The data presented in this chapter support this view, and argue that the intersectional focus is therefore a critical analytical lens in research such as this, which attempts to explore the links between different dimensions and experiences of violence.

Returning to my original argument, ending VAWG will not be achieved through one single entry point, but rather it requires a multilayered approach. The ecology of violence is such that it is sustained by the embedded view that VAWG is normal, which weaves through the many layers of society reaching across the globe. Programming to end VAWG needs to reflect this ecology and connect feminist movements and organisations at each level. Transnational feminist ideals are now beginning to shape the policy discourse of global institutions, and violence is arguably more visible on the agenda than ever before. But in order to be effective, this agenda in turn needs to influence national-level government commitments to the implementation of legalisation and justice mechanisms to promote women's rights and to hold perpetrators accountable. At the local level, networks and organisations of women need to direct agency across and above in order to remind governments and stakeholders of the prevalence of and urgency to end violence, as well as reach out to peers who are struggling to accept that violence is abuse. In other words, autonomous women's networks and organisations must keep VAWG on the agenda and strive to make the issue ever-more visible while highlighting the widespread impact it has on well-being and also economic productivity.

In Nepal there is reason to be optimistic. The 2015 constitution enshrines a commitment to gender equality, which is widely regarded as a major step in the promotion and achievement of women's rights. This is reflected in a national gender equality and social inclusion (GESI) framework launched in 2017 and designed to support the achievement of this constitutional goal. The framework seeks to support the coordination of all stakeholders and donors in such a way that efforts and energies are effectively utilised for the purpose of improving the lives of marginalised people. It advocates working across levels, including through the district network of local government. However, given the evidence emerging and cited in this article regarding the critical need to maintain the autonomy of women's networks and organisations, a word of caution is needed. If the GESI framework is to really bring about the much-needed structural changes in Nepal, it should not attempt to institutionalise women's groups, but should instead actively work to maintain them as a civic space outside of state government instruments. These spaces and the collective women's knowledge inside them should be seen as a crucial resource to guide and course-correct the path towards ending VAWG.

5 | APPLYING THE INTERSECTIONAL LENS: THE EXPERIENCES OF PROFESSIONAL MIDDLE-CLASS WOMEN IN NEPAL AND PAKISTAN

Introduction

The international development literature on women's economic engagement and on violence against women and girls (VAWG) tends to focus on the experiences of women at the lower end of the socio-economic spectrum. However, the research conducted in Pakistan and Nepal that is presented here included interviews with women from a range of different income groupings and income-generating activities. This approach is a critical part of uncovering the differences between various income contexts and supports an analysis that weighs up the extent to which earning an income, in and of itself, may or may not alleviate or exacerbate the various types of violence that women face.

In this chapter, all of the women interviewed were educated to at least university graduate level, most held a master's degree and some also held a PhD. The participants had studied a variety of subjects, ranging from social sciences, business, medicine and humanities. The women were engaged in a wide range of professions, including in the corporate sector, education, NGOs, the public sector and government organisations, medicine, and private enterprise. The findings are contrasted against those of their peers from poorer and less-educated backgrounds, and revealed a striking lack of social and cultural capital from peer networking. In previous chapters, I have argued that drawing on peer spaces and local organisations is a key part of building the resilience of lower-income women to violence. These resources seem largely absent from the lives of middle-class women, particularly in the case of the interviews with women in Kathmandu. The result of this lack of a support network means individual women are potentially left isolated and without the psychological support necessary to build resilience to violence, and indeed to challenge it. This chapter explores the distinct experiences of a group of higher-educated professional women, and in doing so highlights the benefit of taking an intersectional approach to the study of women's empowerment, and specifically violence.

As stated previously, the intersectional approach was pioneered by Yuval-Davis (2006) and enables the simultaneous differentiation of various groups of women according to a variety of factors and/or dimensions. It resists the tendency to homogenise women into a single category as if they all experience the world in similar ways and face the same challenges. While crossovers will exist, not least because VAWG is not unique to a single category of women or girls, responding to abuse must also be responsive to individual context. It is also critical that women are able to tell their own stories of how and why abuse happened, and through their narration assert their agency and resilience. In order to apply the intersectional approach and to understand how earning an income may impact differently on the lives of various groups of women, and how in turn this may feed into increasing or decreasing forms of violence, 30 middle- and upper-class women engaged in professional occupations, all of whom were residing in Nepal or Pakistan, were interviewed. A smaller, more focused sample of eight female entrepreneurs in Pakistan were also interviewed. In both countries, some of the women interviewed were married and some were not. Some lived in joint families while others were in a more nuclear set-up, and some had children and others did not. Many of the women claimed not to practise any religion, but originated from Hindu or Buddhist families in Nepal and from Muslim families in Pakistan. In Nepal, the ethnicities of the women ranged from Brahmin, to Chettri, to Newar. It needs to be stressed that although the sample is diverse, the size is too small in both cases to draw any rigorous evidence, but saturation in responses was achieved. Nonetheless, the picture that emerges from the data is important in terms of challenging assumptions that richer and more educated women automatically have greater resilience and better resources to fight violence.

While differences between women's experiences of work could be seen within this group, what was specifically captured was the impact forms of violence had on and for women's general well-being and mental health, which in turn affected their productivity at work and ability to progress in their careers. A link could be seen between violence, mainly in the form of psychological harassment, at home and instances of prejudicial behaviour in the workplace. Women deemed to be too successful or work-focused reported tensions at home. If married, it was most commonly reported that mothers-in-law and husbands frequently commented that work was compromising their ability to be a good wife, daughter-in-law and mother (if they had children). Women took these tensions with them to work, where the psychological strain was intensified through work-based harassment, mainly at the hands of more senior male colleagues.

This chapter begins by comparing the different work contexts for women in Nepal and Pakistan, and the second section presents the findings thematically, exploring the most striking issues emerging from the data in both countries. The third section focuses in on the experiences of female entrepreneurs in Pakistan, whose stories offer an interesting comparison to women working in other sectors, and also helps to build the comparison with the poor home-based workers discussed in Chapter 6. The conclusion then draws out some comparisons between the two country contexts.

Different work contexts: comparing Nepal and Pakistan

In Nepal, the law is reasonably well formulated in its approach to gender concerns. However, women's organisations warn that official attitudes to implementation – spanning employers, police and the courts – remain relatively indifferent. Women's organisations also report that patriarchal attitudes remain deeply embedded in the general population, and that intimate partner violence (IPV) is often considered "normal." A recent study of women with disabilities in Nepal (Hawkes, Misra & Puri, 2015) found that 57.7 per cent have experienced violence, including emotional violence (55.2 per cent), physical violence (34 per cent) and sexual violence (21.5 per cent). Women in paid employment were more likely to have experienced violence. As noted in the previous chapter, only 1.5 per cent of employed women work in the formal sector (ILO, 2010, p. 9). There is also a marked urban/rural divide, with women in cities significantly less likely to be working. Work-based harassment is common, as illustrated in the previous chapter, and though the long-awaited National Law on Sexual Harassment at the Workplace came into force in February 2015, people working in the informal sector – 92.6 per cent of workers – have no recourse to its provisions.

Some labour unions in Nepal have strong women leaders and have clear policies that promote gender equality. In many sectors, however – notably the entertainment and construction sectors (see previous chapters) – women lack a common platform from which to represent their issues. Rural women are significantly more likely to work compared to urban women, and the highest proportion of working women reside in the rural mountain zone, while the lowest proportion reside in the urban Terai zone. Poverty plays a significant role in women's employment in Nepal, with over 95 per cent of women from the poorest households engaged in work (both paid and unpaid) compared to 61 per cent of women from richer households. In addition, a multivariate analysis that explored the determinants of women's work participation has indicated that after accounting for other variables, such as residence in a specific ecological zone, household wealth, age, and involvement in family decision-making, have a significant influence on women's participation in work (see the Nepal country report published on www.genderinsouthasia.org). While factors such as the age of the woman and involvement in family decision-making were positively associated with women's employment, household wealth was negatively associated.

In Pakistan, according to the Demographic and Health Survey, 39 per cent of married women aged between 15 and 49 have experienced domestic violence. However, Human Rights Watch states that reliable estimates actually range from 70 per cent to upwards of 90 per cent (HRW, 1999), and the Global Gender Gap Index ranks Pakistan 141st out of 142 countries for its level of "economic participation and opportunity" for women (WEF, 2014). At a national level, there are quotas for women in political positions: 60 seats in the National Assembly and 129 (of 758) in Provincial National Assemblies. But despite having equal voting rights, Pakistani women remain poorly represented in formal governance. Although it is illegal, women within certain cultural and geographical boundaries are often stopped from voting, either by their families or through signed agreements endorsed by religious leaders between male political candidates and village committees (USDS, 2014).

Pakistani law has been shaped for more than 30 years by a religious legal structure that has operated alongside the existing penal code. Although changes have been made in recent years (such as a move to prevent raped women being tried under religious law for adultery), the law has not yet been sufficiently transformed. Despite some recent legal reforms, a woman's testimony is still given half the weight of a man's in rape cases. It is certainly notable that, according to data provided to the US

Senate by Pakistan's Ministry of Interior, there were no rape convictions at all in the Capital District Authority (Islamabad) in the five years preceding 2013 (USDS, 2014). In addition, other legal ordinances essentially make honour killings viable under the law. For example, heirs of murdered women can pardon their relative's killer for financial compensation; this means a son can pardon his father and any money exchanged stays in the family. A specific domestic violence law is lacking at the national level, though some regional laws have been passed to address this (in Balochistan and Sindh), but these do not yet cover every province.

The most important change in Pakistani legislation has been the National Law on Sexual Harassment at the Workplace. In it, "harassment" is defined as:

> Any unwelcome sexual advance, request for sexual favours or other verbal or written communication or physical conduct of a sexual nature or sexually demeaning attitudes, causing interference with work performance or creating an intimidating, hostile or offensive work environment, or the attempt to punish the complainant for refusal to comply to such a request or is made a condition for employment.
> (Shirkat Gah, 2014, p. 34)

Women make up 22 per cent of the labour force, and this figure remained consistent throughout the 15 years before 2014 (World Bank, 2014). Of the 12.1 million women in the labour force, 8.3 million work in agriculture or fisheries, 2.2 million in other elementary occupations, and 1.4 million in crafts and related trades (Mustafa Ali, 2011). It should be noted that these are almost always informal job roles and are not covered by labour legislation.

The research presented here focuses on whether affluence and status have any impact on women's experiences of violence, and if working in an organisation that has adopted anti-violence and sexual harassment laws or instituted mechanisms that provide safety to women at work have any impacts for them. Some questions asked were: Are professional women harassed more at work compared to other groups of women? Does earning a higher income mean a woman has a greater self-confidence and agency to challenge violence when it happens? Does this agency reduce a woman's vulnerability to violence in the first place?

In Pakistan, an important and highly successful campaign was launched in 2000. The Alliance Against Sexual Harassment (AASHA) campaign, together with the government, developed a "Code of Conduct for Gender Justice" within the workplace, and the campaign persuaded more than 300 organisations to adopt it. As a result of AASHA's campaigning, the Protection Against Harassment of Women in the Workplace Bill was passed by the government in 2010, which made sexual harassment an offence and required all organisations to adopt and implement the Code of Conduct. The research findings presented in this chapter were supported by interviews with founding members of AASHA.

The AASHA campaign has since been disbanded, but one of its organisations, Mehergarh, continues to provide training to organisations across the country on establishing the required policies and practices. Importantly, AASHA is one of the only initiatives in Pakistan that has addressed both women's economic empowerment (WEE) and VAWG, and was responsible for developing, helping to pass, and then implementing the 2010 National Law on Sexual Harassment at the Workplace, activity that has been widely characterised as being among Pakistan's most successful pro-women campaigns. Interviews for this research were conducted with employees of five organisations who have signed up to the Code of Conduct. The additional eight interviews with entrepreneurs were all with women who own different businesses in and around Lahore and Islamabad. This provides an added dimension to the research as it allows for experiences of women who own their own small businesses, as well as their understanding of empowerment and vulnerability and their experiences of violence, to be compared and contrasted to those of women in other forms of work.

Key themes emerging from the data

Women's motivation to work

Many women shared that they enjoyed and even loved to work; they found it to provide confidence and a sense of being in control. One example is Nida, who worked as an investigative reporter and producer at GEO TV, where she had spent many years covering challenging and controversial stories. Her husband also worked for another media channel. They had two daughters and – though they lived independently – Nida's mother lived with them. Nida had an M.Phil. degree in mass communication and was hired by GEO right after her graduation. She talked about her refusal to slow down, even when pregnant:

> If I sit at home, I will not know what is happening and will not have exposure – I learn a lot and apply it. When NGO Sahil did a report on child sexual abuse, my daughter was only 1 year old – it really grabbed my attention. I told others to take care of their children. What I learn I apply. If something cannot be aired because it is controversial, I still inform people about it, and that is my contribution.

Nida was very clear that her role was not one of being a housewife and mother:

> I spent one week with my daughter and then I found out that anyone can do this, like a maid, but professional work is something only someone like me can do.

And she valued women who worked, as she said:

> I told my brother not to get a professional wife and then ask her to sit at home – this would be wrong. If someone tells me to quit my job, I won't like it. I am respected because I am a supporting hand.

A second woman interviewed in Pakistan was Fatimah, who was divorced and had two children, and worked at Attock Oil Refinery Limited (ARL), one of the companies that had adopted the Code of Conduct. She worked in the human resources department and had been a part of this organisation for many years, joining the company before she got married:

> I joined ARL before I got married, and what really helped me out was that my company gave me accommodation close to my office. When I had my two children, it was easy for me to go home ... they also gave me 24-hour help ... this was 30 years ago.

She was very appreciative of her organisation, both at a personal and professional level, as she said that even though this was mostly a male-centric profession, they had many women who worked alongside men in a very safe and friendly environment, and she was very proud that ARL had adopted the 2010 National Law on Sexual Harassment at the Workplace and trained its staff on it.

Both women shared positive experiences of work, feeling that it reflects an essential part of their identity and one they take great pride from. Both also work for organisations that have embraced the anti-harassment Code of Conduct. These happy experiences contrast against those of some of the women in Nepal, where such a code has not been so strictly enforced. In fact, the sample of women interviewed in Nepal revealed that a majority had experienced forms of work-based harassment, ranging from name-calling to more serious sexual assault. For example, one woman shared the following account:

> At times, once in a blue moon, it happens. When it happens, it's just like my previous job situation with the general manager of a bank who gave me advice over how to get promoted. He told me that I had to start hanging out with him, and if I did that, he would help me. I felt uncomfortable – I did not feel his intentions were good. He said I could not expose him because he had done a good thing for me and it would make me look bad. I had no choice but to avoid him as best I could.

While many of the middle-class women interviewed were able to either drive themselves to work or had drivers, those that did have to take public transport reported very similar accounts of harassment as those recounted by poorer women (see previous chapter). For example, one of the women interviewed in Lahore, Pakistan, made the following comment:

> It might be when travelling at night that the feeling of unsafety is there. I feel unsafe when I have to travel in a taxi. Even though I feel like nothing is going to happen, I feel risks. When I know that a person has bad intentions and I have to travel and work with that person, I feel uncomfortable.

In Kathmandu, another woman shared the following:

> Apart from that, travelling to my work is very hard; it's a very long process. I travel in a scooter and people come up to me. It has happened so many times. They say nasty comments, and after listening to them I get angry. I feel like reciprocating – there is so much confusion at these times. So many questions are also raised in my mind that by the time I reach the office, my mind is full of questions, and I am so occupied that I cannot work or function in the office. Commuting back from my work is also very scary because it is a night shift.
>
> At night, I leave office at 1 or 2 a.m. I have to go back home, even though they say it's not safe for women. No matter how many precautions I take, it is out of my hands. Even though

I take precautions, I don't know if other people are taking them – I cannot guarantee that. So, while returning back in the evening, I feel very scared because I don't who is hiding in the dark, I don't know. Nowadays, there are news sections such as "Crime Patrol" that fill my brain with disturbing things after watching them.

In Pakistan, a woman said:

I feel 100 per cent safe at the workplace. However, being a female, there is some harassment, like how boys overtake my car on the way to work. If they see it's a woman driving, they try to surround her – this kind of harassment is a common thing.

Difference in experiences of violence across employment contexts

In terms of the above findings, no differences between ethnicities, marital status and migration status can be seen in either country, but some differences do emerge across sectors. Women employed in the corporate sector (e.g. IT and banking) and in government recorded higher levels of work-based harassment when compared to those working with international non-governmental organisations (INGOs) and civil society organisations (CSOs), or in medicine or teaching. As the sample is relatively small in this research, this points to areas that require further research. In work settings where gender policies existed (such as separate toilets and maternity leave), these measures did not reduce the violence women experienced. Fear of harassment was higher than concerns of pay inequality or lack of maternity rights, though participants who were employed in government and the corporate sector also recorded concerns over promotion (or lack of it).

Family acceptance of women working

Most of the participants had supportive families who were liberal in their attitudes towards women working. In fact, many of the women described how their mothers had also worked in professional roles. A few cases of IPV were captured, and these were reported to have been triggered by resentment that the wife works and is independent. However, harassment from other family members was the most prevalent form of violence at the household level. Levels of this type of harassment seem to increase the more successful a woman is, and particularly if she has reached a more senior level than her husband. Harassment often comes in the form of accusations that the woman is not fulfilling her domestic role because she is working. Work-based harassment was widespread among those women (the vast majority) who were not home-based for work, and those women who lived in a more conservative family recorded higher levels of harassment at home, with a number of them reporting instances of IPV and also psychological harassment from other family members. For example, one woman in Kathmandu talked about the suspicion her employment raised with her family:

> If I am home late because of a meeting or a work social event, my mother-in-law will interrogate me. She will accuse me of not fulfilling my obligations at home. My husband also questions me, suspecting me of having an affair. I have to attend social events – how else will I get promoted? It is never a problem for my male colleagues – they do not face this level of harassment. It torments me, makes me angry. I do consider it to be a form of violence.

All the participants in both contexts felt that things had changed for them compared to their mothers in that they now have more opportunities available, and they also conveyed feelings of optimism about the next generation of girls and their daughters. But there was also a sense that they were having to endure a level of backlash as a result of this shift. In the words of one woman in Pakistan:

Sometimes I just want to give up work. It feels too much. I work hard all day in the office and then I come home and face abuse and accusations. I am not respected by my family, even though I bring home a good salary. But I look at my daughter and think I must carry on for her. Things will be different for her – I will make sure that she does not suffer as I have.

Another woman in Pakistan shared her story about earning a lot of money; her husband would take it from her without her knowledge and use it on things without her permission, which caused psychological distress for her. She mentioned that many years ago, she had brought home a large sum of money that went missing. When she asked her husband, he said he had used it all to buy groceries for the house:

I said to him, "What are you talking about? When I pay for everything, why would you spend so much on groceries?" This disturbed me a lot, and I thought to myself I will not keep a joint account; neither will I bring money home. Later I found out that he had given the money to his sister so she could build her house.

This was the beginning of the break-up of their marriage. Rubina shared that she did not even realise he was having an affair with the maid; another woman told her about this, so she kicked the maid out. When asked if she ever confronted her husband, she replied:

He was really something. He had a bad temper. If I asked him something, he would prolong the discussion. If the discussion was for an hour, he could drag it on for days. And if it was for days, he would drag it on for weeks, so I stayed quiet.

She went on to say that her CEO had tried to patch up their marriage, but eventually they divorced and the husband married another woman. She was clear that earning an income had given her options that she otherwise would not have had. Employment and her career were too important to her, and when her husband failed to support her, she just decided to leave, knowing that she could cope on her own. What would be interesting to explore is the extent to which working in a safe, supportive environment increases women's self-assurance and makes them more likely to leave situations that become intolerable. This particular woman worked for a company that had signed up to the Code of Conduct and clearly took the view that being happy at home would have a positive knock-on effect for productivity at work, which is further discussed later in this chapter.

In the sample, a number of husbands married to middle-class women who worked were interviewed. In general, they said they were happy with the idea of their wives working. However, most also said that their wives "have to be careful not to stretch themselves too much because of the demands of also looking after the home and children." The perception here is that women can only work up to a level that leaves them relatively free to still fulfil a domestic role. Concerns were expressed over women working in roles that took them away from home for a period of time or that involved evening meetings or socialising with colleagues. These views feed into the harassment, as detailed above, whereby some women reported that relatives would often accuse them of being unfaithful or being irresponsible if they were out too late. Some of the men did share that they hit their wives, but claimed that it was necessary in order for them to assert their authority and remind their wives of it. These instances, though they were in the minority, demonstrate that there has been a degree of male backlash. Women's engagement in professional occupations does seem to be accepted, or at least tolerated, by men to a certain level. However, in instances where homes become tense and potentially violent, women outperforming their husbands appears to represent a tipping point. This relationship between the comparative status of women and their husbands and VAWG warrants further research.

Income and self-esteem

The vast majority of women felt that earning an income gave them more power to influence household decisions – not just how to spend household collective income, but also over the direction of family life. Some of the women directly stated that having greater influence over decisions was a key motivation for earning money themselves – the money was not as important as this leverage. Despite the variety of positive and negative experiences across contexts, earning an income was vital for all the women interviewed. All participants linked income to increases in self-esteem and confidence. While most acknowledged that the risk of violence is not reduced by earning income, but instead increases the range of violence they are exposed to, they would not give up work because of it. As one woman put it:

> Sometimes I feel exhausted with the battle. I wonder how much longer I will be able to stay strong enough to withstand harassment at work and at home. Maybe I should just give in and stay at home like my family want me to.

> If I was given the choice not to work and I was getting the same amount of salary without working, I would take the choice – take that money and look for another job – because I cannot live with this stress, but I would still want to work as it gets me away from boring domestic tasks. I could not just do nothing.

The confidence gained through working, as with women in lower socio-economic positions, is evident in this group of middle-class women in both Nepal and Pakistan:

> It is because of my position that courage is built within me slowly. Before, I used to be scared of speaking, but now I do not feel that way. In front of everybody, if that person has done something bad, I scold them, but I appreciate them as well, especially females – they need a lot of grooming. They need to give more opportunities to them as well. Yes, I think

when you have stability, that courage comes to you on its own. Throughout the course, I felt it myself.

I think, yes, the financial independence that I have, my mother does not feel it, but she never got the opportunity to feel it. At times when talking with her while sharing, I think they have a lot more money than us, but because they did not earn it themselves, they feel that is also what I think. In terms of decision-making, for us, we can make our own decision, but for them they have to at least ask once.

You have your own recognition, you have to respect that, and also your personal satisfaction after working for the money, I guess that is it. There is a saying: instead of stealing and eating, it is better to do and eat.

Today, since I am economically independent in whatever I do and whatever I want to do, I can pursue my dreams, because at this stage of life I am not dependent on my father – my father cannot say anything to me. He cannot say, "Do this and don't do that," because whatever I am doing, I am doing it with my own money. I also feel confident; accordingly, I have learnt to save as well, and I have understood the value of everything. To become independent among men and women of the community as a youth is very important, in my opinion. If we attain economic independence from an early age, I feel we develop a different perspective as well.

For many of the women, work was not just about income; they were also vocationally driven and motivated by feeling that they were making a difference, which also helped to build self-esteem.

Another woman who worked as a journalist talked about the risks she faced and threats she sometimes received as a result of some of the stories she reported. She shared that the nature of her profession, investigative reporting, meant that she had been threatened many times by land-grabbers and human organ trafficking mafias who did not want their stories to be aired:

To take risks and to go into the field for reporting is an adventure. Before a story, I always think, "Let's see what happens this time!"

Female entrepreneurs in Lahore and Islamabad

There is a growing body of literature looking at female entrepreneurs in developing contexts (e.g. see Brush & Cooper, 2012; Carter, Cinnéide, Henry & Johnston, 2006; Chamlee-Wright, 2002). While microcredit and collective banking schemes that specifically target poor women mainly in rural communities have been around for some time, entrepreneurship is a relatively recent area that has captured the attention of development and business actors. Given the problems many women face in terms of accessing professional occupations, setting up an enterprise that can potentially work around other duties and be flexible enough not to intrude too much on family life offers an alternative route for many women. However, that is not to say that pursuing and setting up a business is not fraught with the same risks as paid employment. For example, women who are deemed too successful may threaten the income-earning potential of their husbands, or rather their status as the main breadwinner, and this could trigger tension. Also, as a business becomes more successful, the entrepreneur may increasingly be pulled away from family duties. This section will review the experiences of women who have set up their own businesses in Pakistan. In a highly conservative context such as Pakistan, women living independent lives is often frowned upon, and so setting up businesses that can – in the beginning – be run from home can circumvent the social norms surrounding and limiting the professional options available to women.

Eight women entrepreneurs were interviewed in Lahore and Islamabad. Securing interviews with this group of women was relatively straightforward, but it was challenging to enter into conversations about VAWG. It was clear that none of the women felt comfortable talking about their personal experiences of violence. As I will discuss in more detail in the conclusion to this chapter, among the middle-class women interviewed, there seemed to be a sense of shame in admitting to experiences of violence. This potentially means that it is massively under-reported among this group, and as such understanding the challenges and barriers faced by middle-class women is critical, and it could point to a gap in provision. The entrepreneurs set up their own businesses for a variety of different reasons, ranging from wanting to be significant and unique (through fashion design or jewellery making) or as a reaction to a failed marriage so as a means to achieve financial independence. One example is a woman who was obese at one point in her life and had health issues. She joined a gym and was so inspired by the trainer that they became business partners. Soon thereafter, he left for another country and she bought out the business, and now owns two successful gyms in Islamabad and Karachi. Being able to overcome her body image issues and owning a successful business gave her immense confidence in herself.

The reasons home-based workers gave for their decision to work and earn an income were very different to those reported by entrepreneurs. There is a clear difference between the experiences of middle-class entrepreneurs compared with the home-based workers who work to make ends meet, as will be discussed in the next chapter. But to summarise, where poor self-employed women are in constant survival mode, this group of women are interested in unleashing their potential and creating a niche for themselves. For example, a wealthy woman from Lahore who ran her own power-generating company stated, "Earning is important in order to eat well, have a good lifestyle ... I am an opportunist, I want to learn from whatever I can." Another entrepreneur who had a small set-up of a mobile waxing service (door-to-door hair removal and other cosmetic services), earning about 10,000 rupees per month, said, "I am happy that I am earning – the main reason that I am earning is for my children."

Another woman interviewed, seen as a celebrity stylist, had been in this field for 35 years. Her first husband died, so she decided to bring up her son as a single parent. She got her certification from London and started her beauty salons and clinics with support from her parents. Currently, she has several beauty salons across Pakistan. Her personal experience of IPV in her second marriage led her to do charitable work for other women, particularly those who suffer disfigurement of the face or body as a result of acid being thrown on them or from stove burns. This included providing free reconstructive surgeries and employing survivors at her salons.

Another entrepreneur was a ceramist and ran a clay factory that made tableware and crockery. She was unmarried and lived with her mother. She described her work as follows: "My business is my passion and I really enjoy it. I could take any other job and not be happy ... I can purchase what I want to, I can do whatever I want to."

A divorced restaurant owner had set up her business in an exclusive locality of Islamabad catering to middle- and upper-middle-class people. She was supported by her father throughout her education and then later in starting out in the culinary business. She made an average of about 300,000 rupees per month. Another respondent, who was a gold medal winner in entrepreneurship and had trained in the UK and the US as a consultant in aesthetic and anti-ageing medicine, said, "Half of the secret of success is perseverance. I am happy the way I earn as I believe that your earning should be halal [kosher]."

The work environment of the women entrepreneurs was extremely comfortable and lavish. They had their own offices or beauty clinics in expensive and secure areas of Lahore and Islamabad. Compared to the home-based workers, their monthly earnings were quite impressive. They had immense backing and support from their parents or wealthy relatives and were well known by virtue of their businesses.

For the entrepreneurs who had been working for many years and were educated, the focus was on their career. While the money was appreciated and provided added luxury, it was not needed for survival; the benefit of working was more to do with identity, self-worth and purpose. The challenges were also different. For example, some experienced difficulty relating to pressure from children to spend time with them and help with homework. When one woman was asked how she reconciled this emotional pressure, she stated, "I felt it at a psychological level, but I think that instead of making daal at home, it is better to bring interesting news to people." Some women reported not being able to tell their husbands how much they earnt for fear that they would take it from them, as the following comment shows:

> The woman is not a machine that does everything – this disturbs one's piece of mind. And if the woman is honest and tells him everything about how much she makes, what benefits she gets at work, etc., he will think of ways to get the money out of her.

In the experiences of this woman, it was clear that her husband was taking her money without her knowledge. She stated, "He would use my money and I would not even know it."

In some of the stories, then, there were indications of a strong link between economic engagement and emotional and psychological stress, which can be seen as a form of violence. The difference is perhaps that with successful businesses, these women could leave, and some in fact had. They are in a position to rebuild their lives with their children, and they are also psychologically strong enough to be able to do it on their own, in part due to the self-determination gained from running their own businesses.

Comparing the life stories of this group of women to the home-based workers in the next chapter, we can see that female entrepreneurs were not only protected and felt safe in their work spaces, because they had both created them and also controlled them, but also had the financial means and confidence to leave a situation of violence of any type. They exercised clear autonomy over their well-being. Unlike these entrepreneurs, women who are home-based workers do not have legal or written contractual agreements and usually work on a piece-rate basis. They have few exit options, if any, and are often stuck in a cycle of oppression and exploitation. The stories to come are harrowing, not just because of the levels of violence endured, but because of the extent to which such violence has been normalised. So, while female entrepreneurs often, according to the global evidence, do have to navigate a violent backlash as a result of their success, and are confronted by the same accusations at home in terms of not being present, they seem – as a group – more confident and empowered to leave, even compared to their middle-class counterparts in other professional occupations.

Conclusion

In drawing over all conclusions, two elements are striking. First, many of the women in employed contexts who reported suffering from harassment at work stated that they were less productive at work as a result. Undoubtedly, violence experienced at home – and the trauma associated with it – will carry through to work and affect a woman's ability to concentrate and be productive. Coupled with the fear associated with travelling to and from work, as well as harassment at work, this means that women potentially have to negotiate multiple types of violence simultaneously while still also fulfilling the obligations of work. In addition to the usual male bias in the workplace, these layers of violence and the related psychological impacts represent barriers to women's chances of promotion.

Some of the women shared very personal accounts of the fear they felt travelling to and from work using public transport. This was often in addition to ongoing harassment at work or violence or harassment at home that was at times a result of working. A significant number of women described the effect of violence in terms of their performance at work. Some talked about the personal impact that this fear had, but all talked in general terms. The psychological stress women must endure was noted by a significant number of the participants. For example, one woman shared:

> It hampers your concentration, and also one type of insecurity it generates in an employee is fear – if I have to take any work from him, I would not in front of him. The gap increases – I feel something, and I cannot even express it. So, obviously, yes.

Another woman recounted the following experience:

> By the time I get to work, I have already been subjected to sharp remarks by my in-laws and husband asking me when I might get home, and wanting every detail of what my day might entail, who I might be meeting with, who might I have lunch with. Then I go on to catch the bus – I pray I can get a seat and be sitting next to a woman. If I have to stand, I will have to suffer the looks and the hands of men standing near. Then, finally, I arrive at work, and I begin to field the subtle and often unsubtle references to my gender from male colleagues. Some days, it is just all too much.

In Pakistan, the impact of work-based harassment legislation is evident, with codes of conduct being enforced in a number of employment settings. The women interviewed who worked in these settings reported an environment in which they felt safe and relatively supported. This highlights the importance of introducing and enforcing such codes as they convey a clear ethos around respect. In some cases, this concern went as far as to offer support and strategies to women when tensions and stress occured outside of work. The evidence is building that protecting and nurturing the well-being of employees, both male and female, will have a positive economic impact on an organisation. That said, the motivation to protect employees from violence and harassment should not be motivated by economic considerations, but should instead be a morally driven action. And given the extent of the harassment recorded, even in the very small sample size in this research, something drastic needs to change if women's participation in the labour force is to represent a real step in gender equality and female empowerment.

A second element that stood out in the interviews with middle-class women in both contexts was the very low membership of women's organisations. In the previous chapter, looking at the experiences of women working in the construction sector of Nepal, and the chapter to come, which records the harrowing stories of poor homeworkers in Pakistan, many of the women were members of networks and organisations that offered them support and advice and advocacy. As noted in the introduction to this chapter, none of the middle-class women interviewed in either country belonged to women's organisations. This meant – and can be seen in the testimony cited above – that their resilience to violence was directly linked to the empowerment they felt they had acquired through earning money. Yet for poorer women, the combination of the agency and confidence brought by earning an independent income was bolstered by membership of peer networks, which in turn linked into other forms of local and specialist support, either in the form of social mobilisers or formal organisations. There seems to be an association between the level and amount of social and cultural capital available to a woman and resilience to violence. This resilience then needs to be further strengthened by enabling an environment of effective legislation and codes of conduct, as well as safe travel to and from work.

As pointed out at the beginning of this chapter, applying an intersectional lens to research on women, work and violence is critical, which allows for similarities and distinctions to be identified between different groups of women who engage in a variety of types of income generation. In doing so, their unique experiences of violence at home, travelling to and from work, and in their working lives, as well as more general patterns of abuse, can be uncovered. As this chapter has illustrated, differences exist, but it is possible to learn lessons by considering the ways in which women in a range of circumstances respond to the violence they encounter, as well as the resources they have available and are able to utilise in doing so. Among the middle-class group, no clear differences stood out in terms of age, marital status, ethnicity, religion or migration status. When applying the ecological approach, as in questioning the extent to which different women may confidently engage with actors in the various spheres from community through to district and state, women in this group appear to be more engaged with district and state apparatus through their professional lives, and so perhaps better understand how power operates at these levels. However, even with this knowledge, they do not seem to be using it to challenge the violence they experience. This may be due to the fact that their ability to influence decisions at higher levels is constrained by their gender. So, while they are confident working in the public sector, for example, they may still encounter a glass ceiling with a disproportionate number of female employees at lower administrative levels. Related to this is the gendering of professions and of power distribution, which is seen at the household level (particularly in relation to women earning more than men or not fulfilling "family duties") and is then reproduced in the workplace. This gendering blocks women from progressing equally and generates tension, and potentially provokes violence or harassment, at home and at work.

Entrepreneurship is the most accepted form of work for women, specifically because it is perceived as something that can be built around domestic responsibilities and can be done at home. As the accounts in this chapter show, once they are successful, the entrepreneurs increasingly prioritise work over "family duties." The idea that they are taken away from it suggests they do not have a choice. However, this stress is – to some extent – mitigated by the greater sense of self-confidence and liberty experienced by financial success.

Attitude change can be seen across generations. Many of the women reported that things would be different for their daughters, but challenges still exist. For example, the lack of engagement with local organisations is very apparent, meaning women in this group do not access support from women's organisations, and instead draw on their own self-confidence and the support of friends. Given the very high level of harassment and fear recorded as a result of work, it could be argued that greater attention needs to be placed on developing a network of support targeting this group of women.

6 | THE EXPERIENCES OF HOME-BASED WORKERS IN PAKISTAN

Introduction

This chapter offers a contrasting picture of women's lives, focusing on a group of poor, home-based, self-employed women in Lahore, Pakistan. The aim is to develop the intersectional perspective by adding the experience of another distinctive group of women who live and work in a challenging conservative gendered context. The experiences presented and analysed in this chapter are those of 20 women who fall under the remit of HomeNet Pakistan (HNP), created in 2005 as a network of organisations working for the recognition and labour rights of home-based workers. All of these women live below the poverty line and, as their stories reveal, all have experienced brutal structural violence and exclusion on a daily basis. Of the women interviewed, ten are from Shadipura and ten are from Gulberg Town, Lahore. The experiences of this group of women need to be placed within and analysed against the broader political and economic context. Pakistan arguably has one of the most deeply discriminatory legislative and criminal justice systems in the world, and these structural issues contribute to levels of violence against women and girls (VAWG), helping to deeply embed the normalisation of violence at every level. The relatively recent return to democracy in Pakistan raised hopes that the state would become more proactive in its efforts to empower women. But to date, progress on relevant legal reform and attention to problematic normative practices and beliefs have been limited. As such, it is important to consider the experiences of these women within this wider political and social reality.

The chapter begins by reviewing the country context, focusing specifically on worker rights and the position of homeworkers. The second section then summarises the work and living conditions of home-based workers, and the third section provides more detail of the organisation HomeNet and its role in raising the profile of workers in the informal sector who work from home. The fourth section then presents the findings from the research. The conclusion draws some critical comparisons between the different groups of women discussed in this chapter and those in previous chapters.

Reviewing the country context

At the community level, especially in rural areas, the formal governance system is often sidestepped in favour of the *jirga* system, whereby elite (mainly male) members of the community form a council to set local rules and hand out punishments. These judgements are underpinned by traditional customs and beliefs, and are often illegal in terms of both common law and sharia law (Shah & Tariq, 2013). The violation of human rights is endemic throughout these formal decision-making bodies but is especially evident in matters concerning morality and the control of women's sexuality (Iqbal, 2007). One manifestation of women's human rights being abused by these local councils is called *swara* or *van*, which is the use of women as "payment" or compensation for crimes committed or using women as a bargaining chip in dispute resolution. Moreover, *jirgas* are not held accountable to higher authorities, and their decisions usually go unchallenged (Iqbal, 2007).

The impact of such discriminatory gender systems is that women's freedom of movement is seriously curtailed. The safe and free movement of women is, as noted in the research presented earlier in this volume, often linked negatively with issues relating to *izzat* – personal and family honour. However, the impact of public space norms on women's experiences of violence is complex and requires a nuanced intersectional analysis. For instance, one study of women's mobility found that for poor women, unaccompanied travel leaves them at risk of sexual violence, but similar movement among richer women does not have the same effect (Mumtaz & Salway, 2005). In terms of empowerment, factors that may help to challenge and change the limitations women face vary from place to place. For example, access to education varies significantly by location. This relates to the local availability of physical resources, such as schools and training centres, but also depends on the attitudes of local communities in relation to women's and girls' uptake of such services. In some places, the risk of religious fundamentalism impinging upon women's opportunities to seek education or skills training must also be considered.

At the household level, as in many parts of the world, patriarchal norms characterise decision-making power and economic control as masculine preserves. According to Ali (2011), men are usually the decision-makers in the family, with strong egos and aggressive temperaments, which are considered socially acceptable. Religious doctrine is regularly invoked to inculcate the belief that women cannot and should not challenge their husbands. According to the same study, socio-economic status notwithstanding, the overarching belief is that a "good woman" does the household chores, cares for her children, the husband and the in-laws, hides her emotions, and "sacrifices her dreams" (Ali, 2011, p. 3).

Statistics have already been given on women's labour force participation in Pakistan and the division between urban and rural areas (see Chapter 5). To reiterate, women are more likely to work if they do not own valuable assets such as land or their homes, but this association is only significant among rural women. In other words, owning land or a home reduces the likelihood of working, but not significantly. Also, rural women are less likely to work if they live in female-headed households when compared to male headed households, but in urban areas this is reversed. Women in rural female-headed households are almost twice as likely to have been employed in the previous 12 months. In urban areas, women who work tend to be older than those who do not, and the odds of working significantly increase with each year of age, but this association is not significant in rural areas.

In rural areas, better-educated women were less likely to work, and the odds of working decreased significantly for each additional year of education. However, in urban areas, the association between female education and employment was not significant. In both urban and rural areas, the education of women's husbands was significantly associated with female employment: the better educated the husband, the less likely the woman was to work. For each additional year of their husband's schooling, the odds of women working decreased significantly. Discrepancy in educational status between husbands and wives was also significantly associated with women's employment in both urban and rural areas. In rural areas, in households in which both partners were uneducated, women were significantly more likely to work. This was the case when compared to households where the man was better educated than the woman, where both partners were educated to the same level, and where the woman was better educated than the man. In urban areas, the trend was similar but was only significant among households in which men were better educated than women.

The number of living children was significantly associated with female employment in the last year in rural areas, but not in urban areas. In rural areas, the odds of women working significantly increased with each additional child. In both urban and rural areas, women were more likely to work if they were not currently in a union, but differences were not significant. Being involved in household decisions, making them alone or together with the husband, was significantly associated with female employment; women who had the most say in decisions were more likely to work when compared to those who had none. In urban areas, for example, women who had the most say were 3.7 times more likely to work when compared to those who had none.

In rural areas, women were less likely to work the more they agreed with norms justifying wife-beating, but in urban areas this trend was reversed – a higher proportion of women who agreed with three or more statements justifying wife-beating were employed when compared to women who said there was no justification for wife-beating. The association was statistically not significant.

In the report published on www.genderinsouthasia.org, multivariate logistic regression models examining the odds of working in the last 12 months show that geographic variation remains statistically significant for both rural and urban areas, and that female employment is significantly associated with poverty. After controlling for variables at the individual and household level, women remain significantly less likely to work in rural Khyber Pakhtunkhwa, Baluchistan and Baltistan when compared to rural Punjab, and also in urban Khyber Pakhtunkhwa and Baltistan when compared to urban Punjab. Women from the poorest households are much more likely to work when compared to those from the richest. In urban areas, women from female-headed households are twice as likely to work as those from male-headed households, but this is not a significant factor in rural areas. Women with higher levels of education are more likely to be employed in urban areas, while higher education of husbands significantly decreases the likelihood of women working. But in rural areas, neither a woman's education nor her husband's are significantly associated with female employment. Women's age is significant in urban areas, with the odds of working increasing with age. Finally, in both urban and rural areas, the odds of employment are significantly associated with the number of household decisions a woman is involved in. The more say she has, the more likely she is to work.

Women's occupations or the sector in which they work varies significantly depending on urban or rural residence. Urban women are most likely to be employed in services and clerical jobs at 49.1 per cent, followed by professional, managerial and technical professions at 21.3 per cent, while almost half of rural women are employed in agriculture, and a fifth have unskilled manual occupations. Type of employer, seasonality of work, type of remuneration, and location of work also vary significantly with urban or rural residence. While the majority – 82.3 per cent – of both rural and urban dwelling women report that they decide (either alone or jointly with their husband) how their money is spent, this is almost universal among urban women at 91.3 per cent. The difference between urban and rural women is statistically significant.

When it comes to experiences of violence, about one in three women have experienced physical violence since the age of 15 (not only intimate partner violence), and 19.2 per cent have experienced it in the last year. Unadjusted odds ratios show that rural women are significantly more likely to have ever experienced all forms of violence and are also more likely to have experienced it in the last year. Experience of most forms of violence considered alongside employment status shows that women who had worked in the 12 months preceding the survey had experienced significantly higher levels of violence than women who did not work.

The data presented here show that rural women are significantly more likely to work than urban women. Factors significantly associated with the outcome were controlled for in the analyses. The model included data on factors ranging from alcohol consumption, having witnessed father beating mother, the respondent's age, education, number of living children, whether their husband is employed (yes or no), husband's education (continuous, single years), province, and household wealth. The odds of experiencing IPV for rural women who worked remained elevated but not significant. One factor that increased the odds of IPV in rural areas was the number of living children: compared to those with no children, women with children were significantly more likely to experience violence. Those with five or more were over three times more likely to experience violence compared to those with none. Violence was also associated with poverty, with women from the poorest households experiencing a significantly higher incidence of violence. Whether a woman had witnessed her father beat her mother was also significantly associated with her experience of IPV. In urban areas, the number of living children, poverty, witnessing parental violence, consumption of alcohol, and having an unemployed husband increased the odds of experiencing IPV.

Work and living conditions of home-based workers

Reports published by HomeNet (see details below) claim that home-based women workers in Pakistan comprise 70 per cent of the informal workforce, and as such represent a significant but largely invisible sector in the country's economy. According to government estimates, there are about 8.52 million home-based workers in Pakistan. The women who are home-based workers usually possess very little or no education. The proportion of women workers who work at home is 65 per cent, in contrast to only 4 per cent of all men. Most of the female home-based workers in the country are "piece-rate" workers, meaning they receive work from subcontractors or intermediaries and are paid per piece completed, according to the number of items produced. They do not have any direct contact with the markets for the goods that they produce. These women usually come from lower- or lower-middle-income backgrounds and are from various age groups:

Aged from 6 to 14 years work and help their mothers in making and finishing the tasks assigned to them by the middleman, earning extremely low wages, even after working 12 to 16 hours a day under conditions that are harsh, unhealthy and hazardous. (HNP, 2011)

Home-based workers are involved in different activities, such as carpet-weaving, bangle-making, football-stitching, sewing, knitting and embroidery. According to HomeNet, there are no local laws or rules to support or protect these workers:

> They are not even recognized as a labour force despite the fact labour laws in the country exist, but they don't give any coverage to them. The labour protection, social security coverage and provision of safety and health services and benefits are not extended to them. They are unable to access the services, facilities, rights and benefits, including a fair remuneration under national laws. They have no easy access even to basic civic facilities like that of health and clean drinking water. The areas where these workers normally dwell are poor areas in terms of civic facilities like availability of clean drinking water, access to health care centres, hospitals, schools, recreational parks and even sewerage system. (HNP, 2011)

In the wider academic literature, research notes the chain of exploitation made possible through globalisation and liberalisation, resulting in the deregulation and privatisation of state-run businesses. Lund-Thomsen (2013) describes how the outsourcing of labour-intensive activities to the developing world has led to the creation of global production networks. In his research, Lund-Thomsen focuses on football stitchers whose labour is home-based and seasonal depending on demand. Factory owners have pushed this labour out from the factory setting in order to reduce costs and allow for flexibility in supply to meet the fluctuating demand for the product.

This leaves homeworkers vulnerable in terms of an unstable wage and leaves them open to exploitation in terms of wage levels and conditions of work. Understanding how the work environment is shaped by processes of globalisation is a critical step towards explaining why the home-based sector is so large in Pakistan. Kazmi and Khan (2003) presented research that argued the global production network pushes down the wages earned by workers. In other words, they are denied the value of their work by the bigger production chain.

In summary, home-based workers live and work in poor conditions with little stability in the medium or long term. With economic growth pushing forward in Pakistan, home-based workers and their communities face the constant threat of eviction as the land on which their temporary homes are built is cleared for "development." Home-based workers then face violence of different types and in the various spheres of the web presented in Figure 2 in Chapter 1. The state affords them very little rights and frequently uses violence in moving them from their homes. This can bring tension into the home, leading to high levels of domestic violence exacerbated by drug and alcohol addictions that are common among poor men in these communities. Azman and Hassan (2014) conducted qualitative research that found home-based workers in Pakistan are often invisible and have little understanding of their own rights. Yet they state that the home-based sector in Pakistan is so large that it is a fundamental part of the country's economic development. The gendered reality of this sector also challenges the assumption that Pakistani women are economically inactive. As stated earlier, the home-based sector is made up almost entirely of women. As such, greater attention to and recognition of homeworkers, as well as the improvement of their rights and working conditions, could potentially increase the productivity and quality of output from the sector, and in turn drive greater economic growth.

Details of HomeNet Pakistan

With this context in mind, let us now turn to the focus group for this chapter: poor home-based workers in Lahore. As stated in the introduction to the chapter, HomeNet Pakistan (HNP) is a network of organisations working for the recognition and labour rights of home-based workers. HNP is a member of HomeNet South Asia, which also operates in Bangladesh, India, Nepal and Sri Lanka. HNP is working for women who work at home and who – regardless of the nature of their work – are exploited and poor. Since its inception, HNP has been organising and mobilising home-based women workers, as well as advocating and lobbying for their issues and rights. It has outreach in 86 districts all over Pakistan and currently has approximately 538 registered organisations representing approximately 58,262 women home-based workers. On its website, HNP gives the following broader and gendered contextual information to explain the importance of its work:

> An estimated 50 million out of 151 million are currently living below the poverty line in Pakistan and the poverty level is rising sharply. The capacity of the poor to improve their conditions of living is constrained by their powerlessness within political and social systems and is linked to inappropriate government policies, no access to information and resources, poor quality of social services and gender inequality.

> It is also increasingly evident that women and girls in poor households bear a disproportionately high share of the burden of poverty. Their greater deprivation is due to a host of factors, including restricted mobility, lack of education and training, lower access to or ownership of resources and assets, and limited access to credit and social services. As a result of this Pakistani women have limited participation in decision-making in all spheres of life from family to state. This is, however, a vicious cycle as this state of affairs persists because women have no say in decisions affecting their economic and social status in society.

A national survey generating gender disaggregated poverty data is required for a systematic gender analysis of the processes of poverty and the specific determinants of the economic burden on poor women. However scattered evidence that is available suggests that due to unequal access of women over productive resources and prevailing gender norms within traditional households, women bear a disproportionately higher burden of poverty: Gender discrimination in access over markets, institutions and resources constraint women from overcoming poverty. At the same time lack of autonomy with household restrains them from increasing and consuming income from even the existing very limited market opportunities.

Poverty has increased sharply during 1990s. The percentage of population below the poverty line increased from 26.6% in 1992–93 to 32.2% in 1998–99. Similarly, estimates in terms of the poverty gap and in terms of the severity of poverty, both indicate a worsening of the poverty situation during the 1990s. Likewise poor women in Pakistan have double burden: the poverty burden and the burden of gender bias against them in social and economic life. This gender bias is reflected in national income statistics which fail to adequately account for the economic contribution of women.

Due to gender discrimination against women in work roles as well as social restrictions on mobility, women have a relatively poorer access over education, skill training and health facilities as well as over labour markets. Consequently, the ability of women to access productive resources, increase their income, improve their health and social status is more limited as compared to men.

Women participation in labour markets is adversely affected by the prevalence of traditional gender role norms, restrictions on women's mobility and occupational segregation. Consequently, female labour force participation rates in remunerative employment in Pakistan as a whole are extremely low at 13.7% compared to 70.4% for men.

Reliable estimates about the size of this sector are not available. According to Economic Survey of Pakistan (2000–2001) of a total working population of approximately 49.1 million, 80% or 39.3 million are employed in the informal sector. Of these workers, more than 50% or over 19.7 million are women. At the national level of all employed women, 77% to 83% operate in the informal sector. These women are not considered workers and do not come under any laws or social security coverage. (HNP, n. d.)

HNP is committed to raising the visibility of female home-based workers, striving to see them achieve decent living conditions and a fair wage for their labour. The organisation seeks to raise awareness among its membership of the economic, political and human rights they are entitled to, and also focuses on campaigning around fair trade practices and greater stability for its members. It has acted as the gatekeeper for the research presented in this chapter, overseeing the safe spaces for speaking with some of its members across two sites in Lahore and ensuring a referral mechanism was in place should any of the women require support as a result of engaging with the research process.

Findings

The data presented here were collected in May 2016 and were conducted in urban and peri-urban areas in and around Lahore. Two focus group discussions were held at Shadi Pura and Gulberg Town, and these were used in part to identify the specific sites for further interviews. One site is Shadi Pura (peri-urban),[1] which has a large population estimated at 69,359 people. This area is deprived and lacks government health facilities or colleges, and while there is a private hospital, it is beyond the means of this poor community. In emergencies, people must take public transport, which again comes at a cost they can hardly afford. There is only one government school, located 1.5 km from the residential area, which is not sufficient for a population this size. Drinking water was reported to be polluted and was seen as the main reason for the ill health of residents. The home-based women interviewed through HNP were mostly involved in embroidery and, depending on fluctuations in demand, their income varied. The 20 women came from a variety of ethnic groups, religions, marital status, age groups and levels of education. Most of the women were engaged in work ranging from making badges for the police, fancy embroidery, sewing clothes, making paper bags, sewing pants and making noodles. All the women were engaged in subcontracted work in which the order was brought to their homes by the contractor, who then gave them a certain amount of time to complete the order before returning to collect it. Most of the women had been involved in this type of home-based work for a number of years.

The interviews revealed multiple forms of exploitation as a result of this home-based work. The work itself represents a form of economic violence due to the very low pay the women received for their work. The subcontractors expected very long hours of work for very little pay, and quick turnaround times put immense pressure on the women. The income that women earned was not enough to help them leave an abusive or violent situation, and if and when they could, they did so without having any economic security. Some women interviewed had left their abusive husbands and/or in-laws without the economic means to be independent, and so they returned to their parents' house and became home-based workers.

The main reason that women gave for being involved in home-based work was poverty. One woman shared the following:

> Everyone works here. One person's earning is not enough to run the house. Everything is expensive – wives have to help out by doing embroidery and making *paranda* [a hair accessory].

Another participant stated:

> For people who earn 30,000 rupees per month, it is even difficult for them to make ends meet, so how can anyone making 200 to 400 rupees per month do it? My man brings home 200 rupees and he brings vegetables. Then I have a sister, four children. Out of two sisters, one died, so I have to work.

Another woman recounted her experiences of working in different places:

> There was poverty in my home ... when I worked outside, that was my home for ten years. I washed clothes in other people's homes, I used to give Koran lessons, and another bit of work where I earned 80 rupees, so that was enough for the children.

Other reasons given as push factors into subcontracted work were to either support their families or to supplement the income of their husbands. In some cases, women started working after their marriage when the husband's income was not enough to sustain the family. Some women shared that they did not work when they lived with their parents. Many of the women had assumed that marriage would bring a level of financial security and they expected to continue being provided for in the same way they had been in their parents' home, but this did not happen. Most of the women interviewed looked despondent, claimed to be exhausted, and described a variety of health issues.

One home-based worker made her living by clipping off the extra thread on bed sheets and made about 250 rupees per day. She shared her experience of the double burden of work, doing household chores and home-based work (reproductive and productive labour), and its repetitive nature:

> I forget things – I place something in one place and then forget where it was. The repetitive nature of the work tires me out, not that I don't have the strength.

She shared how she also engaged in other work, ranging from shelling peanuts to packaging biscuits. This pointed to the irregular and sometimes seasonal nature of home-based work. The unpredictability of the work became apparent in the interviews. The women had no control over what work they might be asked to do by the contractor or how much. The women could not guarantee a steady income as they were dependent on the contractor, who could choose to give them more or less. Another woman who was divorced and lived with her parents sewed *shalwars* (pants) and spoke about how important it was for her to work, but she appeared sad:

> I have been earning for a long time and now I don't feel like working anymore ... the repetitive nature of the work makes me angry.

She shared that she liked to work at home because it gave her a sense of ease and freedom and she did not have to cover herself up. And despite the complaints she had about her work, she said:

> I have changed due to earning my own money, in the sense that I can spend my money where I want.

The level of freedom expressed by this woman may be due to the fact that she had left her abusive husband and was living with her supportive parents. She, unlike many of the women interviewed, had control over how to spend her income. In terms of work-related challenges, many of the women shared their experiences of being deceived by men as they had little experience of dealing with them outside their homes. A woman shopkeeper (own-account worker) shared an incident regarding a man who came to her shop and asked for cooking oil. She did not have cooking oil for sale, but gave him a packet of oil that she had for her own use, thinking that he needed it more. The man asked for

900 change from 1,000 but never handed over the money. And when he was given the change, he ran away with his money, the change and the oil!

Another woman who did bridal embroidery shared a similar experience of how she finished a whole order of ornamental embroidery for a shopkeeper who did not pay her. She needed the money for her own daughter's wedding:

> He told me with a lot of love, "I will pay you, don't worry, you know where my shop is." It's been nine years and he has not paid me 35,000 rupees.

If they had the choice, most of the women interviewed for this research said they would not work. They described life as being good when the man was earning and took care of the family. There were only a handful of women who linked work to economic security and autonomy over life choices. One woman stated:

> I think working women are good, they should work. Any catastrophe can happen in her life and she should stand on her own two feet, not be dependent on anyone.

As the workplace was also the home, we found that women carried out their work in very small spaces, with no proper lighting or equipment that would make their work easier and more productive. One woman we interviewed continued doing her work, which was to make noodles out of dough, in highly unhygienic conditions. Another respondent showed us a small, dark room in which she carried out very intricate embroidery, and another woman's hands were bent out of shape and the skin was damaged from using toxic glue for making badges.

Despite the conditions, the repetitive nature of the work and the low rate of pay, women considered this to be their lifeline and were prepared to continue to work under highly exploitative conditions. That said, there are examples of women exercising agency in trying to negotiate a better deal. One woman of Shadipura who sewed together different pieces of cloth to make *shalwars* shared with us that she and another woman who did the same kind of work had once decided to stop working if the contractor would not raise their rate from 4 rupees per *shalwar* to at least 8 or 9 rupees. The contractor raised it to 5 rupees and they accepted, so there were no further negotiations.

In terms of spending, women used their income for a variety of purposes. If the husband worked and their income was supplemental to his, it could either be saved or used to pay bills, school fees or for medical treatment. In most cases, women made the decision on how and where to spend their earned money. None of the women spent much money directly on themselves, but instead prioritised their children and their education. The decision to prioritise the education of their children often came at a cost to their own personal safety, as will be discussed in more detail later in this chapter, and all of the women had suffered or continued to suffer violence at home. However, apart from in one case, the women did not save their money in order to leave, but spent it to further the life chances of their children.

In both areas where the interviews were conducted, many NGOs were active, mainly giving microfinance loans to women. In the conversations, it was clear that while the women often applied for and took out loans, they almost immediately handed them to their husbands or their brothers-in-law. It became apparent that women in the area regularly took out these loans that were only available to them, but the money was then used to support male ventures. This handing over of the capital is well documented. For example, in the work of Goetz and Gupta (1996) (see also the Introduction), a similar pattern of behaviour with regard to microloans was recorded in rural Bangladesh. The realities of how these female-targeted loans are used has to call into question the extent to which they contribute to the empowerment of women.

The women interviewed stated that they felt safer and more in control working at home compared to working in outside contexts. One woman reported trying to go out to work but was consistently harassed at the workplace. Other women told stories of friends being forced into sexual relations with their male bosses when working outside of the home. Fear of travelling to and from work also emerged as a major barrier to the women who wanted to take on employment in more formal settings, even when the income-earning potential was greater. Some of the more educated women interviewed spoke of the suspicion cast over women who leave their home to work. For example, one woman stated:

> Women who get on public transport and travel far to work risk being accused of having an affair and of bringing shame to their families.

Avoiding this suspicion seemed to be another strong factor in motivating women to work at home. The issue of stigma came through in the experiences of one woman who felt she had to keep her work secret from her husband. She stated:

> Women who earn sitting at home have more blessings. Those who go out to work will be under the suspicion of their husband.

Among the home-based women interviewed, it was clear that there was a shared perception that women who step outside of their home will immediately get harassed. Some women reported that when they had worked outside of their homes in the past, they had been under increased scrutiny and judgement from their relatives and neighbours, and also faced sexual harassment on the way to and from work. A few reported that sometimes relatives would comment on them working a tedious job, but most felt they did not have any other earning options since most were uneducated or inexperienced or lacked the confidence to go out and look for work. With regard to community perceptions of women working, one woman said:

> The *baradari* [community] talks. They say, "She goes out by herself," "She goes to the bank" ... When I go to the shops, they respect me. They address me as "mother" and give me respect.

Another woman shared the following:

> Women work in my neighbourhood. Someone's daughter works, someone's wife works. Some weave for beds, some make bed sheets. Everyone works hard; no one has free time.

She added that her family did not ask her to work, but rather she chose it as she liked to do it. However, she hid it from her husband as they were relatively well off and her income was not needed. The fact that she needed to hide her work from her husband indicated that he did not have a positive perception of women who work. When asked what would happen if he found out, she said:

> I won't let him find out. If he finds out that I do embroidery work, I'll say that this other woman, who lives two houses down from me, comes to chat and brings her work, so it belongs to her.

A young woman, in her early twenties, in a love marriage stated:

> I don't like to go out of the house to work. Those women who do get harassed, they get boyfriends. Working hard means you do it at home. Even if you work outside of the home, you should be careful of your honour.

One respondent shared that her family got upset with her that she worked:

> I ask them, "What should I do?" I have five children. I won't let my daughter get into this work; I will educate her. *Baji*, women's life is hell.

Another shared:

> Community people are jealous of those women who work – they don't support it at all. They say that women are our honour and they should not go out – husbands don't allow their wives to work in factories or hospitals.

The operation of honour and shame appeared to be keeping women in low-paid and economically exploitative income activities. Added to the harsh working conditions, in most cases, the respondent's immediate family or in-laws did not appreciate their work. One woman stated:

> My in-laws don't like it that I work.

Another explained:

> My in-laws don't think that working women are good. My relatives talk and my sister-in-law says that those women who work are not good. But they go out to earn because they are looking after their children. They are doing it for them – the whole world does it.

Women's experiences of violence

The types of violence mentioned by women ranged from sexual violence to physical and psychological abuse. In every interview, violence was a part of life. The domestic violence described was not just perpetrated by husband against wife (IPV), but also by the woman against her children, the in-laws against the wife, and even the wife against her mother-in-law. There were many stories of beating and abuse.

In the interviews conducted with home-based workers, the most common forms of violence were physical and verbal. Interestingly, none of the women identified their economic exploitation by the subcontractors as a form of violence. The economic exploitation that women suffered was, to a certain extent, either normalised or just not seen as violence. However, the level of instability of the work combined with often needing to hide their work from their husbands, as well as the lack of decision-making power, all contributed to maintaining women in a vulnerable position that arguably left them exposed to other forms of physical and sexual abuse. A further troubling factor is the extent to which women are locked into a cycle of working long hours for little money that still did not give them the sufficient resources to leave if they chose to.

These home-based workers endured more extreme and intense forms of violence compared to the experiences of the middle-class professional women interviewed in the previous chapter. Most of the violence, reflecting the global norm, was perpetrated by a husband and/or the in-laws. One respondent shared that her husband hit her on her head and face because she answered back to her mother-in-law. Another respondent shared that her husband broke her knee because she did not wash clothes that day – she was bedridden for many days and still felt the pain. This particular case was representative of many others – the husband beat her regularly over issues that seemed insignificant. When asked how it started, she said:

> This was written in my fate. When I got married to him, his maternal uncle came to attend the wedding as well as his four paternal uncles. They fought over something and the conflict got out of hand. My brother got involved and so did I. I took a stand and said, "I will not meet some of your relatives," so he started to beat me.

The woman also talked of having low self-esteem, which was reflected in her view that violence was part of her fate. She said:

> I was not as good-looking as my brothers and sisters, so my parents did not love me as much as I deserved.

When asked about why she put up with it, she said that she had children to consider and no place to go if she left her husband. Regarding the reason for the violence, she said:

> One day, I downed a bottle of poison when I got tired of my life. When my children were little, if someone said something to my husband [meaning something negative], he would hit me. The fault would lie with someone else, but he would take it out on me, even though he knew that it was wrong to do this. Then I tried to take my life. I took rat poison. I was taken to the hospital, where they pumped my stomach and saved me. Sometimes I just want to leave the world, but then I think about what people will say. They will say, "She left the world for some guy."

She did not think this was a good way to be remembered, and added:

> He hits me whenever he has a fit of rage. In the fourth month of 2015, he broke my knee ... it took me two or three months to get better. My sisters came and took me to my mother's place.
>
> He uses bad words for me. If he wants me to do something for him, he won't ask me to do anything without cursing me ... a woman gets married because she wants love, not abuse.

The only reason the frequency of violence had decreased was because one of the boys had grown up and could take a stand for his mother.

Another respondent shared her experience of physical violence, recounting the following during an interview:

> One day, we came back from attending a wedding – we were happy. At that time, I had two children. I was going to my

bedroom for prayers. I don't know what my mother-in-law said to my husband, but he hit me so hard that my whole being was shaken. When he used to hit me after that, I would not say a word. It was my mother-in-law who'd instigate this. He has also given me a verbal divorce twice. Then he says that verbal divorce is not valid if you do it in anger.

When asked why she put up with this abuse, she stated:

I am tired of putting up with it. I work hard to make ends meet, but even then he does not respect me. A woman works hard, and if she does not get anything in return, then what is the point of that work?

She went on to talk about being stressed, and specifically the difficult combination of "working hard and then putting up with my husband."

An interviewee who was 28 years old and divorced shared details about her marriage and the sexual violence she had endured:

My husband harmed me a lot – I have scars. He burnt me with an iron and my eardrum is damaged. He used to hit me on my back and would not give me food.

She said that he resorted to violence because she did not agree to do what he wanted her to do, which was prostitution. She elaborated on her experience as follows:

He had this number two business [meaning prostitution]. That is why I didn't agree to do it. I told him, "Even if you kill me, I will not agree." He tortured me in many ways. I had a son then, and he would also hit him and create a scene in the neighbourhood. I hoped that my marriage would work out, but it didn't.

He used to take sex enhancement medicine [Viagra], and then he would beat me and have sex. I used to wish for the night not to come. I wished for it to be daytime all the time. I didn't want him to be close to me – I still think about it all, I remember it all. I feel that my life is over. My life is only for my parents and my son. I do not think about remarrying.

There were all kinds of reasons for violence given by our respondents, and there were also instances where women had to face mental stress or physical violence due to having earned their own money. For example, women whose husbands had substance misuse issues or suffered from drug addiction reported being beaten and having their money taken to buy drugs.

A strategy commonly shared by the women was to stay quiet, tolerate the violence, and do all that was required to be a "good wife." The women interviewed described how they would be beaten because they failed to finish their required chores or because they answered back to their husband or in-laws. For example, one woman said:

> If a man is angry, it is better that the woman stays quiet.

Another woman illustrated how silence was a strategic choice:

> One-time silence equals one hundred times being happy.

There was also a clear sense that a woman, once she marries, is on her own. As one woman put it:

> My parents taught me, "Once you go to his house after
> marriage, only your dead body should come back to our house."

As an illustration of the amount of violence women endure from multiple perpetrators, a few of the women also shared that they suffered violence at the hands of their sons. One shared:

> My sons fight with me because they think that I support my
> daughters-in-law. They beat up their wives. Wives should also
> take care to do their responsibilities.

Conclusion

As noted in the Introduction, the link between economic engagement and women's empowerment is thought to be critical and central to women's improved status and gender equality. But the extent to which earning an income can help to mitigate and build resilience to violence is still relatively unknown; we certainly do not have a comprehensive picture across different socio-economic groupings. What the experiences of the home-based workers interviewed for this research tells us is that income for these women is necessary for their survival and that of their children. Their husbands did not earn enough for the family, so the women's income was critical. Some of the women talked of having to hide their income and their work from their husbands and in-laws in order to avoid a violent backlash and the accusation of dishonouring the family. However, many of the women felt that their husbands should be happy they were earning an income because "if women are working, they are not a burden on their husband." When asked, the women said that income did not reduce violence. In fact, one woman said that violence "exists even if the woman is working." Another stated, "It does not matter whether one works or not. If the husband finds fault with something, he will be angry regardless." A third woman shared, "You can earn as much as even 10,000 rupees, but if he wants to hit you, he will." In one case, a woman who was earning and had hid it from her husband shared that if he found out that she was earning, he would be very angry and would hit her. This woman suffered physical violence perpetrated by her husband, who used pipes and chains to beat her in the early phase of their married life. While the violence had stopped, she was sure it had nothing to do with her income, but more to do with a change in attitude in him. In two cases, the continuous cycle of verbal and physical violence ended not because of the women's income, but because the women's sons had grown up and could stand up for them.

As evidenced in previous chapters and differing contexts, income may not automatically build resilience to violence, but it does increase a sense of independence and self-satisfaction. Most of the women did mention that having their own income gave them a sense of confidence and well-being. For example, one woman said:

> I am happy that my circumstances have changed for the better. My children are doing better, Allah is the master, and I have never complained. Whatever is in our fate, we are happy with that. I have never asked for help from my relatives, not even for 1,000 or 2,000 rupees. I have never told anyone that we are ill.

Another woman said:

> If I want to eat something and it is not available at home, then I can just buy it with my own money. So, if there is money, there is no tension.

There is undoubtedly a psychological benefit to earning income across different socio-economic contexts, even in very poor and violent situations such as those faced by home-based workers.

The role of organisations such as HomeNet is significant both in terms of negotiating better work and pay conditions but also in generating peer support and advice. The critical role of local specialist NGOs has already been argued in previous chapters, but we see again here that women would be even more vulnerable without such support and representation. In the context of Pakistan, the strict monitoring of women's movement does bring a level of isolation into the lives of women that is not seen, for example, in the lives of women working in Nepal's informal entertainment sector or in the construction sector in Kathmandu. The strict policing through the concepts of honour and shame regarding women's movement outside of the domestic space is oppressive, and it acts as a mechanism to maintain the normalisation of violence at every level. Applying the web introduced in Chapter 1, we can see that violence is legitimised across each level. Communities operate through a system of reporting and monitoring that maintains the social and cultural norms prohibiting women from moving freely in public. The low reporting and application of any form of justice is also evident in the experiences of home-based workers who do not see the police service as accessible or responsive to their injustices. Given the hostility of the environment and the limited employment options open to women because of the norms tying women to a domestic role, there remains a limit to what organisations such as HomeNet can achieve.

7 | THE GLOBAL DRIVE TO END FEMALE GENITAL MUTILATION: IS AN END IN SIGHT?

Introduction

In this chapter, I explore the global evidence on female genital mutilation (FGM), what we know about why it persists, and what works best to end it. FGM is a highly complex issue that varies significantly across the countries where it is practised in terms of why it is observed and how it is conducted. The specifics of context matter enormously, shaping and changing the ways in which FGM happens as well as determining the likelihood of a particular intervention being successful in ending it.

According to a recent review of global evidence published by the Population Council in Kenya, an estimated 130 million women have undergone female genital mutilation in the 29 highest-prevalence countries, many of which are in Africa. This is a worryingly high figure, and – as the fact sheet goes on to state – 30 million more girls under the age of 15 will be at risk in the coming decade (Population Council, 2015). The pressure is on to understand what works in order to see an end to FGM, and we are at a particular moment in history when more money than ever has been directed towards achieving this goal. Even more is being pledged by bilateral and multilateral donors as well as government agencies. For example, the UK's Department for International Development (DFID), or UK Aid, has just allocated a further £50 million to take its current global programme into a second phase. The original hope was that the first round of funding would be enough to see both FGM and child marriage end by 2018. While this goal has not been achieved, we are able to claim that we now know far more than ever before about the prevalence and the geographical diversity of the practice, as well as the different forms it takes. Additionally, research has been strategically focused on gathering data around the interventions designed to end FGM in the hope that activities can be identified as critical to end campaigns.

To take a step back and to ensure readers understand that FGM does not manifest in the same form, but instead will manifest in a variety of forms in different contexts, I will summarise the most recognised categorisation of FGM. In 2014, UNICEF categorised female genital mutilation into three main types. Type I, also known as clitoridectomy or "Sunna," consists of the partial or total removal of the clitoris and/or its prepuce. Type II, also known as excision, consists of the clitoris and labia minora being partially or totally removed, with or without excision of the labia majora. Type III is the most severe form, also known as infibulation or "pharaonic" type. The procedure consists of narrowing the vaginal orifice by covering, cutting and positioning the labia minora and/or labia majora, and stitching, with or without removal of the clitoris (UNICEF, 2013, p. 45). In addition to these thee main types, Type IV can include pricking, piercing and pulling, and though there is some debate around whether Type IV should be seen as harmful and violent as Types I–III, those who have experienced it claim that it carried significant pain and psychological stress. While I agree with the equal inclusion of Type IV within the broader definitional categories, in this chapter I mainly focus on Types I–III purely because in the country case studies given, Type IV is not observed.

This chapter begins by reviewing the most recent evidence and understanding of why the practice continues. This will include consideration of the differences in how FGM is observed, and why, in different cultural and country contexts. The examples of context will briefly cover Sierra Leone, India and Sudan. This section argues that narratives about the why and how of FGM cannot be treated as uniform, and that understanding the specific political, economic and cultural context of FGM is an essential starting point for any campaign that seeks to end it. This has been a key lesson emerging from the last wave of resourcing into end FGM interventions. The chapter will move from consideration of context to explore the most common interventions, most of which focus on public health and human rights campaigning now channelled through social movements and utilising social media. The third section explores the practice in the context of Sudan, both in terms of the prevalence and national diversity of the practice and the impact of internal migration. The focus on Sudan is largely due to the reality that it is among the countries with the highest prevalence rates but also displays ethnic differences that determine the likelihood of whether a family and community will cut their daughters. This final section will also reflect on the various campaigns and social movements that are resourced in Sudan in an attempt to reduce rates. The chapter concludes by presenting recommendations on how the new wave of resourcing might be best directed.

What do we know about why FGM happens?

Cultural discourse is thought to be the strongest influence in maintaining the practice. Culture is commonly cited by both men and women as the key reason for observing FGM, claiming that it is an important marker of tradition and identity. This can be seen in the data on attitudes towards FGM in the UK presented in Chapter 2, in which supporters of the practice across different cutting communities claim it is an essential part of what it is to be a woman. This is even the case when a woman remembers the pain and trauma of the practice. For example, one woman from Gambia stated:

> I went through the practice when 5 years old back in Gambia, it was very traumatic, I can still recall it now. I do not blame my mother but just accept it is part of my tradition. It is very

painful and problematic for women, but if I have a daughter, I would put her through it because it is part of our cultural identity. (Bodian, 2015, p. 8)

For this woman, culture and tradition are the most dominant influences. While the emotional and physical pain and medical implications are acknowledged, they are not sufficient to trigger a reversal in mindset. For her view to change, the medical and rights-/legal-based discourses need to be strengthened, diluting or even squeezing out the cultural dimension both in her own memory of the practice and how she views it continuing into the future. This can certainly be seen in the context of Sudan, where the cultural discourse dominates. In countries where FGM prevalence is high because it is seen as a cultural necessity, the audibility and visibility of medical and rights-based discourse is severely muted. The challenge faced by local activists and organisations is how to reconstruct the "cultural" in order to remove the violent abuse that FGM represents. The helpfulness of the medical, rights-based and feminist discourses in triggering this process of change is unclear and its real impact remains largely unknown, but I argue they are unlikely – either individually or in combination – to have any significant impact unless the language that shapes them comes out of the local context. In other words, they must be shaped by the change agents who live within the cultural contexts that the programmes wish to transform.

Feminist activists and scholars involved in the global movement, such as Hilary Burrage (2016) and Leyla Hussein (2019), describe the practice as one of the most brutal forms of misogyny that exists to maintain a gender ideology that renders women inferior. FGM represents, so they say, the operation of power and prestige through concepts of shame (if a woman does not conform) and honour (because a sexually pure woman can secure a better marriage). These strongly oppositional feminist readings of why FGM happens exist alongside explanations emerging from in-country research in places such as Sudan that record a range of views, most of which suggest that FGM produces positive results for women. For example, in Sudan, communities have been documented claiming that FGM will improve fertility and prevent stillbirth. It is also believed by some that it gives husbands greater sexual pleasure, thus giving women more power to sexually manipulate men to obtain material advantages. A further belief is that FGM enhances a woman's femininity by removing the clitoris, which is deemed to be a masculine part of the body. In the case of infibulation, it is thought to achieve a smoothness that is considered beautiful. Religious reasons are also mentioned and are sometimes used by pro-FGM groups (Bedri, 2013). However, it should be noted that (as discussed in Chapter 3) a growing body of research argues that the influence of religious leadership in ending FGM is more limited than previously thought (e.g. see Østebø & Østebø, 2014).

The cultural reasons that suggest FGM has a positive value are the main challenge to feminist discourse. At present, the feminist discourse which asserts that FGM commodifies women in places such as Sudan is struggling to be heard among the communities where it is practised. This discourse, when applied in Sudan and other African countries, links FGM to bride price, a practice that reduces women to bartered goods traded at marriage – the purer the woman (or girl), the more her family will be given. Campaigns to end FGM are met with a tangled set of abuses. Across FGM contexts, it is part of a deeply embedded marriage system that is projected through cultural values and economic necessity. There are many activists at the community level in places such as Sudan that articulate similar feminist arguments. However, they often find it difficult to be heard above the noise of both the international campaign and the national conservative backlash against the end FGM programme. Of course, mindset change takes many generations, but the danger is that rather than coming together, international, national and local end FGM activists – if they are not careful – will speak in silos and even silence some positive efforts at the grassroots (see Bedri & Bradley, 2017).

The importance of understanding context

In addition to the need for all campaigning to be driven not by celebrity, but by the grassroots, so too should efforts be shaped by the realities of context. It is important to be sensitive to context when analysing why FGM happens because of the often missed diversity across cutting countries in both how and why it persists. In a context such as Sierra Leone, a nuanced approach to understanding the roots of the practice generates distinctions with other countries such as Sudan. For example, in Sierra Leone, FGM is practised by the bondo, a secret society for women, and undergoing FGM is a key part of the initiation into the society. This makes FGM in Sierra Leone exceptionally difficult to end, so much so that the context is regarded by some as ground zero with regard to eradicating the practice. The bondos' primary function is to exert power and influence over the spirit world, which in turn commands economic and political power. The secrecy and associated ability to appease the spirit world enables members to use fear to intimidate non-members. Girls are initiated from a young age, marking their transition into adulthood. It is understood that girls learn what it is to be a woman from adult female members. This process of education represents a central part of the coming of age acknowledgement; in other words, you cannot claim to be a woman until you fully understand certain key sources of knowledge and insights and are able to perform certain skills. A central function of the society is the education of girls, who learn dance, storytelling and healing, as well as cooking and other domestic tasks that are deemed to be the domain of women. It is reported that the educational aspect of the society has now lessened, mainly due to the growth in the state and private school system and the accompanying legislation that insists girls and boys attend school at least through to the end of primary level. However, it is important to note that despite the decline in the need for girls to be educated through the bondo, FGM has – if anything – become more important. Initiation to the society and the education provided through it used to involve many weeks in the forest, at the end of which FGM was performed as a marker of the now completed transition. Today, only a few days are needed, with the focus on FGM rather than on the learning of new skills and knowledge.

Entrenched power and politics play an important role in the continuation of FGM in Sierra Leone. The outer societal power enabled through the bondo is heavily gendered. The strength of the society is in its preserve as a female-only space, and within this space women are able to gain a level of authority otherwise denied within the wider patriarchal society. Not becoming a member, and thereby not going through FGM, is not a viable option for most girls. To be outside the bondo means that a girl or woman will have even less room to navigate male authority in her everyday life and will be vulnerable to other forms of violence seen to be far more life-limiting than being cut as a child. The society is also able to operate as a tightly constructed voting bloc at election time. No president will be voted in without the support of the bondo, whose membership obviously makes up a significant proportion of the electorate. This power and leverage seem to contradict the high level of gendered inequality in Sierra Leone and the recorded prevalence of FGM at 90 per cent. The position of women across different measurements in Sierra Leone, from access to education and healthcare to employment, falls far below that of their male counterparts. And the poor and marginal position of so many women in Sierra Leone also adds an economic dimension to the practice, which also helps explain its continuation. When considering the bondo in the context of FGM and the economic dimension, it is notable that membership and initiation to the secret society involves a cost, making it a means for senior women to make a living (Mgbako, Saxena, Cave & Farjad, 2010).

Given this context reality, approaches to end FGM in Sierra Leone need to be tailored to reflect them, and neglecting to dialogue with the bondo will almost certainly result in failure. At the same time, approaching such conversations will require immense understanding of the operation of and power relations within the society, as well as the role of FGM in maintaining them. This, in part, involves understanding who the main cutters are, which in the bondo is women designated as *soweis* (Almroth, Bergström, Bjälkander, Harman & Leigh, 2012). While the *soweis* visit families of girls prior to cutting, it has been noted recently that fathers do have some influence (Hernlund, Moreau, Shell-Duncan & Wander, 2010). The involvement of men in the decision-making process goes against the prevailing assumption that FGM is something that women do to each other, and that the practice therefore lies outside the influence of men. What we are beginning to see more clearly in research is that families and communities make decisions together, and that – through a web of power relations – these decisions are influenced by many different factors, ranging from political to economic issues and social status to concepts of honour. As we will see in the context of Sudan, fathers and brothers do have a view on FGM, and in many cases they are the first to insist that it should end. Digging deeper into understanding male views and perceptions around this practice may well represent a key and largely overlooked entry point in campaigns to end FGM.

We will move now to consider how FGM has manifested – and continues to manifest – in the very different context of India. A relatively recent movement has emerged in India driven by women from the Dawoodi Bohra Muslim community who have openly shared their cut status and have called for the practice to end. The Dawoodi Muslim community in India live mainly in Maharastra; with a large community in Mumbai and also in Gujarat, the population size is around 1.2 million. As a sect, the Bohra consider themselves a subsect of the Ismaili Shia Muslims, of which there are around 2 million in the world. In terms of understanding why the community practise FGM, it is thought that they originated in the Yemen, where the practice was – and still is – common, settling in India from the sixteenth century. The cutting the Dawoodi Bohra Muslims perform conforms to the definition of Type I and is called *khatna*. In terms of the prevalence of the practice, Sahiyo, the organisation founded by women from the Bohra community in 2015, conducted an online survey in January 2017, finding that of the 400 women who responded, 80 per cent disclosed their cut status (King & Parry-Crook, 2018, p. 15; Taher, 2017, p. 4).

Capturing the views of those affected by HCPs such as FGM is not easy, not least because of how secretly such practices are observed. For example, the interview below was conducted with a woman in her early thirties from the Bohra community in October 2014:

Do you think the oppressive acts against women in the Bohra community are due to society's pressure or do they have religious reasons?

I think it is a mix of both. Some things are restricted for women due to religious reasons, and sometimes society or the community pressurises a family. I think it also depends from family to family. In more developed areas like Mumbai, which is metropolitan, the Bohra community tends to be more closely associated, because ours is a smaller community compared to other communities, so we tend to stick close together. So, we know each and every thing about each other and the family, which makes it restrictive. But that does not stop people from doing what they want. I know young girls who would leave their houses in burqas and hijabs, but the moment they reached college they would change into casual wear, or guys will go out to drink. There is a lot of hypocrisy within the community.

Did you ever feel obliged to talk to these people, or about these people, who broke these rules?

No, I never bothered. I understood that sometimes the pressure from families is too much. And kids and young people did it only to please their parents, but never really believed in any of these rules or restrictions. Also, it is common to see that normally, parents of these kids enforced these rules without really understanding them. It was more to show off in the community that they follow and believe in everything, but in reality they did not care that much at all. It was done more to preserve their image within the community.

Can you tell me about the practice called FGM or circumcision?

We call it circumcision. There is no mutilation or anything. It is not like girls' parts are mutilated or damaged. If done properly, it is a simple circumcision. Circumcision is performed on both boys and girls. In boys, it is normally done at a very young age, and medically it is said that it helps – that it needs to be done. In girls, however, it is done at a later age, sometime after 4 or 5 years of age. The maximum age at which it can be done is 8 years. However, medically it is said that it is not really needed, so I am against it because it is unnecessarily putting a child through pain.

My mum believes the same thing. She said after she got mine done, she got to know that it does not really help with anything, nor is it needed. So, she told me that she will make sure it does not happen with my daughter if I ever have one. She asked me to make sure that I do not put my daughter through it. I have a cousin who did not get it done for her daughter, even though her mother-in-law wanted. But my cousin was against it and refused. So, now women have started saying "no" to it and stopped supporting it. And it is not just the younger generation that is against it. My mother tells me that lot of her friends are also against it. They say they will not let their granddaughters go through it. So, views are changing.

Why is circumcision practised in your community? Is there any specific reason? Are there any religious directives?

Well, medically we know there is no significance in girls. But for boys, it is medically said it should be done. But circumcision is practised to control sexual desires. It is said that when we hit puberty, we can become sexually active, that we have a desire for it. To curb that desire, circumcision is practised. There is no religious significance behind it. It is not like our leader asks us to do it. But it is also not something we talk about. If I am against it, I won't go around and talk about it with other people in my community. I will only talk about it with my close friends. Like, I am friends with this guy who is my neighbour, but I won't be able to discuss this or my views with him or his family because I do not know what they think about it. And I don't know if they support it or are against it. I do not know how they will react. So, it is better I do not talk to them about it.

Why did you choose to talk to me about it? Do you expect some form of backlash?

Yes, there is a chance that people will not be happy that I am talking about this issue. They will talk about me. They will say that I said stuff like this against the community. I am talking to you because I think more young people should talk about change and progress. We should not be regressive. There is a gap in our community, where young people do not express their opinions and views. I think we need to fill that gap. Circumcision does not achieve anything. It is unnecessary putting a child through pain. Within my family, my mum and I have decided that we will not get it done for my niece, my brother's daughter.

Have you had circumcision done?

Yes. My mother said she got it done for me when I was 5 or 6 years old, but I do not remember. When I grew up and she talked to me about it, she told me, "Daughter, do not get it done to your daughter. I do not want you to put your daughter through that pain." I do not remember anything from my experience. My mother says it is a simple procedure, but she did say that I had nightmares for some time after – that I couldn't sleep and I used to cry at night. So, she asked our family doctor about it, and he told my mum that there is no medical reason that supports circumcision. Since then, she has been against it.

Did you know that circumcision is not performed on girls outside your community?

No. This is something we do not talk about. It is not only personal, but also awkward to talk about. We are normally very uncomfortable. I have only talked about it with my closest friends, who all belong to my community. So, they understand and we share our experiences.

I used to know an old lady who used to do it, but she has passed away. There are fewer women who do it in houses now. Almost everyone now goes to a doctor.

Do you know if any doctors turn the parents away and suggest against circumcision?

No. I have never heard of doctors recommending against female circumcision or refusing to do it. Unless asked if it is necessary, they do not say anything and perform the procedure.

Do you know if anyone has ever had problems due to circumcision?

We do hear cases of it going wrong. Personally, I knew some girl in my family's village. She was my cousin's friend. We got to know that hers was not done properly and she had bled a lot. Since then, she has had constant problems.

This interview confirms much of what is already known in terms of the motivations and reasoning for continuing with the practice. In particular, two recent studies draw attention to the tensions and contradictions in how women from different communities talk about the practice: those who link pain and medical complications to the practice are more likely to be against it and to prevent their own daughters from going through it, while those who feel that the cultural or religious requirements have strong links to identity and personhood are more likely to remain firm, arguing for the continued necessity of the practice. The woman interviewed above expresses an understanding of why FGM continues, but also seems adamant that she will not put her own daughter through it. One interview is not enough to give insight into the dynamics of a whole community and the tensions between those who hold to FGM as an important part of their tradition and those who feel it is no longer needed. But what this interview does show is that FGM is a reality for women in this community. Feminists I have spoken with and have asked about FGM admit that it happens, but locate its prevalence within tribal and rural communities rather than in India's most populous urban metropolises. The work of organisations such as Sahiyo will clearly help to dispel incorrect assumptions and focus attention on the largely urban-based Bohra community who clearly continue to observe FGM.

The case study of India highlights how, when FGM is performed by a minority community in a context where it is not practised by the majority community, a number of additional factors emerge. First, it often goes longer undetected by both global and national programmes to end FGM. In India, which is a country in which violence against women is very high and prevalent in many forms, FGM seems like less of a priority for activists. But what does seem to have happened is that a national movement focused on FGM has emerged, which has perhaps been encouraged by the global attention now given to the issue. This example highlights the importance of concerted campaigning at multiple levels, from the local through to the national and global.

Comparing the Sierra Leonean context to India and Sudan reveals some key differences. While the practice is seen in all cultures as a marker of womanhood, in Sudan and India it is very much a family and community decision. With an absence of such tight secret societies in Sudan, it is family and peer networks that wield the most influence, with ethnicity also playing a critical part. In some parts of Sudan, ethnic groups have never practised FGM. With regard to the Bohra community in India, there seems to be a level of secrecy that may be enabled by their minority status. In India, FGM has been able to continue under the radar of legislators and activists, though this might now be changing. These differences point to the need for individualised interventions. In Sudan, community-focused approaches have a much greater effect, while in Sierra Leone these more holistic projects are unlikely to work as they would fail to acknowledge and respect the power of the bondo society. In India, it is likely that working with the Bohra community directly, and particularly with the emergent change agents, will have a greater impact.

The medicalisation of FGM

Key to understanding what works to end FGM must be a review of the impact of different discourses and interventions that have been implemented thus far. The medical discourse that first shaped a global understanding of the practice through the identification of four categories of mutilation (WHO, 2008) overwhelmingly influences the work of international organisations. However, from the 1990s, FGM began to be reframed as an issue of rights, which made it possible for the UN Universal Declaration of Human Rights to be used as an instrument in the campaign for its eradication (Shell-Duncan, 2008). Today, the two discourses have become intertwined, with the language of rights tending to be more strongly used to construct a clear – and hopefully pervasive – message that FGM is child abuse. This intersection of the medical and rights-based discourses can also be seen in Sudan and will be outlined in more detail in the fourth section. The public health sector in Sudan is highly developed, not least because of the large number of medically trained professionals who seek work promoting educational messages across communities. The FGM campaign has been able to utilise this capacity and network to effectively link the discourse regarding medical implications of the practice to a rights-based concept of a whole (uncut) girl as being empowered with multiple opportunities otherwise denied (Saleema) (Bedri & Bradley, 2017, p. 28).

In the drive to understand what is working to end FGM, greater attention has been placed on the impact that medicalisation has had on prevalence rates. The term "medicalization" refers to the practice being performed by a medically trained practitioner such as a doctor or midwife, rather than by a traditional so-called "cutter." Much of the campaigning in countries such as Sudan and Egypt has emphasised the harmful impact of the practice, and the result of this campaigning has tended to be an increase in the practice being carried out by medical professions, rather than it ending altogether. In Sudan, for example, medicalisation rates are the highest in the world, with 67 per cent of all cut women having undergone the practice performed by a medical practitioner. In Egypt, rates are the second highest at 42 per cent. Some argue that the shift to medicalisation should be seen as positive given that it will likely reduce the risk of infection and long-term complications. But for those of us active in the FGM movement, medicalisation masks a lack of progress in terms of denormalising the practice (Njue, Moore & Shell-Duncan, 2018). A further worry in relation to the impact of current interventions is a shift between the different types. Health messaging and human rights campaigning has impacted on medicalisation rates but also on shifting the type observed away from what is seen as the most harmful – Type III to Type I. In fact, Type I is regarded by many in cutting communities as not FGM at all (e.g. see Boddy, 2016).

What is clear is that FGM will only end with further sustained and coordinated efforts to understand the diversity of how and why it continues. We also need to do more to evaluate the impact of different grassroots interventions that the evidence increasingly tells us need to include youth groups and movements.

FGM in Sudan

So far in this chapter, I have reviewed at least some of what we know about why FGM happens as well as some of the efforts to end it. I have also argued that understanding the specific context of FGM is critical in the design and positioning of such efforts. I will now go on to explore FGM in more depth from within a single context. Sudan, as I will describe, has been the focus of UK Aid's pilot intervention programme, which makes it a useful context within which to reflect on the relative success of different approaches. Also, it is a useful platform from which to exercise caution regarding some of the competing discourses that surround the practice and that can unhelpfully clash and inhibit dialogue. Before I go further, I need to outline the FGM picture in Sudan. According to the 1990 Sudan Demographic and Health Survey, 89 per cent of married women in the northern, eastern and western provinces had undergone either Type I or Type II (15 per cent) (i.e. partial or total removal of the clitoris) or Type III (85 per cent) (which is the most severe form, involving infibulation, narrowing of the vaginal opening through the creation of a covering seal). There is, as expected, internal variation in prevalence and type observed across Sudan. The first Sudan National Household Survey (SNHS) conducted in 2006 among women of reproductive age (15–49) recorded an average prevalence of 69 per cent in the 15 northern states, ranging from 40 per cent in West Darfur to 84 per cent in River Nile (SNHS, 2006). The 2010 SNHS recorded a national prevalence of 66 per cent for any type of FGM, with internal differences ranging between 46 per cent in West Darfur and 84 per cent in the northern states. Though this information is useful, there are problems with the collection of quantitative data and also with the types of questions asked (SNHS, 2010). This means the picture is far from clear, but what these statistics do tell us is that FGM prevalence is high across Sudan, with some states exceptionally so. We can also say that very little change has occurred, with only tiny reductions in average rates that are so slight that they could simply be down to the margin of error expected.

The difficulties involved in gaining a clear picture of the problem add another dimension to the uphill struggle campaigners are faced with. Above, I offered a summary of the prevalence of FGM in Sudan and highlighted how averages map differently across states. However, the survey results looking at FGM in Sudan have been criticised for two reasons: first, for the use of different age cohorts; and second, because most of the existing prevalence rates are based on self-reporting by the respondents. Using different age cohorts can influence results. For example, the 2006 SNHS showed a prevalence rate of 69 per cent based on the circumcision status of all women aged 0–50 years. This was then recalculated using UNICEF's standard indicators for women aged 15–49, which eventually gave a prevalence of 89 per cent (Ahmed, Al Hebshi & Nylund, 2009). Moreover, self-reporting has previously been shown not to be accurate, meaning the statistics may not reflect the real situation on the ground. Evidence indicates a discrepancy between types practiced and self-reports by women and cutters. For example, a study in Sudan (see Almroth, Elkhidir, Elmusharaf & Hoffman, 2006) found that at least half of the women who stated they had Type I (clitoridectomy) and Type II (excision) FGM/C were actually subjected to Type III (infibulation). Another study (see Magied & Ahmed, 2002) focusing on midwives asked them to describe the operations they had performed, and while it was recorded that Type I had been carried out, the descriptions given more closely resembled Type II and Type III. What these results show is that statistical research alone cannot tell us the whole story, and can in fact paint an inaccurate picture. Given the huge diversity of Sudan, it is no surprise that this is the case, not least because cultural understanding of the practice varies. The results also highlight that the medical classifications of FGM are not necessarily used by women and girls to describe the practice performed on them, and when they are used it is not always in line with the accepted definitions of types. Interventions to end FGM need to respond to these realities because a lack of clear statistical data, combined with women's own confusion over what level of cutting they have experienced, obscures attempts to get a clear picture upon which to build social change.

In Sudan, efforts against FGM started in the early 1940s in the form of state legislation banning the practice (Predie et al., 1946 cited in Bedri, 2013). In the 1970s, community awareness programmes were introduced, run in the first instance by a few NGOs. Community engagement remains a key approach today, where we see greater engagement from government and other institutions through to the UN.

In addition to the drafting and passing of legislation as a key mechanism in the end FGM programme, media campaigns also exist designed to push for mindset change. The campaigns exist at federal and state levels, utilising radio programmes through which key messages are delivered, usually made by religious and community leaders. Role play and songs have also been developed for use in this campaign. Television channels have increasingly covered the issue, highlighting the key statistics on prevalence and the consequences of FGM. Media approaches feed into the national Saleema campaign, a social movement used to build momentum from the grassroots through to the legislative structures. Saleema is inspired and named after the Arabic word that means "whole, healthy in body and mind, unharmed, intact, pristine, in a God-given condition and perfect." Activists involved in creating the movement chose the word Saleema to create a new field of positive association of expectations for uncut girls and women.

Analysis conducted by the UNFPA on the type and nature of the media campaigning used by the end FGM programme between 2000 and 2010 identified articles stressing the legal position in relation to FGM, as well as many that focused on the medical message. In terms of the discourses shaping the interventions, we see an integrated approach combining medical and legal activism motivated by a commitment towards gender equality. This carries through into the DFID intervention programme being implemented by UNICEF, WHO and the UNFPA. A combination of behavioural change approaches are being used, including peer education, supporting positive deviants and community conversation. Early evidence suggests that each of these approaches has some impact in terms of changing views on FGM, but it is too early to know if they will bring dramatic and sustained change. What we still do not know is what the main and lasting triggers are for long-term mindset change. Until we can generate evidence that helps to pinpoint answers to these questions, an integrated approach is the best way forward. The approaches used are essentially directed at altering the cultural discourse that still holds firmly to the idea that FGM is necessary. But presenting "culture as the problem" is fraught with ethical complexity not least because it tends to lead to misrepresentation of a country's cultural diversity. Furthermore, it assumes there are no change agents inside communities already challenging harmful practices and reinforces global and national hierarchies of power between those that claim to know and those positioned as victims or perpetrators (Bedri & Bradley, 2017, p. 35).

Since its inception in 2015, the Free Sudan programme has evolved into a complex web of interlocking projects. All the programmes together are referred to as Sudan Free from Female Genital Cutting (SFFGC). Five key outputs of the programme can be identified: social norm change policy, legal reform, evidence on what works, community mobilisation, and capacity-building. SFFGC is coordinated by NCCW (which runs the National Task Force), WHO (the end service provider that is also responsible for drafting the research strategy identifying gaps in knowledge in relation to FGM in Sudan), the UNFPA (acting as the capacity-building coordinators) and UNICEF (responsible for the social norm change policy).

The United Nations Joint Programme (UNJP) (which DFID also supports) has three outputs: legal and policy reform, mobilisation, and interventions to end FGM. In relation to the third output, UNICEF coordinates Saleema as a national social movement that will run for four years in total, targeting states with high prevalence through radio and print-based advertising (such as posters, leaflets and T-shirts). In addition to the Saleema movement, The Girl Generation also launched their movement in Sudan, focused on raising visibility of the issue at the community level.

In order to understand if these interventions actually affect any change, it is important to listen to the voices of women and men from within cutting communities. Listening to these voices makes it clear that the campaign to end FGM must be guided by those from within, and it will not work if actors from the outside merely push uniform messages across potentially very different contexts. Voices in Sudan raise specific concerns that the multiple interventions outlined above might not converge sufficiently enough to have any real impact. As one participant told us, "If campaigns are not led by local activists, they will not be taken notice of and have little impact" (interview conducted by author, May 2015). Another local NGO worker admitted that "some organisations are reorienting their focus to take advantage of the additional funding for FGM" (interview conducted by author, September 2016). This viewpoint echoes arguments made earlier in this chapter: the discourse on policy relations has to be contextualised around the politics of resource allocation, which often unwittingly leads to a distortion of discourses for the purposes of organisational survival. Applying Bacci's critique of policy discourse analysis to the FGM discourses reviewed here reveals that at one level, we do accept and support her call to understand the terrain as one in constant flux and fraught with change tension (Bacci, 2000). But these tensions are influenced not just by macro-actors; they are also shaped by community mindsets that reject global discourses as insulting and for failing to reflect their experiences of the practice (e.g. see Malmström & Van Raemdonck, 2015).

It is also necessary to draw attention to the change agents that bridge the gap between the global and the local and facilitate dialogues across and between different discourses. However, we also have to recognise that a significant amount of money is also in play, which produces a power battle between the different discourse policy approaches (see Boyle & Preves, 2000). The political tensions that emerge utilise constructed and essentialist cultural images to further their campaign. With this in mind, I return to arguments made in Chapter 3 in which I applied anthropological theory to a critical deconstruction of how objects of pity can (unintentionally) manifest themselves unhelpfully in movement politics, and consider if this has or is (even slightly) apparent in the case of the global FGM campaign. The anthropological theory helps to frame our cautionary note that builds on, I believe, the work of scholars such as Bacci. Analysing what works involves peeling back the layers of construction that may create multiple myths around why and how FGM continues. For example, Harding (2008), James (1998), Mohanty (2003), Wade (2009) and Yuval-Davis (1997) have all argued that writings on the suffering of black women often create (intentionally or otherwise) a binary between "modernised Western women" and "backward, yet to be liberated African women" (see also Nader, 1989; Volpp, 2000). Thus, the challenge faced by many in the world of end FGM programming is how to navigate a path that is respectful and supportive of the experiences and activism of those most affected while still taking real steps towards ending the practice. In other words, how can we learn and respond to the voices of women affected, rather than impose, assume and further entrench unhelpful racial stereotypes? Wade (2009), in her analysis of the media coverage of FGM, talks of the orientalist gaze through which the media reports stories about the brutality of the practice, parading victims in a way that verges on voyeurism. For Wade, it is not the documenting of the violence that is the issue, nor is it an issue that forthright empowered survivors are given the space to speak. Instead, it is the way in which these experiences may not be heard as empowered rallying cries, but as evidence of the backwardness of the traditions from which the women belong. I argue that there is a danger that the voices of survivors are lost within a more dominant and culturally essentialising response.

In Chapter 3, views were presented ranging from local community groups in the UK to activists in Sudan, all of whom articulated their concern that interventions were not listening to the voices of people already working at the grassroots level to end the practice. As highlighted in Chapter 3, in order to be effective in ending FGM, it is necessary to acknowledge some challenging perspectives that see FGM not just as culturally necessary, but as a practice that enhances female sexuality. This detailed and in-depth analysis makes it possible to appreciate the range of views that need to change if FGM is to end completely.

Conclusion

Digging into what the critiques as well as the statistics tell us, with a focus on what works to trigger change, the following is revealed. A shift in the perceptions of the youth, especially those who are educated and urban-based, is occurring, with an increasing number regarding FGM as a human rights issue. Research capturing youth perceptions of FGM in Sudan recorded that both young men and women use terms such as "torture," "pain" and "unfairness" to describe the practice (e.g. see Abdalla et al., 2018; Ball et al., 2010). Clearly, it is necessary to tap into this by introducing new discourses, approaches and messages that reflect and enhance this stance and empower young people to voice such opinions and reject the practice.

One of the main barriers to decreasing the prevalence of FGM is its strong cultural link to marriage, specifically the view that a girl must be cut in order to preserve sexual purity and family dignity. Young men, so recent research suggests, seem more open in declaring they do not want to marry cut girls. They are beginning to declare in greater numbers that they prefer uncut girls because they are healthier and stronger. This view is echoed by many young women who use the language of sexual rights to argue that FGM violates their sexual identity and expression. However, these views are often hidden by an aggressively conservative discourse that rises in a backlash against suggestions that FGM must end. Finding and encouraging networking between those that carry these strong anti-FGM views will be critical if we are to see an end. It is also critical that support is increased for girls who continue to be cut. The stigma associated with FGM is beginning to work both ways, with cut girls feeling stigmatised by the human rights discourse while uncut girls still feel the pressure to hide their status in case it brings shame on their family (e.g. see Bedri & Bradley, 2017).

While all of this highlights just how complex the issue of ending FGM is, and indeed how much more work we need to do, it also shows that we are beginning to see more clearly how we might better target resources for ending FGM. Efforts need to be directed at the grassroots and towards those that no longer want to be a member of a community or family that cut daughters. This means identifying positive deviants, change agents and grassroots organisers who are already influencing their own communities from within to move away from FGM. It also means ensuring that positive discourses regarding "whole" uncut girls and women do not simultaneously contribute to stigmatising and potentially further marginalising those women and girls who are most vulnerable or who have already been victimised.

8 | VIOLENCE AGAINST WOMEN AND GIRLS IN CONFLICT SETTINGS

Introduction

In this chapter, I will present a review of research on violence against women and girls (VAWG) in times of humanitarian crisis, mostly as a result of conflict. In recent years, much attention has been placed on rape as a weapon used during war as a way of humiliating the enemy. Studies suggest that as many as one in five women displaced due to humanitarian crises experience sexual violence (Adam & Wartz, 2014). As a result of global campaigning, the relationship between rape and war has been recognised and has been condemned as extreme brutality. While the brutality of rape during conflict is beyond dispute, research now asserts that in the broader context of conflict and post-conflict settings and against the spectrum of violence against women and girls, it is not the most prevalent form of violence, even in such extremely externally violent settings. Research conducted in South Sudan (What Works, 2017) recorded that while many women (33 per cent of respondents) reported instances of rape by strangers during the conflict, which in most cases were committed by military combatants, IPV remained the most common form of violence, and prevalence spiked during unrest. In fact, the research recorded that a staggering 73 per cent of women had experienced sexual violence by a partner in some parts of the country (e.g. the state of Rumbek). The report stated:

> While women and girls were often subject to sexual violence by armed actors, they also felt the impact of conflict in a number of other ways. Experiences of displacement,

the breakdown of rule of law, increases in crime and the normalisation of violence also affect VAWG. These indirect experiences of conflict have an impact on violence in the home. (IRC, 2017, p. 12)

This evidence is important in terms of ensuring that resourcing is directed towards responding to the full spectrum of violence women and girls experience during conflict and other humanitarian crises, which includes ongoing domestic abuse, rather than focusing too heavily on conflict rape. The report also stated:

> Recent studies indicate that intimate partner violence (IPV) may be more common than conflict-related sexual assault; however, both IPV and conflict-related violence are under-reported in these settings. Though several studies have collected robust data on VAWG in humanitarian settings, many experts argue that our overall understanding of the issue remains limited. (IRC, 2017, p. 6)

The importance of evidence-based interventions in responding to and preventing violence is illustrated in conflict settings, where it would be relatively simple for practitioners to latch on to the most talked about and globally championed form of violence, namely rape as a weapon of war. This chapter seeks to explore the multiple forms of violence women are subjected to during and post-conflict by comparing a number of settings, but with a specific in-depth focus on South Sudan. The country has been labelled by some activists as one of the worst places in the world to be a woman, largely because of the very high levels of violence that women frequently experience in multiple forms and throughout their lives.

Analysing and indeed capturing the multiple levels of violence women and girls suffer in conflict is made even more complex by the ongoing reality, even outside of conflict, that VAWG is one manifestation of the oppressive cultural and institutional structures that come together to preclude women's empowerment. As such, preventing violence requires a detailed understanding of its origins in sociocultural structures of oppression, and of its situational triggers. These should be conceptualised as a web of intersecting causes and effects. In the 1970s and 1980s, VAWG was analysed through relatively blinkered theoretical lenses. The perspectives of criminology, sociology, psychology and feminist theory led to single-factor explanations of IPV, characterising it as a result of socio-economic disadvantage, social learning from parents, psychopathology and patriarchy, respectively (Heise, 2011), sparking fierce debates about what the "real" cause of violence actually is. In the 1990s, however, it was increasingly recognised that violence – as a manifestation of women's disempowerment – is multifaceted; it results from the interaction of various social, economic and political factors. When conflict is added to this heady mix, the already underlying structures of oppression that render women vulnerable to violence are magnified. With this in mind, unpacking the prevalence and forms of violence during conflict requires the same approach as in non-conflict settings, with the added sensitivity to the potential for conflict to introduce more forms and be a highly toxic trigger for a greater intensity of VAWG.

The acceptance of universal risk factors for VAWG, even in conflict, is highly contentious. Some theorists do argue that universal (i.e. cross-cultural) risk factors for VAWG can be identified. Based on the findings of multiple VAWG studies in different communities, Heise (1998) identified numerous "universal indicators" for IPV, including – but not limited to – witnessing domestic violence as a child, male alcohol consumption, low socio-economic status, and "hypermasculinity." However, this view is problematic in that it generalises findings from numerous studies conducted in singular locations (many of which were in the developed world). To assume that something found to be a risk factor in one setting is also a risk factor in another is certainly ill-advised, and other research that has tried specifically to uncover universal triggers for violent behaviour through direct comparisons of multiple contexts has yielded mixed results. For instance, Ansara, Hindin and Kishor (2008) studied ten countries' Demographic and Health Surveys (DHSs) and found only two universally relevant risk factors for IPV: a man's excessive alcohol consumption and exposure to inter-parental violence. However, it has since been suggested that the lack of success in locating universal factors may be attributable to the DHSs' non-standardised data collection and measurements.

In the context of defining VAWG in conflict, it is imperative to understand local perceptions and interpretations. The key question should be: Is VAWG a category that shapes local discourses? Given the diverse and numerous forms of violence women and girls are subjected to across the globe, it is also important to understand which forms of violence, as categorised through global definitions, are recognised as such at the local level, and how these might change as a result of conflict. For example, is intimate partner violence (IPV) recognised as such or is it widely normalised by women and men? If it is normalised, appreciation of the extent to which conflict exacerbates its prevalence will be hard to evidence. It also means that implementing any form of justice will be difficult.

The first section of this chapter will review what is known about VAWG in conflict and post-conflict settings, and will consider how – and if – a spectrum of violence and associated triggers have been captured by existing research. The second section will introduce the specific context of South Sudan and what we know and understand about VAWG at the national as well as more localised levels. The chapter will conclude with some recommendations on how policymakers and practitioners may be sensitised to the realities of how VAWG emerges in conflict and post-conflict settings, and the best ways to respond.

Review of research on VAWG in conflict settings

Most of the early literature on rape as a weapon of war emerged during the 1990s and focused on the Yugoslav Wars, in which it is estimated that between 20,000 and 50,000 were raped, most of whom were Bosnian (Kohn, 1994). Diken and Lausten (2005) also list the genocide in Rwanda (see also Reid-Cunningham, 2008) and the civil wars in Liberia and Uganda as horrific examples of the use of rape as a weapon. Other examples include the nationalist war in Bangladesh, anti-Chinese uprisings in Indonesia, and Japanese soldiers raping women in China and Korea during the Second World War (see Watts & Zimmerman, 2007). Diken and Lausten (2005) state that "the prime aim of war rape is to inflict trauma and thus to destroy family ties and group solidarity within the enemy camp" (p. 111). This now is widely understood to be a powerful motivating factor behind the use of rape during conflict. Eriksson Baaz and Stern (2013) argue that while the realities of war rape are grim, there is some hope in the fact that it is now acknowledged not as an inevitable result of war, but as a security issue. Rape during conflict is not haphazard and inevitable, but is instead planned and systematic, and the responses to it are now beginning to be planned strategically and – at the global level at least – determined. Eriksson Baaz and Stern (2013) go on to describe how various discourses have emerged around rape, some of which suggest that rape is a conscious strategy and is asserted down the line of command. Other discourses see it as a sign of disorder and a lack of strategy. They go on to state:

> Our exploration into the underlying logics and scaffolding of the rape as a weapon of war discourses emerges out of a concern with the ways in which a generalized story of rape in war limits our ability to analyse and redress instances of sexual violence in specific war scapes as well as to attend to the people whose lives are circumscribed by such. (p. 4)

I would extend this concern to other forms of violence that intensify as a result of war but do not get acknowledged to the same extent, either because of the humanitarian focus on rape as a weapon of war or because other forms of violence are simply normalised and seen as part of everyday life. So, even when they increase as a result of conflict, such normalised forms of violence may remain invisible to outsiders.

In another publication, Eriksson Baaz and Stern (2008) present research from the DRC, dubbed by some commentators as the murder capital of the world. The research presented argues that rape in the DRC was very much framed by international discourses and gendered through them in such a way that it became the focus of most attention, despite the array of many brutal forms of violence, ranging from mass murder through to systematic homicides. A report published by the *American Journal of Public Health* (Bredenkamp, Palermo & Peterman, 2011) revealed that 12 per cent of women had been raped at least once and that 3 per cent of women across the country were raped between 2006 and 2007 alone. Around 22 per cent had also been forced by their partners to have sex or perform sexual acts against their will. The study also revealed alarming levels of sexual abuse in the capital, Kinshasa. The findings led the authors to make recommendations that abuse within families should be the key focus of interventions, with parallel activities aimed at reducing the systematic use of rape by the militia. As the case study on South Sudan given below highlights, women who suffer from rape as a weapon of war very rarely have only experienced this form of violence, and indeed the conflict itself merely increases the likelihood of an array of different forms. Excessive focus on one instance or one form of violence a woman experiences will therefore do little to remove the threat of violence from the lives of women and girls in general.

As stated at the beginning of this chapter and also in the Introduction, understanding why rape and other forms of violence occur requires a close and critical understanding of gendered power, specifically masculinity. Violence is seen as a sign of hypermasculinity, a display of strength that – across contexts – materialises as men having control over women. Eriksson Baaz and Stern (2009) observed in relation to sexual violence during conflict:

> The soldiers explicitly linked their rationale for rape with their inabilities (or "failures") to inhabit certain idealized notions of heterosexual manhood. The soldiers posited the discord between their embodied experiences and their expectations of themselves as soldiers (men) in the armed forces as a site of frustration, anxiety, negotiation and an underlying incitement to sexual violence. (p. 497)

There is clearly a need to not isolate war rape from other forms of VAWG. Instead, the normalisation of violence should be seen as a stark reality in all settings, with the acknowledgement that in times of stress and tension, it will intensify and manifest in new and ever-more brutal forms. Humanitarian responses need to be guided by a more nuanced political, economic, historical understanding of the context. It is only with this complex knowledge that the links between rape and conflict can be gained and used to inform interventions.

A good early example of the kind of in-depth analysis needed was produced by Jok (1999), who focused on Dinka communities in South Sudan. Jok writes:

> The existing studies of gender violence in Africa pertain almost exclusively to statistics of rape in war-torn regions such as Rwanda, Somalia, Liberia and Sierra Leone. The studies of sexual abuse under conditions of civil strife suggest that as young men become machines for violence, random mindless sexual demands become almost an inevitable payment that they expect to receive for their sacrifice for the nation. (Jok, 1999, p. 66)

In South Sudan, male military personal are expected to be violent: "no one can control them when they are off duty," and sex is something young military men expect as compensation for the risks they take (Jok, 1999). Jok (1999) urges the need for a comparative historical perspective in order to challenge assumptions that increased violence against women during conflict is only linked to the intensified hypermasculinity driven by militarisation, because while this may represent one reason, two further contributing factors can be identified. He writes that the strong nationalist sentiment that often goes along with civil war also fuels violence. He cites a quote:

> The war is a responsibility for all; some must die in order for the whole to live ... It is a war to be fought from all fronts and for generations, and women's front is reproduction ... If we fail on that front, we lose the war. (Jok, 1999, p. 67)

The view, then, is that women must procreate to maintain the ethnic population. If they are not seen to be doing this adequately, then rape may be used. While during the early days of the civil war between Sudan and South Sudan women were enrolled as combatants, for reasons Jok records as unknown the female battalions that existed were disbanded. Women's role as being submissive and domestic became entrenched, and reproduction came to be seen as women's nationalist service.

A third reason emerges in the historical context of South Sudan that contributes to explaining the very high levels and acceptance of violence against women: it is necessary for men, according to the Dinka, to regularly force themselves sexually on their wives (Jok, 1999). Marital rape is not recognised as such due to the normative belief that sex is a husband's right in marriage, regardless of whether a wife consents or not. Forced sex is instead seen as a way for husbands to remind wives of the importance of remaining faithful to them. In other words, it is fuelled by jealousy, which in part may be due to the extended periods of time that men involved in war spend away from home. If a husband is denied his marital sexual "rights," this can be taken as proof that his wife is sleeping with another man. Besides the clear ethical and moral issues and the psychological impact on the women who are raped by their husbands, the physical health implications of rape are well known, and these are especially dangerous in a context where health provision is minimal, if accessible at all.

In summary, three interconnections between rape and conflict emerge. First, young military men see rape as their right due to the sacrifice they are making to the nation. Second, part of the role of women is considered to be reproducing the national or ethnic population. And finally, jealous husbands see rape as a marital right, and when they are fearful that their wives cannot be trusted, it is used to "prove" that they have been faithful. The links will no doubt differ according to the nature of the conflict and pre-existing patterns of violence against women, but no single explanation for increase in sexual violence can – or should – be sought. For comparison, in the context of the 1994 genocide in Rwanda, rape was used as a systematic tool designed to "provoke maximum terror by damaging and destroying multiple aspects of human life including social bonds, cultural practices, bodies and psyches" (Nyirazinyoye & Zraly, 2010, p. 1). As such, studies do not tend to report that the genocide worsened already normalised forms of violence in the way the civil wars in places such as the DRC and South Sudan seem to have, but rather it fed into and helped to intensify fear in the "target" Tutsi group.

The nuanced analysis produced by Jok (1999) is in contrast to the messaging emerging as a result of the "celebrity factor," whereby celebrities become involved in promoting or advocating for particular causes. In recent years, we have seen a surge in celebrities taking up development issues, especially in relation to the plight of children – for example, Madonna in Malawi and Angelina Jolie in Cambodia, spurred by her experiences filming there in 2000 (Piknerova & Rybakova, 2017; see also Brockington, 2014; Goodman & Barnes, 2011). Rosamond (2016) details the transformation of Jolie into a "global mother" figure, swapping her vamp image for something more serious and demur in keeping with the responsibilities of raising and caring for children. The global reach of her campaigning is, of course, welcomed, but needs to also be considered with some caution, particularly in relation to war rape. The particular celebrity discourse developed and created in part by and because of the strong following of these figures tends to present universal interpretations of contexts. In turn, the emerging discourse presents a uniform list of reasons and triggers for atrocities and human rights breaches, which often silences local voices and overshadows more nuanced and accurate readings of how and why such things occur. The humanitarian sector rightly sees a certain pragmatic value in working with celebrities, as doing so obviously draws international attention to issues in order to support fundraising. Jerslev (2014) cites Kapoor (2013), Marshall (1997) and Turner (2004), and states that the reciprocal benefit for celebrities seems to be: "At the same time, through the very same activity, celebrities are marketing themselves as humanitarian celebrities, creating a sellable brand identity and possibly thereby improving their general value in the entertainment business" (p. 171).

The context of South Sudan

VAWG is an epidemic in South Sudan. The report cited in the introduction to this chapter also documented that in South Sudan, 65 per cent of women and girls have experienced sexual violence at some point, putting the country at the top of prevalence tables. However, and in contrast to the complex realities of how different forms of violence tend to weave together and trigger each other in times of conflict, newspaper reporting on

VAWG in South Sudan is rather limited. In the English international press, the main focus has been on the high instances of stranger rape as a result of the conflict. As already reported in this chapter, the instances of rape by army personnel is indeed very high at 33 per cent in recent studies, but IPV is still far higher, estimated at 73 per cent in states such as Rumbek. If VAWG is to end or even be reduced in South Sudan, a critical starting point is to develop a more nuanced and accurate picture of how violence impacts on the lives of women and girls in the country.

Before going further, it is important to briefly consider the history of South Sudan. The country gained its independence in 2011 after 50 years of civil war with what is now Sudan. The Sudan People's Liberation Movement (SPLM) signed the first Comprehensive Peace Agreement in 2005, providing the base for the arrangements for South Sudan's independence, which was finally realised in July 2011. However, peace was short-lived, and in December 2013 a new wave of conflict – this time internal to the newly independent South Sudan – broke out between the president, Salva Kiir Mayarditt, and the vice president, Riek Machar. The dispute opened up along ethnic lines as the ruling presidential party was made up of the Dinka ethnic majority while the opposition consisted primarily of the second largest grouping, the Nuer. The conflict that unfolded saw tens of thousands killed and 3 million people displaced, both to neighbouring countries and also internally, with around 200,000 people being forced to move into UN "Protection of Civilian Camps" (PoCs) set up within South Sudan's borders. In its short history, the country has appeared to stumble from one peace agreement to another, with little hope of long-term stability in sight. In August 2015, a new peace agreement was signed, but was short-lived, with violence breaking out again within a year. The July 2016 conflict saw Riek Machar flee the country, opening up an oppositional power vacuum and the installation of a new vice president, Taban Deng Gai, in August 2016 from the Juba-based faction of the SPLM In Opposition (SPLM IO). A further peace agreement was later signed in Khartoum in June 2018.

In addition to political conflict, the country is plagued by inter-communal tensions primarily fuelled by cattle wealth, or rather the drive to accumulate wealth through cattle. This economic reality sees violence erupt through cattle-raiding, which in parallel results in women and girls being abducted for marriage – 33 per cent of the 65 per cent of reported sexual violence by women and girls is said to be the result of non-partner abduction linked to cattle-raiding and displacement. Additionally, and as covered in more detail below, women and girls are subjected to a number of other cultural practices that are in themselves violent or that lead to violence, including bride price, child marriage, polygamy and wife inheritance.

With this context in mind, let us now turn to the most recent figures available on type and prevalence of VAWG in South Sudan. Given the violence that erupted in 2013 and again in 2016, research on the ground in South Sudan became very challenging. In reviewing existing literature, it appears that research stopped in 2013 and is only now being picked up. The South Sudan Household Health Survey states that one in five women have experienced some form of gender-based violence (GBV) (GRSS, 2010). It also records that 79 per cent of people interviewed (both male and female) felt that a man hitting a woman was normal, particularly when married. The UN Mission in South Sudan Human Rights Report (UNMISS, 2014) documents that violence against women during the ongoing civil conflict in South Sudan has notably increased and is widespread across all warring parties and factions. A 2014 report by Care International (CI) also noted, "There are few places in the world where it is more dangerous or disempowering to grow up female than in South Sudan" (CI, 2014, p. 2).

While differences in prevalence and types of violent abuse can be seen across the country, GBV is widespread and often predominantly linked to bride price. This is especially true among the majority Nuer and Dinka ethnic groups. Bride price remains at the centre of much of the customary economy, and effectively reduces women to commodities, to be bought and used – and therefore abused – by husbands who, in effect, feel ownership over them. Levels of abuse and violence suffered by women and girls became profound and entrenched during the conflicts that have been sustained almost constantly since the independence of the Sudan in 1956. In particular, rape has been systematically deployed across warring factions as a weapon of war. The consequences for women and girls' health and well-being are considerable, as are the unmet needs for health and psychosocial care. The many years of conflict in southern Sudan allowed VAWG to become more widespread, and it left behind numerous long-term consequences for women, including health sequelae, psychological trauma and possible HIV infection, and this continues today as a result of the ongoing civil conflict in South Sudan.

Studies prior to the outbreak of conflict in December 2013 recorded existing high levels of GBV. For example, research conducted by Averbach et al. (2013) found that across a number of sites, 69 per cent of respondents knew at least one woman who had been beaten by her husband in the past month. The study also captured that 42 per cent of respondents knew at least one man who had forced his wife to have sex with him (marital rape is not recognised as a crime in the South Sudan legal code). The most recent study into perceptions and prevalence of VAWG in South Sudan was that conducted by Care International in 2014. The study was focused on the Upper Nile and Unity states, the areas most affected by the current conflict. Key findings were that 25 per cent of all respondents (male and female) cited personal experience of physical abuse and 7 per cent reported forced sex: "Given the complexity of GBV, and all that it encompasses, these numbers are likely to be higher" (CI, 2014, p. 6).

In South Sudan, a specific spectrum of VAWG emerges. Springvale Monash Legal Service (SMLS, 2008) identified the following types of violence that women and girls in South Sudan are most commonly subjected to.

Harmful cultural practices (HCPs) essentially operate to ensure that women and girls are kept in an inferior position. This is done through the reinforcement of gendered hierarchies that establish men as the decision-makers. The rendering of women as inferior to men leaves them vulnerable to violence. For example, bride price is a practice that sees women commodified at the point of marriage. Grooms must hand over wealth to a bride's family in the form of cattle and/or material goods and cash in order to take her in marriage. Polygamy is also common, involving men taking on multiple wives. Individual wives in a polygamous marriage often find themselves competing for resources and in a highly dependent position, reliant on a husband whose time and resources are drawn in various directions. Wife inheritance, or rather lack of it, again establishes dependency. Women simply cannot leave a marriage; they do not have the resources to do so, and if a woman tries to, she is expected to repay her bride price, which is not possible given women's low status and lack of independent wealth. "Ghost marriages" evidence again the extent of women's dependency on men. If a woman's husband dies, she is expected to marry a brother-in-law or some other male relative. While female genital mutilation (FGM) is less common in South Sudan compared to Sudan, it is still observed by some communities. In poor families, in order to avoid the pressures of having to raise a bride price, young girls are forced into marriages. Rape is also used by young men as a way of taking a bride. Once a girl is known to have had sex, she is unmarriageable through the bride price market and has no option but to marry her rapist.

Linked to the position of dependency and inferiority, which is reinforced through the practices above, is a basic *lack of rights*; women have no right to land ownership and no property rights. This means that once married, they have very few options in terms of leaving an abusive situation. Bride price is particularly problematic here as it gives husbands a sense of ownership over their wives. Women are simply not seen as independent people; they are joined subserviently to their husbands. This level of complete subservience means women are also subjected to high levels of *sexual harassment occurring in virtually every space of their lives*, including school and the workplace (such as the fields and where women work at day labour) and when collecting water and wood. *Domestic violence*, as the statistics already given show, is very prevalent, to such an extent that it is normalised as part of masculine behaviour. This is often triggered or exacerbated by alcohol, war trauma, poverty and just a need to exert power.

Outside of the domestic sphere, violence exists in various forms and is normalised at a number of other levels. For example, the police are known to perpetrate harassment against women in public. Sexual exploitation is rife, often leading to rape, triggered by conflict but also occurring at the community level (see section above). As noted, abduction during conflict is not uncommon, and it is used as a means of destabilising enemy communities, reducing the ability for a group to reproduce and maintain itself. The 2014 CI (South Sudan) report entitled *The Girl Has No Rights* adds *psychological and economic violence* to this list, with specific reference to the context of South Sudan. *Psychological violence* is described as constant and ongoing verbal abuse within family or community spheres. Unsurprisingly, long-term trauma is left as a result of women and men experiencing and witnessing violence during the conflict, and this materialises in increased violence against women and deeper mental torture for women as a result. *Economic violence* is now accepted as a common form of violence against women globally, and is defined as the denial of financial independence and/or land rights, which gives women no means of escaping a violent relationship. The cultural practices outlined above, as well as the additional circumstances that can trigger violence, mean that many women in South Sudan will experience economic violence alongside many other forms of physical and psychological abuse.

Digging deeper into the normalisation of VAWG in South Sudan

VAWG has to be understood as both a product of a highly patriarchal and misogynistic environment and also as a key mechanism through which male privilege and power are maintained. Each type of violence experienced by women and girls must be viewed in relation to the wider cultural, social, political and economic structures that ultimately sanction and normalise women's inferiority. It is the inferiority of women that is at the root of VAWG. However, as research detailed below shows, different forms of violence emerge at different points and places and out of specific and changing contexts. Given the instability of South Sudan, in terms of the constant threat of violence, food insecurity and large-scale displacement of populations, VAWG continues to emerge in different ways and as a response to the crisis conditions. Benesova (2004) writes that a backlash against changing gender norms occurred following the conflict that ended in 2004. The conflict had caused shifts in traditional patterns of gender relations because with men away fighting, women assumed roles outside of the home. When men returned, they found themselves without work and confronted by wives who were now taking on decision-making roles. The result was a crisis in masculinity and a spike in VAWG (see also Mustafa Ali, 2011).

I have already given a brief outline of what bride price is and how it enforces dependent relationships, but the practice warrants further discussion here as it continues to underpin a large part of South Sudan's economy, especially among the Dinka and the Nuer, the two largest ethnic groups (the Dinka are upwards of 35 per cent of the population and the Nuer 15 per cent). It is a practice dependent upon women's inferiority, and so should be seen as a foundational structural dimension to the patriarchal and misogynistic environment in which VAWG flourishes. The practice places women in a marriage cycle that guarantees their inferiority and legitimises violence against them as a form of discipline. The price comes in the form of cattle, ideally given to a girl's family at the point of marriage, making marriage an important economic resource. Bride price can continue to be a debt for many years. Families want to raise as much as possible in exchange for their daughters, hence associated violent abusive practices such as FGM and forced and early marriage, all of which are designed to preserve the purity of a girl so she may fetch a higher price. Women and girls who are not brought to marriage as virgins suffer extreme stigma, even if virginity was taken due to rape. Educated women are less desirable, which contributes to the low female school attendance rate (Beswick, 2001). Additionally, polygamy is widely practised (estimated at 40 per cent of all unions) and leaves women fighting for household resources and vulnerable to HIV and other sexually transmitted infections. In short, bride price triggers forms of VAWG, as listed above, and so should itself be viewed and categorised as harmful and abusive. It also operates as a foundation that supports the wider social system that treats women as objects of male control.

Abramsky et al. (2011) used a 2005 WHO multi-country study to conduct bivariate and multivariate analyses, and identified several factors that appear to affect the likelihood of IPV across settings. Secondary education, high socio-economic status and formal marriage were found to be protective against IPV, but none of these are available to the vast majority of women in South Sudan. Meanwhile, universal risk factors were found to include alcohol abuse, cohabitation, young age, women's attitudes supporting wife-beating, external sexual relations ("cheating"), experiencing childhood abuse, growing up with domestic violence, and experiencing other (non-IPV) forms of violence in adulthood (Abramsky et al., 2011). In South Sudan, not all of these factors are relevant, but alcohol abuse, the young age of marriage, acceptance of VAWG across society and growing up with domestic violence are clearly risks. While it is possible to fill in gaps in relation to VAWG in South Sudan through applying the findings of these comparative studies, it is crucial to maintain a focus on the culturally specific structures and institutions that shape violence in different places in South Sudan. While considering countrywide factors (such as alcohol abuse) may be helpful, their intersections with diverse features of different sociocultural environments will create contextual particularities that must be understood if interventions are to succeed in different local contexts across the country (e.g. Donnelly et al., 2014).

Cultural practices create a climate of patriarchy that embeds female inferiority as the norm. SMLS (2008) states that men dominate households, and it is expected that a husband will "discipline his wife and children" (p. 12), and Ward (2005) cites interviews during which "a county judge explained if a husband beats his wife, he is trying to refine her, women don't experience it as violence" (p. 47). Ward goes on to highlight the extent to which violence is accepted, recording commonly made statements such as "women are like children – they need to be disciplined" (p. 33). Another study conducted by Averbach et al. (2013) found that 82 per cent of female respondents and 81 per cent of male respondents agreed that a woman "should tolerate violence in order to keep her family together" (p. 101). The majority also agreed that there were times "when a woman deserves to be beaten" (p. 61). Women (47 per cent) were more likely than men (37 per cent) to agree that "it is okay for a man to hit his wife if she won't have sex with him" (p. 23). Though the research also found that acceptance of gender inequality decreased with education, the key point of these findings was that interventions to end violence cannot simply assume that men alone are the problem. This overly simplistic reading of why and how violence happens fails to account for the realities of normalisation in which women, often more so than men, are the ones enforcing violent behaviours against them.

Access to justice in South Sudan in the context of VAWG

The above section reviewed the context of violence against women in South Sudan, detailing types of violence, prevalence levels – as we know them – and the triggers. The complex web of interlocking factors emerging from the conflict context is highly challenging. The operation of some form of justice system is often seen as a critical step in tackling violence. This chapter will now explore what exists in South Sudan and the effectiveness of various different routes.

Justice mechanisms and usage

The lack of a functioning judicial system means that survivors of violence have very little options available to pursue justice or even to report their experience and have it registered. For this reason, it is of no surprise that the common perception is that perpetrators will face no consequences through customary or statutory law in South Sudan; they act with impunity. Prior to the 2013 conflict, there were only 450 practising lawyers in South Sudan and very few criminal and civil law courts, and so 90 per cent of people sought justice via traditional community "Boma" courts (Averbach et al., 2013). It may be that since then, this percentage will have increased due to a widespread mistrust of the government and the state's lack of capacity to implement justice. However, despite more people seeking justice through traditional means, it is also likely that people's access to

Boma courts and other traditional mechanisms will be severely restricted due to the high level of insecurity.

Reliance on customary justice mechanisms is particularly problematic for women, even in relatively peaceful times, because customary law does not afford women equality. In violent relationships, women find themselves stuck without exit options mainly because divorce is so difficult to obtain. Bride price has to be returned at the point of divorce, so families place pressure on women to stay, and given the lack of inheritance or property rights, women – even if a divorce is granted – will struggle to survive outside of marriage. Children are considered the property of the husband, which – emotionally – makes it very hard for a woman to leave her marital home. Moreover, a marriage does not even end with the death of a husband; instead, a widow becomes the property of her deceased husband's brother.

Leonardi (2010) states that statutory (i.e. formal) laws do contain provision to protect women and girls but they are not enforced. A large part of the enforcement problem is that nationally, 80 per cent of women and girls are illiterate and have little or no knowledge of the law. This illiteracy is linked not just to the view that girls do not need to be educated, but – as already mentioned – because educated women are not desirable as wives, they bring a lower bride price. The Child Act 2008 prohibits child marriage. UNICEF (2014) data indicate that 52 per cent of South Sudanese women are married by the age of 18 years old and 9 per cent are married by the time they are 15, with some girls married as young as 12. The Penal Code Act 2008 does not have a specific law against domestic violence, and though rape is considered an offence outside marriage, section 247 of the penal code states that "sexual intercourse by a married couple is not rape" (Bradley & Bedri, 2018). Violence against women is seen as a family matter and is dealt with largely at the clan/chief level, where restorative justice is preferred (Elia, 2007). The Ministry of Gender, Child and Social Welfare has been visible in pushing for greater protection for women and girls from violence.

Findings published in Care International's 2014 report highlighted the weaknesses of the South Sudan justice system as follows:

- Only 7% of survey respondents who experienced GBV said they immediately reported it to the police.
- Only 37% of respondents who said they reported GBV to hospitals or police received any psychological support.
- 43% of GBV survivors said they decided to keep quiet out of fear.
- 57% did nothing because they felt there was no point in reporting cases of GBV. (CI, 2014, p. 3)

This chapter will now explore the possible programmes and interventions that may be able to reverse at least some aspects of this troubling and bleak picture.

In light of the brutal, embedded reality of VAWG in South Sudan, CI (2014) made recommendations that relate directly to how best to respond to GBV. Key to their recommended approach is the need to be survivor-centred. Given the levels and forms that VAWG takes in South Sudan, the assumption that most women and girls are either vulnerable to violence or have experienced it is realistic, and should inform and shape the way in which it is responded to at the level of policy and practice.

All actors who document GBV cases, including UNMISS women's protection advisors, must adopt a survivor-centred approach that respects core international principles regarding ethical data collection while also fulfilling the obligation to provide survivors with access to survivor services. Public awareness campaigns aimed at breaking the culture of silence on GBV, while raising awareness of gender inequality, human rights, the rights of the child, and the importance of women's participation in public life, need to be supported. This requires the close collaboration of community and religious leaders as well as educators, and messaging should incorporate not only mass media, but must also be disseminated to remote communities through networks of partners.

Engaging men and boys as clients, partners and allies, as well as facilitating dialogues to reinforce positive and inclusive relationships between men and women – within and beyond households – will also be critical, as will increasing investment in and support for more effective GBV service delivery. This requires thoughtful, place-sensitive GBV analysis and subsequent mainstreaming in humanitarian response and implementation of a gendered lens in humanitarian funding across design, monitoring and evaluation of emergency programmes. Providing improved care for survivors of GBV by training health professionals, social workers, and educators and community to identify and respond to GBV survivors with medical assistance, psychological and psychosocial support, and/or referral services should be complemented by the creation of safe spaces for women and girls in areas with large numbers of internally displaced person (IDP) camps, as well as fostering the development of support groups.

In the context of South Sudan, using existing data to better understand the main countrywide triggers is an important starting point in the design of access to justice programming (ATJP) for VAWG. From existing research, what we know of VAWG in South Sudan is that excessive alcohol consumption and exposure to inter-parental violence may well be two of the main ongoing triggers. Additionally, hypermasculinities created by and through war, coupled with a backlash against challenges to gender norms, also seems to be a central element contributing to the VAWG we see in South Sudan. For this reason, it is worth considering in the context of South Sudan whether social norm change interventions should be embedded in the ATJP as a way of pushing for mindset changes if justice for women and girls is to be achieved.

Empowerment of women and girls

Ultimately, ATJP should seek to empower women and girls by ensuring and enabling an environment within which the rights of women and girls are respected, and where justice is accessible. Empowerment, in a broad sense, depends on improvements in women's position – alterations in patterns of control. This has often been expressed in terms of the "power quartet": *power over* (ability to influence and coerce), *power to* (organise and change existing hierarchies), *power with* (increased power from collective action), and *power from within* (increased individual consciousness) (Luttrell & Quiroz, 2009: 45).

It is also understood that women in South Sudan (like anywhere else) do not form a singular homogenous group. Gender intersects with other forms of socio-economic discrimination in ways that produce a diverse array of oppressive environments for women, with intersecting issues including, for example, race, nationality, sexuality, class and religious identity. However, the distinction between women's practical gender needs and their strategic gender interests (e.g. see Molyneux, 1985) allows for the development of generalised gender policy by distinguishing between context-specific practical requirements, on the one hand, and a "deductive analysis of the structures of women's subordination," on the other (Kabeer, 2012, p. 6).

Kabeer's (2003) contribution to this overarching feminist politics has been substantial, not least because it offers a specific definition of empowerment.[1] It covers women's sense of self-worth and social identity, their desire and ability to challenge their subordination, their capacity to exercise strategic control over their lives and to renegotiate relationships, and their ability to participate alongside men in the reformation of their societies in ways that lead to more fair and democratic distributions of power and opportunity (Kabeer, 2008, 2012). "Empowerment," according to Kabeer (2003), is dependent on agency, resources and achievement: "Agency encompasses both observable action in the exercise of choice – decision-making, protest, bargaining and negotiation – as well as the meaning, motivation and purpose that individuals bring to their actions, their sense of agency" (pp. 171–173).

Kabeer's definition offers an overarching agenda while simultaneously leaving room for the required analyses of intersecting aspects of social discrimination that affect women differently according to context. Additionally, this definition of empowerment encompasses the need for attention to position *and* condition: the transformation of social and cultural power structures (improving position) must be accompanied by efforts to enable people to benefit from such changes (i.e. people must have good condition – health, economic opportunities, etc. – in order to benefit from the possibilities available). Thus, meeting basic needs is not bypassed by the drive for empowerment. Addressing condition and position must go hand in hand, and care should be taken to combine and sequence both kinds of approach while making sure that they do not become conflated with each other (see also Luttrel & Quroz, 2009).

Conclusion

This chapter has reiterated one of the key arguments of the volume: that programmes to end VAWG need to start from an in-depth understanding of the context because the culturally specific structures and institutions that shape violence will differ from country to country. While considering countrywide factors (such as alcohol abuse) may be helpful, their intersection with diverse features of different sociocultural environments will create contextual particularities that must be understood if interventions are to succeed in different local contexts across the country. According to Care International's report *The Girl Has No Rights*, "There are few places in the world where it is more dangerous or disempowering to grow up female than in South Sudan" (CI, 2014, p. 2). While differences in prevalence and types of violent abuse can be seen across the country, VAWG is widespread and is fundamentally linked to harmful cultural practices, particularly bride price. Bride price remains at the very centre of the economy, and as such reduces women to a commodity, objects to be bought and used – and therefore abused – by husbands who, in effect, feel ownership over them.

9 | EMBEDDING A VIOLENCE AGAINST WOMEN LENS IN DEVELOPMENT

Introduction

This volume has, I hope, made a contribution to the evidence base arguing for the urgent need to make ending violence against women a central focus of development programming. Each chapter explored the specific country and cultural contexts of violence, and a consistent theme has been that – despite diversity both within and across case examples – violence is an embedded and normalised part of the lives of all women. Though it may happen for different reasons and take different forms, this remains true regardless of a woman's social position, economic background and level of education. While taking an intersectional approach does allow for more nuanced appreciation of the ways in which different groups of women understand and respond to violence and the resources available to them, it emerges that violence – regardless of such intersects – is a shared daily reality. This chapter argues that the violence against women and girls mainstreaming tool developed by Bradley and Gruber (2018) needs to become a central part of the design and monitoring of development programmes, regardless of country or sector. In this chapter, then, the model will be summarised and applied to energy access in refugee situations.

The first section of the chapter presents the mainstreaming tool and highlights how and why it will add sensitised value to development programming and monitoring. A sensitised lens helps raise awareness around the ways in which violence can emerge unintentionally and as a response to the changes development seeks to bring. The second section will then apply the tool to two of the most pressing issues concerning women living in refugee contexts: access to cooking fuel and safe, secure housing. The section will explore how the tool may support better, more sensitive programming through the posing of a number of linked critical questions.

What does a VAWG mainstreaming tool look like?

A VAWG lens is a means to improve – and indeed ensure – the sensitive awareness of a range of actors, from development practitioners to policymakers and politicians, to both the ongoing realities of violence and the ways in which change might escalate or intensify these experiences. The approach then requires actors to automatically reflect on *how* and *if* a programme will positively or negatively impact on VAWG. *A series of critical and reflective questions need to be posed*, beginning at the design stage, that consider this. Before these questions can be asked, all involved need to have a detailed knowledge of the current prevalence of VAWG and the evidence base, as it exists, around the main triggers for violence.

The types of critical, reflexive questions suggested are shown in Table 1 and are divided into two main sections: those focused on guiding the design phase and then those to be asked as part of the ongoing evaluation of interventions.

Generating answers to these questions needs to be thought through with reference to each layer of the context. If we refer back to the ethnographic web presented in Chapter 1, we can see how multiple spheres combine in order to maintain violence in the lives of women, but which also hold the potential to bring about positive transformation. The web reflects elements of Heise's ecological model that argues that

Table 1 Design phase questions

Design questions	Programme reflection
• Do we understand the types of violence most commonly experienced by programme recipients who are women and girls? • To what extent are these types of violence commonly talked about and acknowledged to be unjust and abusive? What level of normalisation exists? • To what extent is this normalisation of violence similarly applied by men and women, boys and girls?	Understanding these types of violence should involve an understanding of the contexts in which it occurs (e.g. at home, school and work, or on the way to school or work). If this is not known, should a piece of research be commissioned in order to gather this knowledge?
• Are some groups more likely to project normalised views of VAWG? • Who are the most vulnerable groups? • What material resources and/or social and cultural capital do they have to draw on?	Similarly, an exercise to map out what resources and forms of social and cultural capital already exist (e.g. through established community groups) is needed in advance of programme design. Projects should build, whereever possible, on tried and tested approaches so as to minimise the risk of triggering a backlash (and therefore potentially increasing the vulnerability of certain groups).
• What internal differences scan be seen in patterns and types of violence and in the triggers for it? In other words, are certain forms of VAWG more common in particular areas and under certain conditions?	Can a one-size-fits-all approach to programming respond to the complex contexts of VAWG, even in one country? To what extent will a more locally tailored response be necessary, and if so, is this feasible?

violence exists and is supported by the negative normative views at the level of the household through to the state and national structures. When combined, these spheres can be described as representing the ecology of violence. Change and reductions in violence will only occur once normative views of VAWG at each level are transformed into views that see violence as a violation. The ethnographic web takes the application of the ecology model a step further by adding an intersectional layer. This is because understanding and appreciating within each sphere the differing experiences of groups of women and girls, men and boys, as well as how power is exercised and wielded, is a critical element of the knowledge base needed as the foundation for development planning, again regardless of sectorial focus.

If we also think back to the gender lens introduced in the Introduction, which directs understanding into how decisions are made, the relative freedom of different groups to exercise agency, the differing levels of vulnerabilities across groupings, and how all this links into access issues, we can see the importance of bringing together these various models into a framework that is committed to understanding and challenging VAWG. Appreciating the ways in which decisions are made, who has the power to decide what they can and cannot do with their life? Who has the most access to recourses, such as food, but also medicines and luxury goods? It also leads to a reflection on what happens when individuals challenge these power structures. Is violence used to discipline and maintain this status quo? Is it used to remind household members of the hierarchy of power? How are these structures and behaviours shaped by world views that hold to a status quo that marginalises some, and in doing so create groups who are vulnerable because they have less power? All these questions are significant when it comes to assessing potential and actual levels of violence.

In general terms, the following questions could help to measure the impact of an intervention in relation to VAWG:

- Is there any risk that a development activity may unintentionally increase or spark instances of VAWG?
- Gender- and VAWG-related indicators/targets need to be set and then monitored throughout, including at review points.
- Does the programme have referral mechanisms for any cases of VAWG that emerge as a result of activities? These might be a case of identifying support already in place and ensuring it is accessible to the programme should it be needed.
- Are there any possible opportunities for non-VAWG-focused projects to link into VAWG programming and thereby maximise opportunities to reduce VAWG?
- What new evidence has emerged on the type and prevalence of VAWG and how forms of violence may intersect with other development concerns (e.g. energy, livelihoods, education)?
- What evidence is there of impact in terms of development activities that have worked to reduce VAWG (when not the core focus)? Can examples of good practice be seen, and can they be scaled up, or are the triggers for violence completely context-driven?
- How is knowledge on what works being gathered and communicated? Can it be used to support the work of stakeholders across development sectors to better respond to the issues of VAWG?

Applying the model to the lives of women in refugee contexts

As discussed above, the reasons for an increase in VAWG during conflict and humanitarian crises are complex and multifaceted. Two issues that particularly impact on women and girls living in refugee camps are cooking and lighting; the lack of both renders them vulnerable to violence. These intersections, it could be argued, emerge as a result of the heightened vulnerabilities of the context and are related to an acute scarcity of resources and infrastructure. However, as argued in the previous chapter, it is still important to remember that VAWG is not caused by these extreme vulnerabilities, as such, but rather it is exacerbated by them. The triggers remain the same as in non-displaced settings: the devaluing of the female body and the normalisation of VAWG.

Potential risk factors and feelings of insecurity are frequently noted by women and girls in camp settings, most commonly in relation to poor lighting in public spaces and the need to collect firewood. While reduction in risks does not necessarily lead to a reduction in VAWG, it must be acknowledged that the collection of firewood presents a significant danger to women and girls. The research reviewed here makes it clear that at the very least, women and girls are fearful of being raped and/or attacked while undergoing this activity. The knock-on impact this will have on the psychological well-being of women and girls, regardless of actual harm through rape, should not be ignored. This situation is compounded by the widespread reliance on traditional and less stable energy sources. There are very few data available on the current energy situation, but it is clear that few refugees or displaced people have access to modern energy services, and energy needs are rarely met through humanitarian rationing. So, in most cases, households in camp settings rely on firewood for cooking. According to research conducted by Grafham and Lahn (2015), "80 per cent of the 8.7 million refugees and displaced people in camps have absolutely minimal access to energy, with high dependence on traditional biomass for cooking and no access to electricity" (p. ix). Although humanitarian agencies supply some firewood (or other cooking fuels) at some sites, the bulk of the firewood must be collected or bought. Fuelwood collection is primarily carried out by women and girls, and involves trips outside the camp. The frequency, distance travelled and length of each trip depends on demand and local fuel availability. This activity is highly gendered, with the responsibility invariably falling to women. What is striking, given the anxieties over gathering firewood, is the lack of prioritisation of this issue by donors and implementers. If a gendered lens, such as that presented in the Introduction, had been used and applied, a greater and more immediate appreciation of the vulnerabilities facing women and girls would have been captured. This, in turn, would give partners a chance to identify and respond to risks such as these and to increase the safety of women and girls.

The incidence of VAWG when venturing outside camp settings is well documented in a range of literature on gender and energy access. In particular, in contexts where the collection of firewood outside of a camp is actually illegal and requires travel to remote locations, insecurities of women will significantly increase, and reporting will most certainly be minimal. A rapid review carried out for DFID's VAWG help desk identified some of the key evidence available on the links between access to different sources of energy at the household and community level and VAWG in camp-based settings (Parke, 2015; see also Grafham & Lahn, 2015; Gunning, 2014; Mercy Corps, 2010; WRC, 2006). VAWG may also emerge in relation to firewood in a domestic sense due to an increase in instances of violence at home due to the stress of not having sufficient fuel to cook with. Also, transactional sex occurs as a way of acquiring more firewood (e.g. see WFP, 2013). Overall instances of VAWG are difficult to measure, mainly due to the normalisation of different forms, and it is greatly under-reported for a number of reasons. The lack of safe reporting structures is one key reason, and another is the fear women and girls have of being ostracised or punished by their communities.

As stated above, poor lighting in camp settings is an issue that feeds directly into making women vulnerable to violence. Protection issues, due partly to lack of lighting (along with lack of privacy), are frequently cited as barriers to the use of the communal wash facilities and also as the reason women fear using the communal kitchens. For example, at the Zaatari camp in Jordan, women identified the wash facilities and kitchens as the most insecure locations, and 24 per cent of participants said that safety concerns had stopped them using communal kitchens (Serrato, 2014). Women feel unsafe, and incidents of VAWG are reported to take place in poorly lit areas. IOM carried out two rapid assessment surveys and found that gender-based violence (GBV) prevalence was very high in two internally displaced person (IDP) settlements in Somalia, and also that many of the incidents took place at night in the dark. Safety issues are affected by lack of lighting and also by the design of – and the distance to – the facilities. Poorly designed lighting interventions could also potentially increase protection risks. For example, illuminated communal areas may encourage people to leave their homes at night to walk through previously poorly lit areas (Perkins, 2015).

In terms of responding to increases in intimate partner violence (IPV) that often occurs when families are put under stress, better housing and domestic lighting could well help mitigate increased risks. A significant body of research exists that links good housing to improved family well-being and positive mental health (e.g. see Gibson, Thomson, Kearns & Petticrew, 2011; Nakazato, Oishi & Schimmack, 2011; Thomson and Thomas, 2015). According to Bratt (2010):

> Housing encompasses a bundle of characteristics that are integral to family well-being. This literature review demonstrates that, on a physical level, housing must be decent and safe, as well as present in a family's life. Housing is also critical because of the way in which it relates to its occupants, providing sufficient space so that the family is not overcrowded; being affordable; providing opportunities to create a positive sense of self and empowerment; and providing stability and security. (p. 112)

It should be noted, however, that much of the international research on the link between housing and well-being focuses on Western case studies. Research on housing in poorer contexts, and in particular refugee settings, tends to focus on the more general relationship between housing and health. Digging deeper into what does exist outside of Western contexts, there are some studies that suggest improved housing is more critically linked to well-being in poor families than for more economically comfortable households (Bookwalter & Dalenberg, 2004). The link between sustainable, clean and secure housing and well-being in many ways is obvious, but what is lacking in the literature is how – and if – a better sense of well-being within a family at home reduces the specific tensions that would normally trigger IPV. Research recently conducted by the Moving Energy Initiative in Kakuma refugee camp in Kenya recorded that women living in poorly constructed and lit homes feel very unsafe and vulnerable to violence, including IPV. Participants felt that better lighting would improve their sense of security and promote well-being, thereby helping to build resilience to IPV.

If we take a context such as Jordan – where a significant number of people live in refugee camps – and explore the levels of IPV, we can see how improvements in lighting and housing may well help to reduce violence. A UNHCR and UNFPA joint sexual and gender-based violence (SGBV) briefing paper in March 2014 stated:

> Domestic violence is the most commonly reported form of SGBV both inside and outside the camps. Social workers, psychologists, and lawyers, estimate that over 50% of the survivors seeking support services, are survivors of domestic violence. Syrian women have reported that their husbands are under immense stress and that this increases physical and psychological violence against them and against children within the home. SGBV incidents are most often reported to

have been perpetrated by male relatives (husbands, uncles, and brothers). (UNHCR & UNFPA, 2014, p. 1)

A study conducted by Care International in 2012 also showed that 68 per cent of women in Jordan are subjected to violence in the marital home, 59 per cent are subjected to violence at their parents' home, and 48 per cent had experienced violence outside the home. According to the study, the proportion of women subjected to beatings was 59 per cent, while those experiencing verbal abuse stood at 51 per cent and insults at 42 per cent. These were the three most common forms of abuse (CI, 2013).

News pieces and published research focusing on the violence suffered by refugees in Jordan have highlighted how the past experiences of trauma and violence suffered by both men and women can be triggers for more intense violence within the home (e.g. see al-Shawabkeh, 2014; Parker, 2015). Care International has also reported:

> Many people report being unable to engage in activities outside of the home due to the high costs associated with recreational activity, even visiting friends or family. This survey found that many participants reported increased feelings of depression and negativity, increased levels of family violence (both verbal and physical), and many mothers reported that children were increasingly demonstrating symptoms of distress, including bed-wetting, temper tantrums (shouting, crying, and throwing and breaking things), and insomnia. (CI, 2013, p.4)

Evidently, violence against refugee women is high and is perpetuated by poor living standards and general insecurity. As a result of these concerns relating to increased exposure to VAWG risk factors, energy issues have begun to be incorporated into global humanitarian responses. The Safe Access to Fuel and Energy (SAFE) initiative was originally established as a protection activity:

> to reduce exposure to violence, contribute to the protection of and ease the burden on those populations collecting wood in humanitarian settings worldwide, through solutions which will promote safe access to appropriate energy and reduce environmental impacts while ensuring accountability.
> (WFP, 2012, p. 13)

And since 2014, the initiative has had a wider cross-sectoral remit incorporating humanitarian energy needs more broadly. It is led by the SAFE Humanitarian Working Group, a consortium of key partners including the Food and Agricultural Organization (FAO) of the UN, the Global Alliance for Clean Cookstoves, the UNHCR, UNICEF, the World Food Programme (WFP) and the Women's Refugee Commission, among others. There are some anecdotal claims that GBV incidence has been reduced following changes to stoves, but no evidence has been given to support these statements. It can also be difficult to attribute changes to one project since changes in behaviour or reported incidences of violence could also be a reflection of factors outside the energy project. For example, the WFP SAFE cookstove project at Kakuma, Kenya, revealed some anecdotal evidence that there was a reduction in domestic violence due to less undercooking and skipping of meals, and that some transactional sex may have been mitigated due to the new efficient stoves (WFP, 2013).

New stoves and reduced fuelwood use do not always result in a reduction in fuel collection trips. For example, in Darfur, women still collected wood after the distribution of improved cookstoves, but to sell it rather than to use it themselves. Some studies even suggest that the time saved by such interventions has fuelled the growth of a secondary market for the sale of firewood (Abdelnour, 2010). It is also important to note, as above, that travel outside camps is not restricted to fuelwood collection.

The review entitled *Gender-Based Violence in Humanitarian Settings: Cookstoves and Fuels* produced by the Global Alliance for Clean Cookstoves studied 15 humanitarian energy projects that included reducing GBV as an objective (GACC, 2016). It provided the following findings. First, reducing the need to collect firewood does not necessarily bring down the total number of rapes. Moreover, the most prevalent form of VAWG (as already stated) is in fact IPV, not rape in public by a non-partner (which most firewood rapes are classed as) or conflict rape. Evidence capturing even a decrease in rape as a direct result of firewood collection is flimsy at best. Second, there is a lack of understanding around which cooking interventions are likely to have the strongest protection impacts. For example, only providing firewood that meets household cooking needs may not address all VAWG related to firewood collection.

Although there is a link between lighting (including handheld lanterns and street lighting) and reducing VAWG risk factors, there is little evidence since there are no studies that have monitored the incidence of VAWG before and after the introduction of a lighting initiative. One study tried to assess the effectiveness of solar lamps to reduce insecurity and SGBV in Puntland, Somalia, but the low reporting levels of such cases of violence rendered the task almost impossible (DFID, 2014). However, that survey and other surveys and assessments do show that women often feel safer and appreciate the lights and the reduced risk of fire-related accidents. For example, following the pilot launch of its Light Years Ahead initiative, the UNCHR carried out a survey in three countries, with the findings showing that "60% of respondents feel safer using the bathroom at night" (UNHCR, 2012). However, a study undertaken by the International Rescue Committee (IRC) evaluated the impact of the distribution of handheld solar lights on women's and girls' perceptions of their own safety in two Haitian camps, and found that women did not feel safer (IRC, 2014). Before and after comparisons found that although 95 per cent of the women and girls reportedly used the lamps, the women's own perception of their safety remained the same or worsened (though this was largely attributable to other broader security issues). The lamps did not address the women's primary safety concerns, which included generalised violence, crime and mistrust, and specifically sexual violence and harassment. In another case in the Democratic Republic of the Congo, the UNHCR received feedback of an unforeseen consequence that IDPs did not use their solar lamps at night for fear of revealing their location to rebel groups (IOM, 2011). The IRC study concluded that handheld solar lamps are an important personal resource for women and girls, but the root causes of VAWG are complex and cannot be addressed by a stand-alone distribution of lamps. Once again, the message that emerges is that ending VAWG is tied to complex transformations in mindsets that legitimise the use of different forms of violence across contexts. Reducing risk alone will not result in the necessary shift in attitudes and perceptions.

In summary, most evaluations of energy initiatives conclude that the root causes of VAWG are complex and cannot be addressed by the distribution of energy products. To address VAWG effectively, any alternative energy initiative needs to be part of a much larger long-term risk reduction programme that addresses mindset changes, social norms and cultural practices. However, greater awareness of the extent of VAWG and the resultant feelings of insecurity would greatly improve the sensitivity of energy programming in humanitarian settings and potentially feed into a process of change that could make a positive contribution. By applying a simple framework, it becomes possible to increase awareness of the likelihood of VAWG being triggered or intensified by the immediate context. As already stated, the framework asks questions that cut across different levels and spheres in order to capture where and how vulnerabilities emerge. Table 2 applies the ecology model to an energy programme setting.

Table 2 Operational questions

Ecology/web	Meta-question	Factors to think about for operationalisation
Sociocultural	Are there dominant sociocultural views and norms that might make women and girls particularly vulnerable to violence? For example, not being given enough cooking fuel, making it necessary for women to risk attack by venturing to the outskirts of the camp.	Can safer fuel alternatives be made a priority, thereby reducing the need for women and girls to risk insecurity by going to collect firewood?
Community	What community mechanisms exist to mitigate VAWG or offer security and protection to survivors? For example, what is the size of the police support (or are they in fact perpetrators)? Are there existing community structures or mechanisms that could be better resourced to help combat instances of VAWG?	How effective are the community mechanisms perceived to be, and could they be built upon by the programme? Are there individuals who act as social mobilisers/leaders? To what extent are they sensitised around VAWG issues? Could they be trained to offer support? Is there an effective referral mechanism in place that is focused on tackling VAWG? To what extent are social mobilisers/leaders connected to the referral processes and working alongside the police? What level of trust exists in the effectiveness and responsiveness of these actors and services?

(continued)

Table 2 *(continued)*

Ecology/web	Meta-question	Factors to think about for operationalisation
Household	What dynamics or material circumstances exist at the household level that may support or perpetuate VAWG that relates to energy? For example, poor housing or lack of energy can trigger violence or increase the risk of gender-based violence. Are a high number of households headed by a single woman?	Are there certain intra- or inter- household behaviours that could be eased through improved energy, housing or income opportunities (e.g. improved lighting in the home)? Would this help to ease fear of attack during darkness, particularly in female-headed homes? And would this then reduce the feeling among single women that they need to find a partner (who may be violent) in order to offer protection against sexual attack from strangers? Is there opportunity to use existing programmes to tap into certain pre-existing processes of change?
Individual	What room is there for individuals to challenge and change instances of violence? For example, taking on the role of social mobilisers to support women who find themselves targets for violence either in the home or community.	Is there room for the programmes to utilise individuals who are active in challenging VAWG or have the potential to be? Could the programme in fact employ someone to take on this role as a way of increasing VAWG protection provision but also to monitor and mitigate unintended harm as a result of the programme intervention.

		What potential is there for these individuals, with resourcing, to act as a bridge between instances of violence and structures of support, either inside or outside of the programme? For example, identify households where domestic violence is known to occur and assess if the situation could be eased by in any way by the programme.
Intersectional features	Have particular groups been identified as having greater vulnerability? Has a risk assessment been conducted exploring how and if the programme may bring about unintended increased risk to these groups (and any others)?	Is there room for the programme to utilise individuals who are active in challenging VAWG, building their capacity to act as a bridge between instances of violence and poor energy resources? For example, identify households where domestic violence is known to occur and assess if the situation could be eased by improved energy.

Conclusion

This chapter is intended to highlight how the application of a more sensitised lens may support better contextual understanding of the likelihood of different types of VAWG, acting as a predictive mechanism that can then be used to design responses that may be able to prevent VAWG. The approach requires a level of acceptance that VAWG is normalised and will therefore exist, after which the first step is to seek to understand how and where VAWG exists and to reflect on whether any given activity will make the situation worse or trigger new ways of violence. The feasibility and scoping and design phases of a programme are the ideal times to apply a gendered sensitive lens. An assessment of gender equality can be done relatively easily (i.e. capturing of access to and preference for different services, facilities and products), and doing so at an early stage will allow the programme design to incorporate women and their specific needs from the outset. Combining a gender lens with a sensitivity to VAWG will mean that opportunities to empower women and build resilience to violence should be identified. In the context of the example given above, income opportunities in situations where domestic lighting is poor would enable women to buy lamps and thereby reduce feelings of insecurity.

An important and increasingly expected aspect of interventions is the application of a "do no harm" approach, which will ensure that the programme design does not accidentally exacerbate gender inequalities or violence. For example, an awareness of how some income opportunities targeting women may trigger a male backlash (see previous chapters) or understanding how gendered power relations may play out is a critical way of ensuring an intervention does not cause harm. Finally, prioritising the inclusion of women and taking every opportunity to embed their involvement at each stage and level of energy programming will ensure maximum impact. The concern is that with heightened awareness of the realities of violence against women, donors and implementers may be discouraged from including women for fear of making existing instances of violence worse or causing new ones. The example approach outlined here is intended to demonstrate that by following a multistaged process and asking a series of critical questions throughout, any programme (regardless of sector) can in fact bring about positive change. But doing so effectively without causing unintended harm requires careful planning and the adoption of a gender lens from inception, through planning and implementation, and in monitoring and evaluation mechanisms.

CONCLUSION: TOWARDS A MORE NUANCED THEORY OF CHANGE

The chapters in this volume have each provided examples that show the extent to which violence is woven into the very fabric of the lives of women and girls in a variety of different contexts. The first chapter reviewed what we understand by the concept of normalisation and then considered the various mechanisms through which different forms of abuse become accepted as necessary in order to discipline and to maintain inequalities that benefit some while marginalising others. I unravelled some of the ways in which power essentially acts as the force that determines and ensures that violence is retained as a fundamental part of everyday life for women and girls across the socio-economic spectrum. This volume has applied an intersectional approach and has argued that context matters in developing our comprehensive understanding of why violence flourishes. But it has also shown why understanding context is critical in identifying entry points for interventions and policies. By documenting the experiences of diverse groups of women in different parts of the world and by viewing their challenges within a web of intersecting factors, we begin to build a better, more comprehensive picture of where activism and programming to end violence is. In the Introduction, I summarised some of the main approaches and tools that have been used in efforts to combat violence. While there is evidence that these approaches are the best we currently have and that they do bring about reductions in the levels of violence, reversing deeply ingrained patterns of violence will not happen quickly. The current and increased levels of resourcing will need to be maintained not just for a number of years, but for a number of generations.

CONCLUSION | 221

By comparing and contrasting the different country case studies covered in this volume through applying the web, we can see how highly conservative normative values around gender, heterosexuality and the role of women in the domestic sphere still have a heavy impact in terms of rendering women vulnerable to violence. In other words, in a context such as Pakistan, women working does not seem to bring the same level of freedoms to poor women as it does to women working in the informal entertainment sector in Nepal. In fact, in many families, women working is only accepted if it can be kept hidden from the wider community. If the norm of the husband as the only breadwinner can be upheld, then it is possible for women to earn an income. This invisibility is convenient to the state as it means the appalling working conditions and exploitative terms of labour can be ignored and allowed to exist, fuelling economic growth that benefits the elite but does little to reverse generations of inequality. In Sudan, we see a similarly conservative environment in which women must conform to avoid shaming their family. Tight controls over women's bodies are extreme, ranging from the mutilation of genitals through to the state policing of how women dress in public. In this context, unravelling the multiple threads that maintain violence in everyday life is challenging.

The context described above reveals a very harsh environment in which women must survive. However, even within such extreme situations, individuals exist who represent agents of change. They are able to find the motivation and energy to push for transformation. In Nepal, I gave examples of positive deviants striving to reverse and knock down barriers in order to see women claim justice and political representation. In fact, we see this determination across many contexts, including through the work of women's organisations such as HomeNet in Pakistan, an array of community based anti-FGM organisations in Sudan and India, and the network of organisations working for women in the entertainment sector in Nepal.

Together, the chapters illustrate just how urgently we need to find approaches to women's empowerment that are increasingly sensitised to violence as an ever-present force. Three of the chapters in this volume have explored violence through a focus on income generation. Economic engagement has been heralded as a central route to gender equality, and this volume has not disputed its importance. However, as I have shown, there are no magic bullets, and as such economic empowerment and income generation should be seen as components of a more integrated and nuanced approach to confronting – and ultimately ending – violence against women and girls (VAWG). What is clear is that whatever the entry point to change, and regardless of whether that change is specifically focused on gender relations, an understanding of how violence may act as a crippling barrier to positive change needs to be in place. In fact, this level of sensitisation is necessary regardless of the development forces. This was shown through the application of a VAWG mainstreaming tool to sustainable energy developments and has relevancy to emergency responses to environmental displacement. By applying a tool that lists a number of simple questions, a greater awareness of how an intervention could be tweaked in order to respond better to violence and also avoid doing harm can be achieved. Doing so at the level of inception and implementation also lays a foundation for more effective and sensitive monitoring and evaluation, allowing for changes that might otherwise be overlooked to be captured.

A simplistic theory of change (ToC) would imply that increased ability to earn and increased earnings of women enable them to stop violence against them and/or move out of a situation where they are subjected to violence. This theory presupposes that women who earn their own income have control of the income and/or are able to wield and negotiate power in a different way. It also assumes that this will enable them to exercise their rights and either escape from violence or stop the violence. But it ignores the extent to which powerful social norms operate to maintain stigma as a means of ensuring women conform to family structures of male control, which can leave them stuck in an environment of violence with or without independent earning.

The research presented in this volume challenges the assumption that change is linear or straightforward. It has highlighted the complexities in terms of power dynamics in relationships across a number of settings, from the workplace to the household, and has also discussed some of the limitations caused by a lack of state legislation against VAWG, or the weak enforcement of legislation where it does exist. The contribution of this volume is, I hope, that it feeds into a growing body of research that pinpoints mindset change across genders and socio-economic groups and in differing cultural contexts through a prism of power relations. VAWG will not end until current power dynamics and relationships based on authority are disrupted and replaced by a concept of equality, and there cannot be any single entry point to change – the problem cannot be reduced to a lack of financial independence or education, or even a weak justice system. Instead, it needs to be set within the wider social and cultural environment that propounds a dominant set of values and beliefs that sanctions. The research in this volume sought to understand if and in what ways various strands link together to prevent change, and went on to consider if forms of income earning and specific work/employment contexts may bring about positive change. The volume sought to highlight the types and nature of activities that can support the empowerment of women and bolster the infrastructure needed to build resilience to violence.

Figure 4 depicts a process of change that is true to the concept of transformation in terms of a web: interlocking dimensions must come together if change is to occur and be sustained.

Women's own stories and voices have fed into the picture of change depicted above. At the heart of it are women; they are

Figure 4 Women, work and violence: a theory of change

Source: Reproduced with permission from the illustrator/designer, Louis Netter

vocal in their challenge to violence, and by joining their agency the collective becomes even more powerful. However, without a supportive enabling environment, these voices will have little potential to bring lasting change. A committed government with inclusive representation of the full diversity of the country is crucial. So too is a functioning and well-resourced judicial system and a flourishing civil society with expertise in supporting and advocating for women and girls. We now know that in order to be successful in ending VAWG, these strands need to come together, but what we still know little about is how to make this happen. This, then, is the next – and hopefully final – challenge that will see the goal of a violence-free existence for all achieved.

NOTES

2 Measuring attitudes around harmful cultural practices: the continuum approach

1 Please note that the research summarised in this chapter has been included with the consent of the lead organisation and represents a secondary summary of a report available in the public domain. The volume author worked as a consultant, and was responsible for the research design, data analysis and final write-up of the final published report.

6 The experiences of home-based workers in Pakistan

1 Definition of urban and peri-urban areas is given by the local government or municipality.

8 Violence against women and girls in conflict settings

1 Kabeer's parallel attention to resources and agency (structure and culture) has been incorporated into and/or has informed innumerable research and policy frameworks on women's empowerment, including that of ICRW (Golla, Malhotra, Mehra & Nanda, 2011), and she has worked extensively for DFID.

REFERENCES

Abdalla, T., Badri, H., Barrett, N., Donahue, C., Johnson, A. C. & Evans, W. D. (2018). Qualitative evaluation of the Saleema campaign to eliminate female genital mutilation and cutting in Sudan. *Reproductive Health*, 15(1), 30.

Abdelnour, S. (2010). Fuel-efficient stoves for Darfur: The social construction of subsistence marketplaces in post-conflict settings. *Journal of Business Research*, 63(6), 617–629.

Abramsky, T., Devries, K., Ellsberg, M., Garcia-Moreno, C., Heise, L., Jansen, H. A. F. M., Kiss, L. & Watts, C. H. (2011). What factors are associated with recent intimate partner violence? Findings from the WHO multi-country study on women's health and domestic violence. *BMC Public Health*, 11(109), 1–17.

Abu-Lughod, L. (2013). *Do Muslim women need saving?* Cambridge, MA: Harvard University Press.

Ahmed, S., Al Hebshi, S. & Nylund, B. V. (2009). *An in-depth analysis of the social dynamics of abandonment of FGM/C* (Innocenti Working Paper No. 2009-08). Florence: UNICEF Innocenti Research Centre.

Ali, N. M. (2011). *Gender and statebuilding in South Sudan: A special report*. Retrieved from www.peacewomen.org/assets/file/SecurityCouncilMonitor/Missions/SouthSudan/special_report_usip_december_2011.pdf

Almroth, L., Bergström, S., Bjälkander, O., Harman, G. & Leigh, B. (2012). Female genital mutilation in Sierra Leone: Who are the decision makers? *African Journal of Reproductive Health*, 16(4), 119–131.

Almroth, L., Elkhidir, I., Elmusharaf, S. & Hoffman, S. (2006). A case control study on the association between FGM and sexually transmitted infections in Sudan. *BJOG: An International Journal of Obstetrics and Gynaecology*, 113, 469–474.

al-Shawabkeh, M. (2014, 29 June). Syrian women refugees suffer in Jordan. *AL Monitor*. Retrieved from www.al-monitor.com/pulse/culture/2014/06/jordan-syria-refugees-violence-against-women.html

Alvarez, S. E., Chuchryk, P., Navarro-Aranguren, M. & Sternbach, N. S. (1992). Feminisms in Latin American from Bogota to San Bernardo. *Signs*, 17(2), 393–434.

Anker, R., Korten, A. & Malkas, H. (2003). *Gender-based occupational segregation in the 1990s* (ILO Working Paper 16). Geneva: ILO.

Ansara, D. L., Hindin, M. J. & Kishor, S. (2008). *Intimate partner violence among couples in 10 DHS countries: predictors and health outcomes* (DHS Analytical Studies No. 18). Retrieved from https://dhsprogram.com/pubs/pdf/AS18/AS18.pdf

Appadurai, A. (2013). *The future as cultural fact: Essays on the global condition.* London: Verso.

Askew, I. & Keesbury, J. (2010). *Comprehensive responses to gender-based violence in low-resource settings: Lessons learned from implementation.* Retrieved from www.oecd.org/dac/gender-development/47563490.pdf

Averbach, S., Cornish, S., Hacker, M. R., Merport Modest, A., Murphy, M., Parmar, P., Scott, J. & Spencer, D. (2013). An assessment of gender inequitable norms and GBV in South Sudan. *Conflict and Health, 7*(24), 1–11.

Ayotte, K. J. & Husain, M. E. (2005). Securing Afghan women: Neocolonialism, epistemic violence, and the rhetoric of the veil. *NWSA Journal, 17*(3), 112–133.

Azman, A. & Hassan, S. M. (2014). Social risk management lens: A framework for marginalized segments. *Pakistan Journal of Social Sciences, 34*(1), 1–12.

Bacci, C. (2000). Policy as discourse: What does it mean? Where does it get us? *Discourse: The Cultural Study of Politics in Education, 21*(1), 45–57.

Ball, L., Paluck, E. L., Poynton, C. & Sieloff, S. (2010). *Social norms marketing aimed at gender based violence: A literature review and critical assessment.* New York: International Rescue Committee.

Bank, A., Dutt, M., Horn, J., Michau, L. & Zimmerman, C. (2015). Prevention of violence against women and girls: Lessons from practice. *The Lancet, 385*(9978), 1672–1684.

Basnyat, I. (2014). Lived experiences of street-based female sex workers in Kathmandu: Implications for health intervention strategies. *Culture, Health & Sexuality, 16*(9), 1040–1051.

Basu, A. & Dutta, M. J. (2009). Sex workers and HIV/AIDS: Analyzing participatory culture-centered health communication strategies. *Human Communication Research, 35*(1), 86–114.

Bedri, N. (2013). Evidence based advocacy for ending FGM/C in Sudan. *The Ahfad Journal: Women and Change, 30*(1), 9–21.

Bedri, N. & Bradley, T. (2017). Mapping the complexities and highlighting the dangers: The global drive to end FGM in the UK and Sudan. *Progress in Development Studies, 17*(1), 24–37.

Benesova, S. (2004). Southern Sudanese women in the diaspora. *The Osprey Journal of Ideas and Inquiry, 4*(79).

Berkey, J. P. (1996). Circumcision circumscribed: Female excision and cultural accommodation in the medieval Near East. *International Journal of Middle East Studies, 28*(1), 19–38.

REFERENCES | 229

Beswick, S. (2001). "We are bought like clothes": The war over polygyny and levirate marriage in South Sudan. *Northeast African Studies, 8*(2), 35–62.

Boddy, J. (2016). The normal and the aberrant in female genital cutting: Shifting paradigms. *HAU: Journal of Ethnographic Theory, 6*(2), 41–69.

Bodenner, C. (2015, 1 May). The complexity of female circumcision: Your thoughts. *The Atlantic.* Retrieved from www.theatlantic.com/international/archive/2015/05/complexity-of-female-circumcision-your-thoughts/391841/

Bodian, A. (2015). *Research report: Attitudes to female genital mutilation/cutting in Portsmouth and Southampton.* Portsmouth: Southern Domestic Abuse Service and African Women's Forum.

Bookwalter, J. & Dalenberg, D. (2004). Subjective well-being and household factors in South Africa. *Social Indicators Research, 65*(3), 333–353.

Bourdieu, P. (1977). *Outline of a theory of practice.* Cambridge: Cambridge University Press.

Boyle, E. & Preves, S. (2000). National politics as international process: The case of anti-female-genital-cutting laws. *Law & Society Review, 34*, 703–737.

Bradley, T. (2006). *Challenging the NGOs: Women, religion and Western dialogues in India.* London: I.B. Tauris.

Bradley, T. (2010a). Religion as a bridge between theory and practice in work on violence against women in Rajasthan. *Journal of Gender Studies, 19*(4), 361–375.

Bradley, T. (2010b). *Religion and gender in the developing world.* London: I.B. Tauris.

Bradley, T. (Ed.) (2011). *Women, violence and tradition: Taking FGM and other practices to a secular state.* London: Zed Books.

Bradley, T. (2017). *Women and violence in India.* London: I.B. Tauris.

Bradley, T. & Byrne, G. (2019). Applying a gender lens to humanitarian programming.

Bradley, T. & Gruber, J. (2018). VAWG mainstreaming and framework for action. *Development in Practice, 28*(1), 16–32.

Bradley, T. & Kirmani, N. (2015). Religion, gender and development in South Asia. In E. Tomalin (Ed.), *The Routledge handbook of religions and global development* (pp. 215–230). London: Routledge.

Bradley, T., Martin, Z. & Parliwala, R. (forthcoming). Applying *habitus* to a study of women, work and violence in Myanmar, Nepal and Pakistan.

Bradley, T. & Pallikadavath, S. (2018). Dowry, "dowry autonomy" and domestic violence among young married women in India. *Journal of Biosocial Science, 51*(3), 353–373.

Bradley, T. & Sahariah, S. (2019). Tales of suffering and strength: Women's experiences of working in Nepal's informal entertainment industry. *International Journal of Gender Studies in Developing Societies, 3*(1), 20–36.

Bratt, R. (2010). Housing and family well-being. *Housing Studies, 17*(1), 13–26.

Bredenkamp, C., Palermo, T. & Peterman, A. (2011). Estimates and determinants of sexual violence against women in the Democratic Republic of Congo. *American Journal of Public Health, 101*(6), 1060–1067.

Brockington, D. (2014). The production and construction of celebrity advocacy in international development. *Third World Quarterly, 35*(1), 88–108.

Brush, C. G. & Cooper, S. Y. (2012). Female entrepreneurship and economic development: An international perspective. *Entrepreneurship & Regional Development, 24*(1–2), 1–6.

Burrage, H. (2016). *Eradicating female genital mutilation: A UK perspective.* London: Routledge.

Busza, J. (2004). Sex work and migration: The dangers of oversimplification – a case study of Vietnamese women in Cambodia. *Health and Human Rights, 7*(2), 231–249.

Carter, N. M., Cinnéide, B. Ó., Henry, C. & Johnston, K. (2006). *Female entrepreneurship: Implications for education, training and policy.* London: Routledge.

Caviglia, L. (2017). *Sex work in Nepal: The making and unmaking of a category.* New York: Routledge.

Chamlee-Wright, E. (2002). *The cultural foundations of economic development: Urban female entrepreneurship in Ghana.* London: Routledge.

Chapkis, W. (2003). Trafficking, migration, and the law: Protecting innocents, punishing immigrants. *Gender & Society, 17*(6), 923–937.

CI. (2013). *Syrian refugees in urban Jordan: Baseline assessment of community identified vulnerabilities among Syrian refugees living in Irbid, Madaba, Mufraq, & Zarqa.* Retrieved from www.care.org/sites/default/files/documents/EMER-JOR-2013-Syrian-Refugees-in-Urban-Jordan.pdf

CI. (2014). *The girl has no rights: Gender-based violence in South Sudan.* Retrieved from https://insights.careinternational.org.uk/media/k2/attachments/CARE_The_Girl_Has_No_Rights_GBV_in_South_Sudan.pdf

Clarke, J. & Haque, Y. (2002). The Woman Friendly Hospital Initiative in Bangladesh setting: Standards for the care of women subject to violence. *International Journal of Gynaecology and Obstetrics, 78*(Suppl 1), S45–S49.

Clifford, J. & Marcus, G. E. (Eds.) (1986). *Writing culture: The poetics and politics of ethnography.* London: University of California Press.

Cloud, D. L. (2004). "To veil the threat of terror": Afghan women and the clash of civilizations in the imagery of the US war on terrorism. *Quarterly Journal of Speech, 90*(3), 285–306.

Connell, R. W. (1995). *Masculinities.* Cambridge: Polity Press.

Coyne, J. (2016, 23 May). An anthropologist justifies female genital mutilation. *Why Evolution Is True.* Retrieved from https://whyevolutionistrue.wordpress.com/2016/05/23/an-anthropologist-justifies-female-genital-mutilation/

Crenshaw, K. (1989). Demarginalizing the intersection of race and sex: A black feminist critique of antidiscrimination doctrine, feminist theory and antiracist politics. *University of Chicago Legal Forum*, 1(8), 139–167.

Cruz, A. & Klinger, S. (2011). *Gender-based violence in the world of work: Overview and selected annotated bibliography* (ILO Working Paper 3/2011). Retrieved from www.ilo.org/wcmsp5/groups/public/---dgreports/---gender/documents/publication/wcms_155763.pdf

Dalal, K., Svanstrom, L. & Wang, S. (2014). Intimate partner violence against women in Nepal: An analysis through individual, empowerment, family and societal level factors. *Journal of Research Health Science*, 14(4), 251–257.

DFID (2012). *A theory of change for tackling violence against women and girls* (DFID Practice Paper: CHASE Guidance Note Series, Guidance Note 1). Retrieved from www.womankind.org.uk/docs/default-source/resources/vawg_guidance1_toc11.pdf?sfvrsn=2

DFID (2014). *Review of non-food items that meet the needs of women and girls, June 2014.* Retrieved from https://assets.publishing.service.gov.uk/media/57a089a6e5274a27b20001cf/hdq1107.pdf

Diken, B. & Laustsen, C. B. (2005). *The culture of exception: Sociology facing the camp.* London: Routledge.

Diop, N. J., Johansen, R. E. B., Laverack, G. & Leye, E. (2013). What works and what does not: A discussion of popular approaches for the abandonment of female genital mutilation. *Obstetrics and Gynaecology International*, 348248, 1–10.

Donnelly, P. D., Goodall, C. A., Neville, F. G. & Williams, D. J. (2014). Violence brief interventions: A rapid review. *Aggression and Violent Behavior*, 19(6), 692–698.

Dorkenoo, E. & Macfarlane, A. J. (2015). *Prevalence of female genital mutilation in England and Wales: National and local estimates.* London: City University London and Equality Now.

Dworkin, A. (1993). *Letters from a war zone.* New York: Lawrence Hill Books.

Dworkin, A. (2004). Pornography, prostitution, and a beautiful and tragic recent history. In C. Stark & R. Whisnant (Eds.), *Not for sale: Feminists resisting prostitution and pornography* (pp. 137–148). Melbourne: Spinifex Press.

Easton, P., Monkman, K. & Miles, R. (2003). Social policy from the bottom up: Abandoning FGC in sub-Saharan Africa. *Development in Practice*, 13(5), 445–458.

Elia, L. (2007). Fighting gender-based violence in South Sudan. *Forced Migration Review*, 27(39), 44–58.

Eriksson Baaz, M. & Stern, M. (2008). Making sense of violence: Voices of soldiers in the Congo (DRC)'. *Journal of Modern African Studies*, 46(1), 57–86.

Eriksson Baaz, M. & Stern, M. (2009). Why do soldiers rape? Masculinity, violence, and sexuality in the armed forces in the Congo (DRC). *International Studies Quarterly, 53*(2), 495–518.

Eriksson Baaz, M. & Stern, M. (2013). *Sexual violence as a weapon of war? Perceptions, prescriptions, problems in the Congo and beyond.* London: Zed Books.

Farley, M. (Ed.) (2003). *Prostitution, trafficking and traumatic stress.* London: Routledge.

FPH. (2016). *The role of public health in the prevention of violence: A statement from the UK Faculty of Public Health.* Retrieved from www.fph.org.uk/media/1381/the-role-of-public-health-in-the-prevention-of-violence.pdf

GACC (2016). *Gender-based violence in humanitarian settings: Cookstoves and fuels.* Washington, DC: Global Alliance for Clean Cookstoves.

Gartner, R. & Macmillan, R. (1999). When she brings home the bacon: Labor-force participation and the risk of spousal violence against women. *Journal of Marriage and Family, 61*(4), 947–958.

Gibbs, A., Jewkes, R. & Sikweyiya, Y. (2017). "I tried to resist and avoid bad friends": The role of social context in shaping the transformation of masculinities in a gender transformative and livelihood strengthening intervention in South Africa. *Men and Masculinities, 1*(3), 1–20.

Gibbs, A., Jewkes, R., Willan, S. & Washington, L. (2018). Associations between poverty, mental health and substance use, gender power, and intimate partner violence amongst young (18–30) women and men in urban informal settlements in South Africa: A cross-sectional study and structural equation model. *PLoS one, 13*(10), 1–19.

Gibson, M., Thomson, H., Kearns, A. & Petticrew, M. (2011). Understanding the psychosocial impacts of housing type: Qualitative evidence from a housing and regeneration intervention. *Housing Studies, 26*(4), 555–573.

Goetz, A. M. & Sen Gupta, R. (1996). Who takes the credit? Gender, power and control over loan use in rural credit programmes in Bangladesh. *World Development, 24*(1), 45–63.

Gold, A. & Raheja, G. (1994). *Listen to the heron's words: Reimagining gender and kinship in North India.* Berkeley, CA: University of California Press.

Golla, A. M., Malhotra, A., Mehra, R. & Nanda, P. (2011). *Understanding and measuring women's economic empowerment: Definition, framework and indicators.* Retrieved from www.icrw.org/wp-content/uploads/2016/10/Understanding-measuring-womens-economic-empowerment.pdf

Goode, W. (1971). Force in the family. *Journal of Marriage and Family, 33*(4), 624–636.

REFERENCES | 233

Goodman, M. K. & Barnes, C. (2011). Star/poverty space: The making of the "development celebrity." *Celebrity Studies, 2*(1), 69–85.

Grafham, O. & Lahn, G. (2015). *Heat, light and power for refugees: Saving lives, reducing costs.* London: Chatham House.

Grisurapong, S. (2002). Establishing a one-stop crisis center for women suffering violence in Khonkaen, Thailand. *International Journal of Gynaecology and Obstetrics, 78*(Suppl 1), S27–S38.

GRSS (2010). *South Sudan Household Health Survey.* Retrieved from http://microdata.worldbank.org/index.php/catalog/2588/study-description

Gunning, R. (2014). *The current state of sustainable energy provision for displaced populations: An analysis, research paper.* London: Chatham House.

Harding, S. (2008). *Sciences from below: Feminisms, postcolonialisms, and modernities.* London: Duke University Press.

Harman, J. J., Kaufman, M. R., Menger, L. M. & Shrestha, D. K. (2016). Understanding the experiences and needs of female commercial sex workers in Kathmandu, Nepal. *Health Care for Women International, 37*(8), 872–888.

Harper, C. & Marcus, R. (2014). *Gender justice and social norms: Processes of change for adolescent girls – towards a conceptual framework, 2.* Retrieved from www.odi.org/sites/odi.org.uk/files/odi-assets/publications-opinion-files/8831.pdf

Hawkes, S., Misra, G. & Puri, M. (2015). Hidden voices: Prevalence and risk factors for violence against women with disabilities in Nepal. *BMC Public Health, 15*(1), 261–274.

Hawkins, K. & Price, N. (2002). Researching sexual and reproductive behaviour: A peer ethnographic approach. *Social Science & Medicine, 55*(8), 1325–1336.

Healy, G. & O'Connor, M. (2006). *The links between prostitution and sex trafficking: A briefing handbook.* Retrieved from https://renate-europe.net/wp-content/uploads/2014/01/CATW_handbook_LinksProstitution_Trafficking2009.pdf

Heckert, A. & Heckert, D. M. (2002). A new typology of deviance: Integrating normative and reactivist definitions of deviance. *Deviant Behavior, 23*(5), 449–479.

Heise, L. (1998). Violence against women and girls and integrated ecological framework. *Violence Against Women, 4*(3), 262–290.

Heise, L. (2011). *What works to prevent partner violence? An evidence overview* (DFID Working Paper). Retrieved from http://strive.lshtm.ac.uk/resources/what-works-prevent-partner-violence-evidence-overview

Heise, L., Ellsberg, M. & Gottmoeller, M. (2002). A global overview of gender-based violence. *International Journal of Gynaecology & Obstetrics, 78*(Supplement 1), S5–S14.

Hernlund, Y., Moreau, A., Shell-Duncan, B. & Wander, K. (2010). *Contingency and change in the practice of female genital cutting: Dynamics of decision making in Senegambia Summary Report*. Seattle, WA: University of Washington Press.

HNP (2011). *Empowering home-based workers: End of project report*. Retrieved from https://homenetpakistan.org/wp-content/uploads/2017/03/ending-report.pdf

HNP (n.d.). *What is HomeNet?* Retrieved from https://homenetpakistan.org/what-is-homenet/

HRW (1999). *Crime or custom? Violence against women in Pakistan*. Retrieved from www.hrw.org/sites/default/files/reports/pakistan1999.pdf

Htun, M. & Weldon, L. (2012). The civic origins of progressive policy change: Combatting violence against women in global perspective, 1975–2005. *American Political Science Review, 106*(3), 548–569.

Hussein, L. (2019, 14 February). I know first-hand FGM is one of the worst forms of abuse – survivors like me shouldn't need more laws to feel protected. *HuffPost*. Retrieved from www.huffingtonpost.co.uk/entry/fgm-bill_uk_5c659ce5e4b0bcddd40fa8fb

ICRW. (2014). *Masculinity, intimate partner violence and son preference in India*. Retrieved from www.icrw.org/publications/masculinity-intimate-partner-violence-and-son-preference-in-india/

ILO. (2004). *Sexual harassment at the workplace in Nepal*. Retrieved from www.ilo.org/kathmandu/whatwedo/publications/WCMS_113780/lang--en/index.htm

ILO. (2010). *Labour and social trends in Nepal 2010*. Retrieved from www.ilo.org/wcmsp5/groups/public/---asia/---ro-bangkok/---ilo-kathmandu/documents/publication/wcms_151322.pdf

IOM. (2011). *MRF Nairobi Bulletin, 5(11)*. Retrieved from www.iom.int/jahia/webdav/shared/ shared/mainsite/activities/countries/docs/kenya/MRF-Nairobi-Newsletter-May-2011.pdf

Iqbal, N. (2007). Legal pluralism in Pakistan and its implication on women's rights. In J. Bennett (Eds.), *Scratching the surface: Democracies, traditions, gender*. Berlin: Heinrich Böll Foundation.

IRC. (2014). *Lighting the way: The role of handheld solar lamps in improving women's and girl's perceptions of safety in two camps for internally displaced people in Haiti*. Retrieved from www.safefuelandenergy.org/files/IRC%20Haiti-Solar-Light-Evaluation-Research-Brief.pdf

IRC. (2017). *No safe place: A lifetime of violence for conflict-affected women and girls in South Sudan* (What Works: Summary Report 2017). Retrieved from www.rescue.org/report/no-safe-place

James, S. (1998). Shades of othering: Reflections on female circumcision/genital mutilation. *Signs: Journal of Women in Culture and Society, 23*(4), 1031–1048.

Jenkins, C. (2006). *Violence and exposure to HIV among sex workers in Phnom Penh, Cambodia*. Washington, DC: POLICY Project/USAID.

Jerslev, A. (2014). Celebrification, authenticity, gossip: The celebrity humanitarian. *NORDICOM Review: Nordic Research on Media and Communication, 35*, 171–186.

Jewkes, R. (2002). Intimate partner violence: Causes and prevention. *The Lancet, 359*(9315), 1423–1429.

Jewkes, R., Karmaliani, R. & Mcfarlane, J. (2018). *Right to Play: Preventing violence among and against children in schools in Hyderabad, Pakistan*. Retrieved from www.whatworks.co.za/documents/publications/211-right-to-play/file

Jewkes, R. & Morrell, R. (2017). Hegemonic masculinity, violence, and gender equality: Using latent class analysis to investigate the origins and correlates of differences between men. *Men and Masculinities, 3*(1), 1–25.

Johnson, A., Evans, D., Badri, H., Abdalla, T. & Donahue, C. (2018). Qualitative evaluation of the Saleema campaign to end female genital mutilation and cutting in Sudan. *Reproductive Health, 15*(1), 30.

Jok, J. M. (1999). Militarisation and gender violence in Southern Sudan. *Journal of Asian and African Studies, 34*(4), 427–442.

Jones, B. & Petersen, M. J. (2011). Instrumental, narrow, normative? Reviewing recent work on religion and development. *Third World Quarterly, 32*, 1291–1306.

Kabeer, N. (2003). *Gender mainstreaming in poverty eradication and the Millennium Development Goals*. London: Commonwealth Secretariat.

Kabeer, N. (2008). *Paid work, women's empowerment and gender justice: Critical pathways of social change*. Retrieved from http://eprints.lse.ac.uk/53077/1/Kabeer_Paid-work_Published.pdf

Kabeer, N. (2012). *Women's economic empowerment and inclusive growth: Labour markets and enterprise development* (CDPR Discussion Paper 29/12). Retrieved from www.soas.ac.uk/cdpr/publications/papers/file80432.pdf

Kapoor, I. (2013). *Celebrity humanitarianism: The ideology of global charity*. London: Routledge.

Kazmi, S. & Khan, S. (2003). *Revenue distributions across value chains: The case of home-based sub-contracted workers in Pakistan*. (University of Utah Department of Economics Working Paper, 2003-04).

Keck, M. & Sikkink, K. (1998). *Activists beyond borders*. Ithaca, NY: Cornell University Press.

Kelly, L. (1988). *Surviving sexual violence*. London: Polity Press.

Khazan, O. (2015, 8 April). Why some women choose to get circumcised. *The Atlantic*. Retrieved from www.theatlantic.com/international/archive/2015/04/female-genital-mutilation-cutting-anthropologist/389640/

Kilonzo, N. & Taegtmeyer, M. (2005). *Comprehensive post-rape care services in resource-poor settings: Lessons learnt from Kenya* (Liverpool VCT, Policy Briefings for Health Sector Reform, 6). Kenya: Liverpool VCT Centre.

Kilonzo, N., Theobald, S. J., Nyamato, E., Ajema, C., Muchela, H., Kibaru, J., Rogena, E. & Taegtmeyer, M. (2009). Delivering post-rape care services: Kenya's experience in developing integrated services. *Bulletin World Health Organization, 87*(7), 555–559.

King, S. & Parry-Crook, G. (2018). *Towards an understanding of the current debates on the Dawoodi Bohra tradition of female genital cutting: A synthesis of key issues*. Retrieved from www.tavinstitute.org/wp-content/uploads/2018/08/TIHRsynthesisDB2018.pdf

Kohn, E. (1994). Rape as a weapon of war: Women's human rights during the dissolution of Yugoslavia. *Women's Law Forum, 24*, 199–213.

Leonardi, C. (2010). Paying buckets in blood for the land: Moral debates over economy, war and state in Southern Sudan. *Modern African Studies, 49*(2), 215–240.

Liechty, M. (2005a). Carnal economies: The commodification of food and sex in Kathmandu. *Cultural Anthropology, 20*(1), 1–38.

Liechty, M. (2005b). Building the road to Kathmandu: Notes on the history of tourism in Nepal. *HIMALAYA: The Journal of the Association for Nepal and Himalayan Studies, 25*(1), 19–28.

Liechty, M. (2010). The key to an oriental world: Boris Lissanevitch, Kathmandu's Royal Hotel and the "golden age" of tourism in Nepal. *Studies in Nepali History and Society, 15*(2), 253–295.

Lund-Thomsen, P. (2013). Labor agency in the football manufacturing industry of Sialkot, Pakistan. *Geoforum, 44*, 71–81.

Luttrell, C. & Quiroz, S. (2009). *Understanding and operationalising empowerment* (ODI Working Paper 308). Retrieved from www.odi.org/sites/odi.org.uk/files/odi-assets/publications-opinion-files/5500.pdf

Mackie, G. (1996). Ending footbinding and infibulation: A convention account. *American Sociological Review, 61*(6) 999–1017.

Mackie, G., Moneti, F., Shakaya, H. & Denny, E. (2015). *What are social norms? How are they measured?* New York: UNICEF.

MacKinnon, C. A. (1987). *Feminism unmodified: Discourses on life and law*. Cambridge, MA: Harvard University Press.

MacKinnon, C. A. (1993). *Only words*. Cambridge, MA: Harvard University Press.

Magied, A. A. & Ahmed, S. M. (2002). Sexual experiences and psychosexual effect of female genital mutilation (FGM) or female circumcision (FC) on Sudanese women. *Ahfad Journal, 19*(1), 21–30.

Mahood, L. (2009). *Feminism and voluntary action: Eglantyne Jebb and Save the Children, 1876–1928.* New York: Palgrave Macmillan.

Malik, N. (2014, 13 November). Failing hospitals and private-public fiefdoms: What healthcare reveals about Sudan. *African Arguments.* Retrieved from https://africanarguments.org/2014/11/13/failing-hospitals-and-private-public-fiefdoms-what-healthcare-reveals-about-sudan-by-nesrine-malik/

Malmström, M. F. (2016). *The politics of female circumcision in Egypt: Gender, sexuality and the construction of identity.* London: I.B. Tauris.

Malmström, M. F. & Van Raemdonck, A. (2015). "The clitoris is in the head!" Female circumcision and the making of a harmful cultural practice in Egypt. In C. Longman & T. Bradley (Eds.), *Global perspectives on FGM/C and other harmful cultural practices and their implications for women's rights* (pp. 121–138). London: Ashgate.

Mansbridge, J. (1995). What is the feminist movement? In M. M. Ferree & P. Y. Martin (Eds.), *Feminist organizations: Harvest of the new women's movement* (pp. 27–34). Philadelphia, PA: Temple University Press.

Mansbridge, J. & Morris, A. (2001). *Oppositional consciousness: The subjective roots of social protest.* Chicago, IL: University of Chicago Press.

Marshall, P. D. (1997). *Celebrity and power: Fame in contemporary culture.* Minneapolis, MN: University of Minnesota Press.

McKean, L. (1991). *Divine enterprise: Gurus and the Hindu nationalist movement.* Chicago, IL: University of Chicago Press.

McCloskey, L. A. (1996). Socioeconomic and coercive power within the family. *Gender & Society, 10*(4), 449–463.

Medani, M. (2010). *Criminal law and justice in Sudan.* Retrieved from www.pclrs.com/downloads/1206_criminal_law_and_justice_feb_2010.pdf

Mercy Corps. (2010, 23 March). *In Congo, saving trees and lives.* Retrieved from www.mercycorps.org/articles/dr-congo/congo-saving-trees-and-lives

Mgbako, C., Saxena, M., Cave, A. & Farjad, F. (2010). Penetrating the silence in Sierra Leone: A blueprint for the eradication of female genital mutilation. *Harvard Human Rights Journal, 23,* 111–126.

Mohanty, C. T. (1988). Under Western eyes: Feminist scholarship and colonial discourses. *Feminist Review, 30*(1), 61–88.

Mohanty, C. T. (2003). "Under Western eyes" revisited: Feminist solidarity through anticapitalist struggles. *Signs: Journal of Women in Culture and Society, 28*(2), 499–535.

Molyneux, M. (1985). *Mobilization without emancipation? Women's interests, the state, and revolution in Nicaragua*. Ann Arbor, MI: University of Michigan Press.

Monto, M. A. (2014). Prostitution, sex work, and violence: Lessons from the Cambodian context. *Studies in Gender and Sexuality, 15*(1), 73–84.

Mukhopadhyay, M. (2016). Mainstreaming gender or "streaming" gender away: Feminists marooned in the development business. In W. Harcourt (Ed.), *The Palgrave handbook of gender and development: Critical engagements in feminist theory and practice* (pp. 77–91). London: Palgrave Macmillan.

Mumtaz, Z. & Salway, S. (2005). "I never go anywhere": Extricating the links between women's mobility and uptake of reproductive health services in Pakistan. *Social Science & Medicine, 60*(8), 1751–1765.

Murthy, L. & Seshu, M. S. (Eds.) (2013). *The Business of Sex*. New Delhi: Zubaan.

Mustafa Ali, N. (2011). *Gender and statebuilding in South Sudan* (United States Institute of Peace Special Report, 298). Washington, DC: USIP.

Nader, L. (1989). Orientalism, occidentalism, and the control of women. *Cultural Dynamics, 7*(2), 323–355.

Nakazato, N., Oishi, S. & Schimmack, U. (2011). Effect of changes in living conditions on well-being: A prospective top-down bottom-up model. *Social Indicators Research, 100*(1), 115–135.

Narayan, U. (1997). Forgiveness, moral reassessment, and reconciliation. In T. Magnell (Ed.), *Explorations of value* (pp. 169–178). Amsterdam: Rodopi.

Nayyar, D. (2012). *UN System Task Team on the Post-2015 UN Development Agenda*. Retrieved from www.un.org/millenniumgoals/pdf/deepak_nayyar_Aug.pdf

Njue, C., Moore, Z. & Shell-Duncan, B. (2018). *Trends in medicalisation of female genital mutilation/cutting: What do the data reveal?* (Evidence to End FGM/C: Research to Help Women Thrive: October 2018 Update). New York: Population Council.

Nussbaum, M. (2000). *Women and Human Development: The Capabilities Approach*. Cambridge: Cambridge University Press.

Nyirazinyoye, L. & Zraly, M. (2010). Don't let the suffering make you fade away: An ethnographic study of resilience among survivors of genocide-rape in Southern Rwanda. *Social Science & Medicine, 70*(10), 1656–1664.

O'Connell Davidson, J. (2006). Will the real sex slave please stand up? *Feminist Review, 83*(1), 4–22.

Ong, A. (1988). The production of possession: Spirits and the multinational corporation in Malaysia. *American Ethnologist, 15*(1), 28–42.

Østebø, M. T. & Østebø, T. (2014). Are religious leaders a magic bullet for social/societal change? A critical look at anti-FGM interventions in Ethiopia. *Africa Today, 60*(3), 82–101.

REFERENCES | 239

Otoo-Oyortey, N. (2014, 30 July). Where were the grassroots voices at the Girl Summit? *The Guardian*. Retrieved from www.theguardian.com/global-development-professionals-network/2014/jul/30/where-were-grassroots-voices-girl-summit

Panda, P. & Agarwal, B. (2005). Marital violence, human development and women's property status in India. *World Development*, 33(5), 823–850.

Parke, A. (2015). *VAWG and energy in camp-based settings* (VAWG Helpdesk Research Report No. 94). London: VAWG Helpdesk.

Parker, S. (2015). Hidden crisis: Violence against Syrian female refugees. *The Lancet*, 385(9985), 2341–2342.

Paternoster, R. & Tittle, C. R. (2000). *Social deviance and crime: An organizational and theoretical approach.* Los Angeles, CA: Roxbury.

Perkins, S. (2015, 5 August). *Lighting impacts SGBV but not in the way you think* (UNHCR Innovation Service Blog). Retrieved from http://innovation.unhcr.org/light-impacts-sgbv-but-not-in-the-way-youthink/

Peterman, A., Pereora, A., Bleck, J., Palermo, T. M. & Yount, K.M. (2017). Women's individual asset ownership and experience of IPV: Evidence from 28 international surveys. *Journal of Public Health*, 107(5), 747–755.

Population Council (2015). *Evidence to end FGM/C: Research to help women and girls thrive.* Retrieved from www.popcouncil.org/uploads/pdfs/2016RH_FGMC-Factsheet.pdf

Povey, E. (2003). Women in Afghanistan: Passive victims of the borga or active social participants? *Development in Practice*, 13(2–3), 266–277.

Piknerova, L. & Rybakova, E. (2017). The celebritization of development: Bono Vox and Angelina Jolie as actors in development. *Development, Environment and Foresight*, 3(1): 20–35.

Reid-Cunningham, A. R. (2008). Rape as a weapon of genocide. *Genocide Studies and Prevention*, 3(3), 279–296.

Roomi, M. A. & Parrott, G. (2008). Barriers to development and progression of women entrepreneurship in Pakistan. *The Journal of Entrepreneurship*, 17(1), 59–72.

Rosamond, A. B. (2016). The digital politics of celebrity activism against sexual violence: Angelina Jolie Pitt as global mother. *Popular Culture and World Politics*, 2(3), 76–90.

Saferworld (2014). *"How can you be a marda if you beat your wife?" Notions of masculinities and violence in Eastern Nepal.* Retrieved from www.saferworld.org.uk/downloads/pubdocs/how-can-you-be-a-marda-if-you-beat-your-wife-2nd-edn.pdf

Serrato, B. C. (2014). *Refugee perceptions study: Za'atari camp and host communities in Jordan.* Retrieved from www-cdn.oxfam.org/s3fs-public/file_attachments/rr-refugee-perceptions-study-syria-jordan-020614-en.pdf

Shell-Duncan, B. (2008). From health to human rights: Female genital cutting and the politics of intervention. *American Anthropologist, 110*(2) 225–236.

Shrestha, H. K. (2015). Sexual harassment at workplace act comes into force. *Nepal Mountain News.* Retrieved from www.nepalmountainnews.com/cms/2015/02/18/sexual-harassment-at-workplace-act-comes-into-force/

SMLS (2008). *Comparative analysis of South Sudanese customary law and Victorian law.* Springvale: Springvale Monash Legal Service.

SNHS (2006). *Sudan National Household Survey SMS: 2006.* Retrieved from www.ssnbss.org/home/document/survey/sudan-household-health-survey-SHHS-2006

SNHS (2010). *Sudan National Household Survey SMS: 2010.* Retrieved from http://ghdx.healthdata.org/record/sudan-household-health-survey-report-2010

Sutherland, S. J. (1989). Sītā and Draupadī: Aggressive behavior and female role-models in the Sanskrit epics. *Journal of the American Oriental Society, 109*(1), 63–79.

Taher, M. (2017). *Understanding female genital cutting in the Dawoodi Bohra community: An exploratory survey.* Retrieved from https://sahiyo.files.wordpress.com/2018/12/Sahiyo-Study_Final_12.28.18.pdf

Taylor, G. & Pereznieto, P. (2014). *Review of evaluation approaches and methods used by interventions on women and girls' economic empowerment.* Retrieved from www.researchgate.net/profile/Paola_Pereznieto/publication/263041749_Review_of_evaluation_approaches_and_methods_used_by_interventions_on_women_and_girls'_economic_empowerment/links/0a85e5399d7f058045000000.pdf

Taylor, G., Bell, E., Jacobson, J. & Pereznieto, P. (2015). *Addressing violence against women and girls through DFID's economic development and women's economic empowerment programmes* (DFID guidance note part 1). Retrieved from https://assets.publishing.service.gov.uk/government/uploads/system/uploads/attachment_data/file/444143/Economic-Development-Part-A_2_.pdf

The Girl Generation. (2016). *The Africa-led movement to end female genital mutilation (FGM).* Retrieved from www.thegirlgeneration.org/about

Thomson, H. & Thomas, S. (2015). Developing empirically supported theories of change for housing investment and health. *Social Science & Medicine, 124,* 205–214.

True, J. (2012). *The political economy of violence against women.* Oxford: Oxford University Press.

Trust for London. (n.d.). *Prevalence of female genital mutilation in England and Wales: National and local estimates.* Retrieved from www.trustforlondon.org.uk/publications/prevalence-female-genital-mutilation-england-and-wales-national-and-local-estimates/

REFERENCES | 241

Turner, G. (2004). *Understanding celebrity*. London: SAGE.

UN. (n.d.). *Goal 5: Achieve gender equality and empower all women and girls*. Retrieved from www.un.org/sustainabledevelopment/gender-equality/

UNHCR. (2012). *Light Years Ahead: Innovative technology for better refugee protection*. Retrieved from www.unhcr.org/4c99fa9e6.pdf

UNHCR & UNFPA. (2014). *Sexual and gender-based violence: Syrian refugees in Jordan* (Sexual and Gender-Based Violence Sub-Working Group Briefing Paper, March 2014). Retrieved from https://data2.unhcr.org/en/documents/download/40258

UNICEF. (2013). *UNICEF female genital mutilation/cutting: A statistical overview and explanation into the dynamics of change*. Retrieved from www.unicef.org/cbsc/files/UNICEF_FGM_report_July_2013_Hi_res.pdf

UNICEF. (2014). *Brochures archives*. Retrieved from https://data.unicef.org/resources/resource-type/brochures/

UNMISS. (2014). *United Nations Mission in South Sudan: Conflict in South Sudan – a human rights report*. Retrieved from https://reliefweb.int/report/south-sudan/conflict-south-sudan-human-rights-report

UN Women. (2018). *Annual report 2017–2018*. Retrieved from www.unwomen.org/-/media/annual%20report/attachments/sections/library/un-women-annual-report-2017-2018-en.pdf?la=en&vs=2849&la=en&vs=2849

Van Raemdonck, A. (2016) *Female genital cutting and the politics of Islamicate practices in Egypt: Debating development and religious/secular divide*. PhD thesis.

Vaz, P. (2008). *Sexual violence and HIV/AIDS services: Thuthuzela care centres in South Africa*. Presentation to Office of the US Global AIDS Coordinator, Washington, DC.

Volpp, L. (2000). Blaming culture for bad behavior. *Yale Journal of Law and the Humanities*, 12(1), 89–117.

Vyas, S. & Watts, C. (2009). How does economic empowerment affect women's risk of intimate partner violence in low and middle income countries? A systematic review of published evidence. *Journal of International Development*, 21, 577–602.

Wade, L. (2009). Defining gendered oppression in US newspapers: The strategic value of female genital mutilation. *Gender & Society, 23*(3), 293–314.

Ward, J. (2005). *"Because now men are really sitting on our heads and pressing us down": A report of a preliminary assessment of GBV in Rumbek, Aweil (East and West) and Rashad County, Nuba Mountains*. USAID and University of Missouri.

Ward, J. (2013). *Violence against women in conflict, post-conflict and emergency settings*. Retrieved from www.endvawnow.org/uploads/modules/pdf/1405612658.pdf

Watts, C. & Zimmerman, C. (2007). Violence against women: Global scope and magnitude. *The Lancet, 359*, 1232–1237.

WEF (2014). *Economies: The Global Gender Gap Index, Nepal*. Retrieved from http://reports.weforum.org/global-gender-gap-report-2014/economies/#economy=NPL

Weitzer, R. (2005). Flawed theory and method in studies of prostitution. *Violence Against Women, 11*(7), 934–949.

Weldon, S. L. (2006). The structure of intersectionality: A comparative politics of gender. *Politics & Gender, 2*(2), 235–248.

Weldon, S. L. (2011). *When protests make policy: How social movements represent disadvantaged groups*. Ann Arbor, MI: University of Michigan Press.

Westoff, C. (1988). Is the KAP-gap real? *Population and Development Review, 14*(2), 225–232.

WFP. (2012). *WFP handbook on safe access to fuelwood and alternative energy (SAFE)*. Rome: WFP.

WFP. (2013). *WFP SAFE project in Kenya, Kakuma: Fuel-efficient stoves and gender-based violence*. Retrieved from www.safefuelandenergy.org/files/WFP%20SAFE%20Kenya%20Project%20Kakuma%20GBV%20Report%20FINAL.pdf

What Works. (2017). *No safe place: A lifetime of violence for conflict-affected women and girls in South Sudan*. Retrieved from www.whatworks.co.za/documents/publications/185-no-safe-place-a-lifetime-of-violence-for-conflict-affected-women-and-girls-in-south-sudan-summary-report-2017/file

WHO. (2008). *Eliminating female genital mutilation*. Retrieved from www.who.int/reproductivehealth/publications/fgm/9789241596442/en/

WRC. (2006). *Finding trees in the desert: Firewood collection and alternatives in Darfur*. New York: Women's Refugee Commission.

Young, I. M. (2000). *Justice and the politics of difference*. Princeton: Princeton University Press.

Yuval-Davis, N. (1997). *Gender and nation*. Thousand Oaks, CA: SAGE.

Yuval-Davis, N. (2006). Intersectionality and feminist politics. *European Journal of Women's Studies, 13*(3), 193–209.

INDEX

abduction, South Sudan women, 188, 191
Abramsky, T., 193
Abu-Lughod, L., 65-7, 70, 75
accepted behaviours, sanctions backed, 28
access, inequality of, 13
access to justice programming (ATJP), 5, 10, 198-9
acid throwing, 119
Afghanistan, women's liberation narrative, 62
Africa, research from, 4
African diaspora, Hampshire, 55
agency, 13; agents of change, 221; defiant collective, 32; definition of, 200; differing forms, 43; freedom to exercise, 205; peer ties importance, 40; platforms, 14; speaking up confidence, 14; women's collective, 34; women's employment, 16; *see also*, positive deviants
Al-Bashir, Omar, 46
alcohol violence role, 132, 179-80, 191, 194, 198
Ali, N.M., 128
Alliance Against Sexual Harassment, Pakistan, 107
alternative energy initiatives, 214
analytical web, culture role, 51
Ansara, 180
anthropology: cautionary role, 173; cultural relativism accusation, 20, 66; grassroots audibility role, 80; self-reflexive turn, 64; theory; unheard FGM narratives, 77

anti-FGM campaigns condescension risk, 78; conservative backlash, 175; grassroots silencing danger, 78, 158; movement, 77
attitude(s) "continuum", 49, 51, 55, 60-1; generations change, 125; shifts measuring, 49; transforming entry points, 97
Attock Oil Refinery Limited, Code of Conduct, 109
authority: elite structures, 29; issues of, 28; religious, 75
autonomous women's organisations, importance of, 97
Averbach, S., 189, 194
Azman, A., 134

Bacci, C., policy discourse analysis, 173
backlash(es), male/conservative, 27, 112, 192; resilience against, 35
Balistan, 130
Ball, L., 26
Baluchistan, 130
Bangladesh: 135; nationalist wars, 181; rural microfinance, 142
Basnyat, I., 40
behavioural change approaches, 6, 171; programmes, 5, 34
Benesova, 192
Birmingham, FGM rate, 53
Bohra community: India, 166; urban-based, 165
"Boma", Sudan traditional courts, 195; access to, 196
bondo: FGM women's secret society, 158-9; power of, 166; *soweis* main cutters, 160

Bosnian women, rape scale, 181
Bourdieu, P., 32; *habitus*, 30
Bradley, T., 11, 37-8, 40, 44-5, 202
Bratt, R., 209
Brent, London, FGM scale, 53
bride price, 190-2, 196, 201; FGM link, 157; GBV link, 189; VAWG trigger, 193
Bristol, FGM rate, 53
Buddhist nationalists, extreme Myanmar, 34
burqa, Western liberal narratives, 65
Burrage, Hilary, 156
Byrne, G., 11

Cambodia, informal sex industry, 37-8
camps, displaced peoples: cooking fuel, 203; energy access/initiatives, 202, 216; firewood collection, 213; Haiti solar lights impact lack, 213; insecure settings, 209; intersectional features, 217; Jordan violence, 211; lighting issue, 213; meta questions, 215; poor lighting, 208; women vulnerabilities, 207
Care International, 188-9, 197, 211; *The Girl Has No Rights*, 200
"celebrity factor", development issues, 185; universalising, 186
chains of exploitation, global, 133-4
change agents, 173, 175; FGM, 156
child abuse, FGM, 166
Child Act, Sudanese states ratifying, 74
child marriage, 4, 39, 60, 153; South Sudan law against, 196
children's education, commitment to, 86
China, Japanese soldier rapes, 181
Christian Church, Egypt, 72
circumcision, 163-4; FGM as, 162
City University, London, 53
clitoridectomy, 154

clitoris, post-Freudian Western emphasis, 76
"Code of Conduct for Gender Justice", Pakistan, 107, 109, 114
collective banking schemes, 117
colonial narratives: anthropology involvement, 64; resurgent, 63
community mindsets, global discourse rejecting, 173
Comprehensive Peace Agreement, Sudan 2005, 187
confidence, income link, 89, 108, 151
conformity, as defiance act, 43; codes of, 28
Connell, R.W., 28, 32, 75
conservative gender values, policing by, 22
conservative Islam, Sudan, 34
continuum, violence attitudes change tracking, 49
contradictions, violence complexities, 30, 61
Coyne, Jerry, 69
Crenshaw, K., "intersectionality" term, 52
cultural conservatism, FGM/C, 60
cultural relativism: critical approach, 20, 63, 66-7; lens, 63, 70, 75
"cutting communities", 78; women of views, 77

Darfur, camp fuel collection, 212
Dawoodi Bohra, Muslim community, 160-1
decision-making, 13: employment link, 105, 115; FGM, 160; gendered, 14; income link homeworker lack, 146; interdependent processes, 28; sex workers, 36; women working, 16, 96
Democratic Republic of Congo, 214; international rape framing, 182

INDEX | **245**

Demographic and Health Survey, Pakistan, 105, 180
Deng Gai, Taban, 188
development initiatives/programmes, 32; gender needs embedding, 23; security policies, 49; simplistic theories, 23; unintended consequences, 203
DFID, UK: Sudan intervention, 46, 171; VWAG help desk, 208
dharma, gendered, 45
difference, respect for, 69
Dinka people, 184, 187, 189, 193
discourse policy approaches, money influence, 173
dispute resolution, women as bargaining chips, 127
Ditmore, M.H., 37-8
division of labour: gendered, 87; male ideology, 95; women overburdened, 96
"do no harm" approach, 23, 218
domestic chores, Nepalese male view of, 95
Domestic Violence Act, Nepal, 82
dowry system, 4, 20, 39; women's shifting attitudes, 50-1

ecological approach, 96, 124, 203
ecology of violence, 63, 99; conceptual framework, 4
economic engagement: empowering criteria, 17; women higher levels, 26. *see also*, income; working women
economic exploitation, women normalised, 146
Economic Survey of Pakistan, 137
education, employment links, 130; gender discrepancy effects, 129; girls access to, 26; Nepal women worker levels, 84; programmes impact measuring, 50; women's access to, 128; women's lack, 39
Egypt: FGM "medicalisation", 167; FGM observed, 72
elites, Pakistan law, 127
emotional stress, entrepreneurs, 120
empowerment, 39, 141, 150; concepts of, 37; condition and position, 200; violence sensitised, 222
entrepreneurs, Pakistan women, 117-18; 125: career focus, 120; protected, 121; single parent, 119
Eriksson Baaz, M., 181-3
eThekwini Municipality, 6
Ethiopia, FGM, 75
ethnic/caste groups: FGM differences, 155; Nepal, 84
ethnographic lens, 67
ethnographic web, 203; intersectional layer, 205; lens, 67; model, 71

family(ies): abuse within, 182; "duties", 124; successful women harassment, 112; well-being IPV improvement, 210
FAO (Food and Agriculture Organisation), 212
female peers, Nepal protective, 36
female-headed households: rural Pakistan, 129; work likelihood, 130
femininity, FGM enhancement claim, 157
feminism: FGM activists, 156; transnational ideals, 99
feminist anthropologists, 63, 66; accusations against, 62
feminist discourse, 157
fertility, FGM improvement claim, 157
FGM (female genital mutilation), 1, 4-5, 7-10, 20, 22, 25, 27, 65, 70; abuse perception, 55; affected women voices, 174; age cohorts

statistics, 169; as circumcision, 59; campaigning, 20; community pressure, 164; competing discourses, 168; contexts, 158; cultural identity argument, 55, 57, 156, 171; Egyptian women's experience, 76; fear of social marginalisation, 58; financial pressures for, 46; global funding against, 67; grassroots campaign, 172; Hampshire attitudes, 20; insider status, 68; intergenerational conversations, 80; international campaign noise, 157; interventions data, 154; Islamic discourses, 72; legislation against role, 56; "marker of womanhood", 166; media coverage, 174; medicalised procedures, 46; mindset change tracking, 50; minority communities, 165; no-saying, 162; regional prevalence rates, 52; religion links, 64; sanction preserving, 28; scale of, 2; self-identification, 71; South Sudan, 190; specific contexts, 153, 155; statistical research limits, 170; Sudanese male views, 160; Sudan prevalence, 46; trauma of attitudes, 60; two-way stigma, 175; UK African diaspora, 49, 51–2, 60; women actors, 69; women's support for, 68

firewood collecting refugee camps: highly gendered, 208; vulnerability, 207

FORWARD, 78

frames, range of different, 4

Free Sudan programme, 74, 171

fundamentalism, Hindu, 44

Gambia: diaspora women's FGM concerns, 56–7; FGM practice, 155

gender: -based violence, 25, 33, 190; division of labour mindset, 87; equality achievement inroads, 26; equality assessment of, 218; hierarchies reinforced, 190; IDP Somalia settlement, 209; lens, 11–13, 205, 208; lens interventions assessing, 15; mainstreaming, 11; norms traditional transgressed, 18; social and cultural norms, 47

GEO TV, 108

Gibbs, A., 6

Gilberg Town, Lahore, 137

Girl Generation Africa-led, 9, 172; FGM scale estimate, 52

Girl Summit 2014, African grassroots unheard, 78

girls' education, Bondo role, 158

glass ceiling, women's work, 87, 124

Global Alliance for Clean Cookstoves, 212, 213

Global Gender Gap Index, 105

Goetz, A.M., 142

Gold, A., 43

good housing, family well-being outcome, 209

"good wife", status of, 149

Grafham, O., 207

grassroots: change agents, 64; organisers anti-FGM, 175

Gruber, J., 202

Guinea, 56; conservative diaspora, 58; women FGM attitudes, 57

Gujarat, 161

Gulberg Town, Lahore, 126

habitus, 32–5; structures changing, 41; theoretical lens, 30

hadith, FGM hint, 72–3

Hampshire, UK, FGM/C research, 20, 49, 54

Hanuman, monkey god, 42

INDEX | **247**

harassment: bride-price-related, 4; informal work sector, 82; middle class women's work, 103; working women, 17, 33, 36, 50, 91–2, 110–11
Harding, S., 173
harmful cultural practices (HCPs), 19; attitudes towards, 20, 50; denormalising, 10; gendered lens, 52; prevalence, 49
Harper, C., 26
Hassan, S.M., 134
Heise, L., 179; ecological web, 203
Hindin, M.J., 180
Hindu fundamentalism: effect of, 44; Hindu Bharatiya Janata Party (BJP), 45; right wing politics, 34
Hindu Sena, 45
Hinduvata ideology, everyday life presence, 45
hitting women, normalised, 188
HIV/AIDS, 7
home-based women workers Pakistan, 22, 132; children interests prioritised, 142, 145; economic importance of, 22, 134; eviction threat, 134; income hiding, 150; low self-esteem, 147; non-payment, 141; potential tensions, 18; push factors, 139; self-employed organising, 126; subcontracted, 138; survival mode, 118; textiles, 133; unpredictable income, 134, 140; violence against, 146; visibility raising, 137; wage negotiating agency, 142
HomeNet, Pakistan, 126–7, 132–3, 135, 137–87, 151–2, 221
HomeNet South Asia, 135
honour, disciplining concept, 5, 25, 144, 151; killings, 60, 106; low pay factor, 145
horizontal segregation, patterns of, 17
Htun, M., 97–8

human rights: FGM issue, 174; *jirga* violation, 127; shift, 30
Human Rights Watch, 105
humanitarian funding, gendered lens need, 198
Hussein, Leyla, 156
Hyderabad, Right to Play success, 9
hypermasculinity(ies), 179; militarisation intensified, 184, 198; violence signified, 183; war enhanced, 198

illiteracy, South Sudan women, 196
in-laws, women censoring, 145
income generation, women: access, 31 -empowerment assumption, 222–3; financial independence, 879; sense of freedom, 140; violence creating, 187, 222; wish resilience non-link, 150–1; *see also*, home-based workers; working women
India, 3, 35, 135, 154, 160; community pressure, 166; dowry system, 51; FGM, 22, 221; IPV-income link, 18, 44; VAWM laws implementation, 45; VAWM scale, 44, 165; vocal women targeted, 34
individual behaviours, social norm theory, 28
Indonesia, anti-Chinese uprisings, 181
informal networks, strength from, 96
International Centre for Research on Women, 44
International Labour Organization (ILO), 81
International Rescue Committee, 213
intersectional approach/lens, 4, 22, 52, 84–5, 98, 102, 124, 126–8, 220
interventions: design and evaluation, 48, 203–4; "do no harm approach", 218; gender approaches, 47; possible effects, 15; unintended consequences, 219

IPVs (intimate partner violence), 4, 6, 50, 145–7; alcohol worsened, 93, 134; childhood abuse impact, 194; denormalisation, 96; divorce consequence, 148; drug exacerbated, 149; Indian women, 44; in-laws instigated, 146, 148; limited universal factors, 180; middle class under-reported, 118; most prevalent VAWG, 213; Nepal, 81, 85, 90, 95, 104; normalisation of, 83; Pakistan, 112, 119, 132; resistance to, 94; Rumbek state, South Sudan, 187; single-factor explanations, 179; spousal economic disparities relation, 18
ISANGE, Kigali OSC, 8
Islam: FGM blurred links, 72; scholars, 64
Islamabad, 107, 117–19
Islamic Jurisprudence Council fatwa, Sudan, 74

James, S., 173
Jerslev, A., 186
Jewkes, R., 6
Jirga system, 127
Jok, J.M., 183, 185
Jolie, Angelina, Cambodia role, 186
Jones, B., 75
Jordan: marital violence, 211; refugee camps IPV, 210

Kabeer, N., 200; empowerment model, 39, 199
Kakuma refugee camp, Kenya, 210, 212
Kapoor, I., 186
Karachi, 118
Kathmandu, 110; Dial community school, 91; Manohara district, 83; migration to, 20, 36, 82; prostitution hub, 39; women of, 102

Kazmi, S., 134
Kelly, L., *Surviving Sexual Violence*, 85
Kenya: diaspora FM concerns, 56; Population Council, 67
Khan, S., 134
khatna, FGM cutting, 161
Khyber Pakhtunkhwa, 130
Kiir Mayarditt, Salva, 187
Kinshasa, sexual abuse scale, 182
Kirmani, N., 44–5
Kishor, S., 180
knowledge-attitudes-practice (KAP), 26
Koran, the, 72
Korea, Japanese soldier rapes, 181

Lahn, G., 207
Lahore, Pakistan, 107, 117–19; home-working, 22; work travel harassment, 110
law: -implementation Nepal failure, 104; legal rights discourse limits, 156; Pakistan domestic violence lack, 106; Pakistan religious structure, 105
Leicester, UK, FGM rate, 53
Leonardi, C., 196
Liberia, rape as weapon, 181
libido, women controlling, 76
Liechty, M., 39
Light Years Ahead Initiative, 213
listening, importance of, 20
livelihood schemes, 15
local women's organisations, importance of, 83, 151
Lund-Thomsen, P., 133

Macfarlane, Alison, 53
Machar, Riek, 187
Mackie, G., 28
Madonna, in Malawi, 185
mainstreaming tool, VAWG, 202

INDEX | 249

Malaysia, OSC model origins, 8
male authority, navigating, 159
male backlash, 18, 22, 114, 218; navigating, 121; women's employment, 17
Malmström, M.P., 76
Manchester, UK, FGM rates, 53
Maoist conflict, Nepal, 36, 39
Marcus, R., 26
marginal space, women negotiating in, 40
marital rape: jealousy fuelled, 184-5; non-criminalised, 189
marriage: child, 2; early, 83; FGM link, 175; forced, 1; Nepal arranged, 84; young, 194
Marshall, P.D., 186
media campaigns, FGM, 170-1
"medicalisation", FGM discourse, 166-78, 170
Mehergarh, 107
men: breadwinner status, 33, 86; engagement with need, 198
microfinance, 16, 117, 142
middle-class women: religious background, 103; support network lack, 102; unorganised, 123; work and violence link, 21
mindset change, 19, 170, 214; continuum change, 54; FGM mindset, 60 level of, 61; models, 31
Ministry of Gender, Child and Social Welfare, 196
Mohanty, C., 173
monitoring and evaluation, effective, 222
Monto, M.A., 38
Moving Energy Initiative, Kakuma refugee camp, Ken, 210
Mumbai, 161
Murthy, L., 36

Muslims, Ismaili Shia, 161
Myanmar, 33; military violence, 34

National Council on Child Welfare, Sudan, 74
National Law on Sexual Harassment at the Workplace, Pakistan, 104, 106, 109
National Plan of Action on FGM, Sudan, 73
Nayyar, D., 49
Nepal, 3, 35, 115, 123, 135; anti-VAW law failure, 104; construction sector women workers, 20-1, 36, 81-2, 87-8, 90, 151; employment violence, 21; Gender Equality and social inclusion frame, 82, 99; informal entertainment sector, 43, 221; law enforcement failure, 109; middle-class women, 102; patriarchy, 39 women working, 27
NGOs, resource allocation politics, 172
NHS (UK National Health Service), violence(s) cost, 7
normalisation patterns reversing, 27
normative values, conservative, 221
norms: reversing social movements, 29; "underpinning", 34
Nuer people, 187, 189, 193

one stop centres (OSCs), 5, 7; Malaysia origins, 8
Ong, A., 66
orientalist gaze, FGM, 174
Østbrø, M.T., 75
Østbrø, T., 75
outside work, women's stigma fear, 143-4
outsourcing, labour-intensive work, 133

Pakistan, 3, 115; discriminatory legal systems, 126; family accusations, 112; female entrepreneurs, 102–3; harassment legislation, 122–3; home-working economic importance, 22, 134; "informal" economy scale, 137; IPV rates, 105; poverty increase, 136; rural women work, 129; traditional customs, 127; violence scale, 131; women workers, 27, 106; women's employment violence, 21; work travel harassment, 111
Paluck, E.L., 26
parental violence, children effect, 179–80
participation, access inequality, 13
patriarchy: climate of, 194; household norm, 128; Nepal, 39; sanctioning discourses, 34
peer education, FGM, 171
peer ethnography approaches, 64
peer networks, 101; local membership importance, 21; organic, 41; women, 3
peer violence, boys, 9
Petersen, M.J., 75
"pharaonic", FGM type, 154
"piece-rate", home-based workers, 132
police help, women inaccessible, 152
political economy: analysis, 4, 67
polygamy, 190, 193
Population Council of Kenya, FGM estimates, 153
Portsmouth: African diaspora communities, 59; FGM 'at-risk' communities, 55
positive deviants, 40, 175, 221; concept of, 19; critical catalysts, 35; FGM critiques, 62
poverty, 138–9; family violence exacerbated, 211; gendered, 136; male violence, 191; work incentive, 104

power: gendered dynamics, 12; pervasive nature, 29; "quartet", 199; relational, 75; sanctions use, 29
Poynton, E.L., 26
professions, gendered, 124
programmes, reflection phase, 204
prostitution, 148; social obligations upholding, 38
Protection Against Harassment in the Workplace Bill, 107
public awareness campaigns, 5
public transport, women's fear, 122
Puja, Hindu daily practice, 42; women's space, 43
Puntland, Somalia solar lamps, 213

qualitative data, intersectional analysis, 50

Raheja, G., 43
Rajasthan, passive women image challenged, 43
Rama, hegemonic masculinity symbol, 42
Ramayana, Hindu epic, 42
randomised control trials (RCT), 6
rape: conflict interconnections, 185; excessive war focus on, 178, 182; male marriage technique, 190; Pakistan cases, 105–6; soldier compensation, 184; stranger, 4; weaponised, 23, 177, 181, 189; work travel anxiety, 91
Rashtriya Swayamsevak Sangh (RSS), 45
relative resource theory, 18
relativist lens, justified, 64
religion: FGM context, 71, 73; fundamentalist, 128; rituals women using, 47
Rendille women, 68; Kenya, FGM experiences, 67

reproduction: women's role pressured, 184–5
reproductive health strategy, Sudan, 73
resilience: empowered figures, 41; enabling environments, 40; to violence, 81, 83, 123, 218; women, 44
resourcing, FGM, 155
"restaurants of dance", Kathmandu, 39
Right to Play, Pakistan, 9
rights, FGM discourse, 166
risk, work at home, 18
River Nile, 168
role models, norms reversing, 29
Rosamond, A.B., 186
rural women, Pakistan violence likelihood, 131
Rwanda: genocide rape, 185; National Police and Health Services, 8

"sacrifycing dreams", women, 128
Safe Access to Fuel and Energy (SAFE) initiative, 212
safe reporting, lack consequence, 208
safe spaces: female-only peer networks, 32; IDP camps need, 198; importance of, 85; informal women's organisations, 98; research need, 137
Sahariah, 37–8, 40
Sahiyo, Bohra women's community, 161, 165
Saleem movement, Sudan, 10, 170, 172
sanctions, norms linked, 26
SARCs and SARTs, 8
saving people, rhetoric dangers, 76
savings groups, Nepal women, 94
school-based interventions, 9
SDGs (sustainable development goals), 19; Fifth, 1, 48
secure housing, refugee camps need, 203

self-reporting, FGM statistics, 169
Seshu, M.S., 36
sex: as work, 37; role theory, 28
sex work/workers: better working conditions politics, 38; contexts of, 37; not "frozen in sadness", 36
sexuality: clitoris focus, 76; desire curbing, 72, 163; FGM context, 71
Shadi Pura, Lahore, 126, 137; public resources lack, 138
shalwars, sewing of work 140, 142
shame, 28; family control mechanism, 221; low pay pressure, 145; policing role of, 25, 151
Shell-Duncan, Bettina, 67, 69–70, 77
Sieloff, S., 26
Sierra Leone, 154; bondo FGM practice and power, 158–9; ending FGM approaches, 160; FGM, 22
silence, gendered violence survivors, 197; women's strategic choice, 149
Sita, Hindu figure of, 42
social and cultural capital, 32, 97, 101; resilience making, 123
social ecology, 71; framework, 84
social knowledge, generation of, 97
social marginalisation, fear of, 58
social media, FGM discussions, 79; potential of, 6
social mobilisers: role of, 93; women's groups link, 94
social movements, activist platforms, 10
social norm(s), change measuring tool, 48; definition of, 26; reductive theoretical theory framework, 31; shifts in, 27; theories of, 19, 28; violence link, 28; women income limiting, 36
solar lamps, camp unintended consequences, 214
Somali women, 58; FGM culture attitudes, 59

sons: mother defending, 147, 150; violence from, 149
South Asia, research from, 4
South Sudan, 3, 184; cattle wealth conflict, 188; Dinka community, 183; Household Health Survey, 188; instability consequences, 192; IPV, 177; judicial system lack, 10, 195; laws unenforced, 196–7; media stranger rape focus, 187; multiple violences, 178; police harassment, 191; VAWG, 201
Southampton, African diaspora communities, 59; FGM 'at-risk' communities, 55
Southwark, London, FGM scale, 53
SPLM in Opposition, Juba-based faction, 188
Springvale Monash Legal Services, 190
Sri Lanka, 135
state health system, Sudan impoverishing, 46
Stepping Stones, 6, 34
Stern, M., 181–3
stigma, policing mechanism, 223
still birth prevention, FGM claim, 157
success, backlash navigating, 121
Sudan, 3, 33, 73, 154; anti-FGM efforts, 170; community pressure, 166; conservative Islamic government, 46; Demographic and Health Survey, 168; female battalions disbanded, 184; FGM cultural discourse, 156; FGM practice and opinion diversity, 22, 155, 157, 160, 174; FGM prevalence, 53, 80, 167, 169; Free from Female Genital Cutting (SFFGC), 171–2; military violence, 34; National Household Survey, 168; 1956 independence, 189; organisations, 73, 221; People's Liberation Movement (SPLM), 187; public health sector, 166; Saleem movement, 10; urban-based youth movement, 79
Sudanese Network for Abolition of FGM, 73
survivor-centred approach, GBV cases, 197
Sutherland, 42

textiles, home-based workers, 141
Thamel, Kathmandu tourist district, 39
Thar Desert villages, women of, 41–2
tipping point, women outperforming men, 114
tradition and identity, FGM marker, 155
traditional courts, reliance on, 196
transactional sex, firewood gathering, 208
Trust for London, website, 53
turnaround pressure, home-based workers, 138
Turner, G., 186

Uganda, rape as weapon, 181
UK (United Kingdom), 3; DFID, 84, 153; Faculty of Public Health, 7; FGM scale, 53–4; research from, 4; women training in, 119
UK Aid, 67, 153; FGM programme, 73; Sudan pilot intervention, 168
UN (United Nations): Joint Programme (UNJP), FGM, 172; Mission in South Sudan Human Rights Report, 188; "Protection of Civilian Camps", 187; UNFPA, 8, 171–2, 210; UNHCR, 210, 212–14; UNICEF, 8, 29, 52, 72, 154, 169, 171–2, 196, 212; Universal Declaration of Human Rights, 166; UNMISS, 197; women, 1, 2, 87
Unity state, South Sudan, 189
"universal indicators", IPV, 179

INDEX | 253

Upper Nile state, South Sudan, 189
USA (United States of America), training in, 119

Valamiki, 42
value-for-money, donor demand, 60
Van Raemdonck, A., 72, 76
VAWG (Violence Against Women and Girls), 1, 200; acceptance of, 217; denormalising, 7; economic engagement related, 17; ending of entry points, 98; family matter, 196; female body devaluing, 207; health impacts, 103; Indian rates, 44; intersectional focus, 19; interventions against, 11; IPV prevalence, 23; Nepal, 81, 104; Nepal women's organisations against, 96; networks agenda need, 99; 1970s–80s blinkered lens, 179; normalisation mechanisms, 202, 220; normalisation opposition, 24; normative, 85, 205; patchy data, 2; programmes against, 3, 5, 217–18; public debate marginalised, 98; rates of continuity, 27; social norms legitimising, 25, 48; South Sudan accepted, 194; South Sudan level, 186; South Sudan prevalence, 186, 188; unenforced legislation, 223; universal risk factors, 193; women normalising, 195; women's economic engagement, 18; *see also*, violence(s); women; working women

veiling, 65; globally manipulated image, 70; Western obsession with, 71
vicious circle, home-based workers, 146
victim framing, 173

violence(s), 16; change barrier, 222; contextual understanding need, 63; ecology of, 4, 205; economic, 138, 191–2; gendered, 11–12, 189; global realities of, 19; income link doubt, 150; inter-parental effects, 198; legitimisation, 29; mapping of, 30; middle class shame, 118; narratives of, 20; negotiating, 121; normalcy challenged, 6, 44; normalisation, 126, 152; political conflict situation, 23; poverty link, 132; public health problem, 7; study relational approach, 19; relative, 38; resilience to, 81, 83, 123, 218; South Sudan spectrum, 178; symbolic and physical intersections, 33; web of complexity, 31; women acceptance, 32; women's daily life, 21; women's disempowerment, 179; *see also* VAWG
violent husbands, reactions to, 92–3
virginity, higher priced women, 193
Vishva Hindu Parishad (VHP), 45
vulnerability(ies), 13; differing levels, 205; gendered, 15

Wade, L., 173–4
War on Terror, 65; women's liberation rationale, 62
war rape, 186; trauma, 191
Ward, J., 194
Washington, L., 6
web approach, 32, 34, 152; ethnographic, 35; model, 40, 44
Weldon, S.L., 97–8
West Darfur, 168
Western interests, other cultures denigration, 62
WHO (World Health Organisation), 171–2

wife-beating, norms, 130
Willan, R., 6
women: access to networks, 96; child comparison, 194; class natured labour, 128–30; constant daily violence, 41; decision-making, 16, 96, 105, 115; economic role under-accounted, 136; Egyptian, Western condescension, 77; "inappropriate" dress attacks, 45; income effects, 16, 21, 40, 86, 115–16; inferiority normalising, 191–2; mobility curtailed, 127–8; Nepal labour union leaders, 104; networks autonomy need, 99; -only spaces, 97; organisations, 3; overburdening, 86, 87; own voice, 223; peer networks, 34, 47, 85, 94; personal narrations importance, 102; Rajasthan rural, 41; religious inferiority ideology, 71; safe spaces importance, 85; success resentment, 103, 110; working, *see below*
women's movement, Pakistan monitoring of, 151
Women's Refugee Commission, 212

working women, 16, 96; domestic role expectations, 114; empowerment link, misplaced, 141, 150; family acceptance, 111; harassment at work, 4, 17, 33, 50, 121–2; hidden exploitation, 221; life choices non-link, 141; mother-in-law harassment, 112; Pakistan rural women, 131; Pakistan urban age-related, 129; pay gendered, 87; safe environment effect, 114; success pressures, 103; travel harassment fear, 36, 91–2, 110–11, 143; workplace cultures negative masculinities, 17; workplace violence, 81; *see also*, home-based workers
World Food Programme, 212
www.genderinsouthasia.org, 130

Yemen, 161
young people: FGM voice lack, 163; perceptions shift, 174
Yugoslav Wars, rape focus, 181
Yuval-Davis, N., 102, 173

Zaatari camp, Jordan, 209